A YEAR IN LAPLAND

A YEAR IN LAPLAND

GUEST OF THE REINDEER HERDERS

HUGH BEACH

SMITHSONIAN INSTITUTION PRESS

WASHINGTON AND LONDON

Editor: Jack Kirshbaum
Designer: Kathleen Sims

Library of Congress Cataloging-in-Publication Data

Beach, Hugh.
    A guest in Lapland : a year with the reindeer herders
/ Hugh Beach.
        p.   cm.
    ISBM 1-56098-230-6 (alk. paper)
    1. Saami (European people)—Sweden—Jokkmokk.
2. Beach, Hugh.
I. Title.
DL641.L35B43   1993
305.89′ 4550488—dc20   92-30436

British Library Cataloging-in-Publication data available

Manufactured in the United States of America

96 95 94 93   5 4 3 2 1

∞ The paper used in this publication meets the minimum requirements of the American National Standard
for Permanence of Paper for Printed Library Materials
Z39.48–1984.

Contents

Preface

Maybe in a former life I was a reindeer herder. At times I have felt sure that I was predestined to travel the mountains with the reindeer, although my childhood on the eastern seaboard of the United States certainly contained nothing to anticipate this development. Yet when an experience jumps out of nowhere and grabs hold so strongly that it cannot be denied, instead growing to become the backdrop of all other experiences, then it is natural for one to look back with concepts like destiny and fate. Odd how we try to construct logical progressions and feel the guidance of unseen hands to account for ourselves when, perhaps, we have merely been tossed by chance and buffeted by our own indecision. I suppose that chance caused me to dream, and dreams led on to decisions and more chance, until, in a curious manner, I set out to drift on an unknown current. Nothing is more obvious to me—and more difficult to explain to anyone else— than why I came to live in Lapland. I hope you will come to know why from the pages that follow.

To my family and friends who have borne with me throughout the writing process, this book has come to be termed my "personal Lapland book." In its pages my wish has been to convey something of the people and the country I have come to love. As a professional anthropologist I have written a good deal about the Laplanders and their reindeer herding, but little directed toward a larger, not necessarily academic audience. This is an account composed with the aid of the daily journals I wrote while surrounded by the people and mountains I describe. I lend the reader my eyes and ears for a year of adventure with the reindeer herders of Tuorpon Sameby in northern Sweden. The reader will learn much of the herder's life and his seasonal cycle of work with the reindeer; but I also wish to impart my personal experiences as a guest among these people. The beauty of the highlands, the laughter along the migration route as well as the painful cold that freezes your hair to the tent cloth—everything has its place. I have written out of thankfulness to those who made it possible for me to come to know this land and its people.

The first of my many thanks goes to my grandmother, Inga Bergström Schenck. While touring Sweden with her twenty-three years ago, at the age of fifteen, I wandered into a Saami calf-marking. My grandmother was showing me her homeland, having taught me Swedish as a child. This chance encounter with the Saami infected me with an enthusiasm so great that I still can hardly stand to pass up a calf-marking in the mountains no matter how many I have attended or how distant they may be. After this first calf-marking I was changed thoroughly by the possession of one dominant dream: to get back. Lapland became my special interest, guiding my studies in anthropology at Harvard, and as soon as I could manage release from the obligations and demands of a formal education, I shot forth with one goal in mind: to join the reindeer herders.

Parental generosity, supportive friends (in particular my college mate Ben Moulton), good luck, a stubborn dash of bravado, and a dismal budget are the factors that conspired to the financial soundness of the venture. I was solvent, but hardly, and certainly not for long.

Admittedly I still knew little about the undertaking I had chosen. I was full of out-dated or even false romanticism (I suppose I will always be a romantic) from the things I had read. I was a naïve young man, driven by the dream of a teenager to a wilderness I did not know, armed with a few scattered addresses. I arrived in Sweden in May 1973 and on this first trip stayed for seventeen months.

Difficulties are usually expected when one sets out to meet a foreign culture and people, and I was prepared for stony silence or a change of topic in conversation with any Saami I might meet. My initial difficulties, however, were of an entirely different nature. Everywhere I probed I encountered the veil of tourism wrapped tightly about Lapland. The more tourism is developed, the more difficult it is to leave the artificial and thoroughly beaten track. After all the smiling Saami posters welcoming me to Lapland, how I would have appreciated a Saami not somehow connected with the tourist business, stony-faced or not. When the inland train stopped at a small Lapland town, I managed to escape the Saami posters and grumbled about them at the local cafe.

"It's all over up here," said the man behind the counter, and I felt he had expressed my worst fear. After two weeks of working my way northward into Swedish Lapland, all I had seen were a couple of colorfully dressed Saami on postcards, a few reindeer by the railroad track, and a cheap assortment of Saami reindeer-antler handicrafts at the local shops—made in Japan!

Of course, I was not expecting to find the Saami of the 1600s beating on their trolldrums and falling into a trance, but I had hoped to find the modern Saami still culturally distinct from the modern Swede and not different just for the sake of the tourist trade.

I had seen advertisements in the travel bureaus to join a "real Saami migration" and the Saami would still wear their bright blue, yellow, and red dress to suit any color film. Visitors who were especially lucky might even hear a *yoik,* the traditional Saami form of song, all for only $300. Everywhere I went I seemed to be always one step too late. The man beside me at the bar was apparently a Saami, and he enjoyed the chance to gab with a foreigner. Many of his remarks depressed me. "The last Saami reindeer caravan ground to a stop five years ago. There was an old woman who still used to milk her reindeer in this village, but she died last winter. Wolves used to ravage the reindeer herds in the winter. There was even a bounty on them, but now they say there is only one poor wild wolf left in all of Sweden. My grandfather used to hunt bear with a spear. The bear hunt was a ritualized event. Now we just use a gun and sell the meat to the delicatessen." I felt like an old man longing for the good old days. I felt guilty too, for was *I* not doing what every visitor to Lapland was doing, and was it not this that put the migration in the hands of the tourist bureau and the fake Saami souvenirs in the shops?

One of my heretofore unproductive addresses led me to Jokkmokk and into the kitchen of the Märak family. After weeks of futility,

I was ready to return home only to discover that in Jokkmokk, just above the Arctic Circle, I had found home. When I finally did leave, it was only to prepare for a more extended visit.

With the help of the Ella Lyman Cabot Trust Fellowship, I returned to Jokkmokk in May 1975. With the further support of the American-Scandinavian Foundation, and the Swedish Institute, my "visit" has never really ended. At first I lived the life of a guest and "reindeer hand," able to earn my way through an eagerness to help even if my help was not always so helpful. For four years I enjoyed the herding life with the Tuorpon reindeer herders. The more I came to admire them, the more I came to realize that I could never be one of them even if Swedish law permits a non-Saami to become a herder through marriage.

I did want to stay, and yet I wanted to stay in my own capacity, and not as someone copying an ideal he could never realize anyway. During my four years in the field I turned back more and more to my own training and soon found myself engaged in serious anthropological fieldwork. I became Tuorpon's resident historian, a role that evolved naturally from my constant efforts to learn what was going on around me and to establish my own place among these herders. Later, I registered at the University of Uppsala in Sweden and in February 1981 obtained my Ph.D. degree in anthropology with the completion of my dissertation, "Reindeer-Herd Management in Transition: The Case of Tuorpon Saameby in Northern Sweden."

The present work, however, was written in 1975, five years before the completion of my dissertation, in the transition period toward academia. It remained wrapped in a plastic bag throughout my university years—dissertations are notorious for overriding everything else in their path. In returning to it now, thirteen years later, I recognize myself in the flush of a past dream, as one might upon finding an old photograph. I am in the position now to correct certain errors in the original version, but on the whole, I have not wanted to change anything. Although I would not write this book the same way now, I am glad I did then.

Throughout my changing interaction with Lapland, I could have done nothing without the support and warmth of the Märaks: Johan, Gunborg, Gunnlög, Annika, David, and Gunilla. They gave me their family to have as my own, and it is through them that I have come to know the Tuorpon herders. I want to give a special thanks also to my wife, Annie, who has not only translated this text into Swedish for its initial publication in Sweden, but who has also come to be my companion in Stalo. Finally, I would like to thank the Tuorpon Saami, who despite my wanderings know I would rather warm my hands around their fires, and who, whenever I do manage to join them in the summer camp at Staloluokta, always try to detain me with promises of new adventures.

March 1988

Preface to the English Edition

O nce again I am in a position to make corrections and additions, but as before with the Swedish translation, I do not want to make major changes. Naturally there are small passages explaining points obvious to Swedes that were left out of the Swedish edition but that are reinstated here. Most, but not all, of the photographs in the English version are also in the Swedish. The English edition, however, includes a sampling of photographs in color, so that the reader can get a feel for the Lapland palette. I have slightly expanded the epilogue that I composed in 1988, encompassing those changes of great significance for the Saami that have occurred in Swedish Lapland since then.

It is, of course, gratifying to see the positive reception the Swedish edition of "my personal Lapland book" has met since its publication three years ago. This book is used as a text in some of the Swedish schools and universities, and through it I have even made new friends. Most important for me, those Saami whose way of life it has described have liked it. I am very grateful for the opportunity to bring out an English edition. The original manuscript was written in English, and I am glad that it can now be read by a wider public.

January 1992

Introduction

The Lapland wind can be cruel. Small lakes can be blown to such violence that boats sink, nets rip, and fishermen drown. In the large forest belts, firs and pines are often torn out of the ground and strewn about as if a giant troll had cut a path for himself. And higher up in the mountains where the air is always thinner, the birches are dwarfed and have long since stopped growing toward the sun. Instead they snake along the ground no higher than the grass, bowing to the wind.

The people of Lapland, the Lapps, Saami, or Sapmi, as they call themselves, tell of a monstrous figure, Biegolmai, the mythical Wind Man who long ago wielded two huge shovels with which he scooped the wind and dropped the snow upon Lapland in such torrents that no living thing dared enter his realm. Lapland was a dead land of black rock and white snow. Once, however, in a raging snowstorm in the midst of his fury, one of Biegolmai's shovels broke. The wind abated, and for the first time living things were able to take a timid hold upon the land.

Even with a single shovel Biegolmai is strong and dangerous. To look out upon the frozen wilderness above the Arctic Circle in the dead of winter one would be convinced that the land was still uninhabitable by any living creature if not for the hundreds of reindeer tracks and perhaps some occasional long grooves beside them in the snow made by Saami on skis as they drove their herds toward new

I

winter pastures. It is a wonder that life is at all possible here. The myths do not tell us when the Saami came to Lapland or where they came from, but they tell of something more important: the relationship of these people to their land, a land so fierce and bitter that mankind obtained its chance only through the respite afforded by Biegolmai's broken shovel.

It is a land of extremes, a land where in the summer the midnight sun circles endlessly, only to hide itself in one long night below the winter horizon. Temperatures vary from 68°F to −40°F. The deep evergreen forests wash the feet of the mountains, mix briefly with birch, and are left behind. The lowland birch soon assumes the twisted shape of the mountain birch, which steals up protected hollows until it too must pass on the struggle to the dwarf birch. In the winter everything is frozen, and all the land is white. During the few summer months, however, a brief journey from the mountains to the lowlands can take the traveler through three seasons. On the high peaks the snow is never fully vanquished; tiny delicate mountain flowers spring up in the shadow of a melting snowdrift. The tundra above the treeline is dotted with huge boulders rising from a layer of moss and grass. The ground is almost always wet, and below the spongy moss there is usually only rock or mud. Farther down the mountainside scattered clumps of bushes show the tips of folded spring leaves, and down in the lowland, summer is in full dress.

But the summer is short. No sooner has the ice melted from the lakes, the flooding spring streams and rivers subsided and the flowers bloomed, than the first white powder visits the peaks. The melted snow is never fully drained away and the midnight sun never admired enough before the land is once again at the brink of winter and twilight. Biegolmai's respite is not long.

As the winter is long, so must the other seasons be short; everything must be precisely timed and prepared in order to survive. Reindeer calves are born just as soon as the first patches of bare ground appear on the mountain slopes uncovering the moss required for food. Calves born any later will be that much younger when winter begins, and that much less likely to live through it.

The Lapland wind blows across four countries: Norway, Sweden, Finland, and Russia's Kola Peninsula. For thousands of years the Saami traversed this land on their hunts and migrations, long before the founding of these modern nations. It was all their land, Lapland.

Although the national borders have given rise to such terms as Swedish Lapland, Norwegian Lapland, Finnish Lapland, and Russian Lapland, there are other older categories that divide Lapland along more natural boundaries. Not so long ago the Saami inhabiting one valley had little if any contact with their neighbors to either side of them. Those who were nomadic traveled their respective valley routes in more or less parallel directions, northwest in the spring, southeast in the fall. Each district developed a distinct dialect, dress, and form of reindeer herding.

Lapland encompasses broad topographical diversity. Seldom has it been better described than by the tenth-century viking poet Egill Skallagrimsson, who wrote that in northern Norway one finds the wide flat tundra land called the "vidda," and along the Norwegian coast there are deep fjords that penetrate into the heart of the mountains. Finland's broad forests are broken by innumerable lakes and waterways. All along the western frontier of Sweden there is a massive mountain chain. These mountains continue into and cover most of northern Norway, but in Sweden the land drops into a broad lowland forest district of pine and fir before meeting the Baltic Sea.

The Saami number about 60,000 (the exact figure is unknown and depends largely on how one defines the category) and inhabit Arctic and subarctic regions in all of these countries. In the past they extended much further south as well, but the increasing waves of Finns and Scandinavians pushed them to the northern districts.

No one can say where the Saami came from, nor is it known how long they have inhabited Lapland. Some say that they moved westward from the Ural Mountains, others that they moved northward with the reindeer as the ice receded from the last Ice Age. The prominent Saamiologist K. B. Wiklund proposed that the early Saami may have "wintered" this most recent glacial period along the coast of the Arctic Sea, surrounded by the massive European ice sheet that isolated them from the rest of mankind. Although these questions stir the imagination, it is doubtful whether they will ever be satisfactorily answered.

Cultural similarities with other Arctic and Siberian peoples hint at

Agricultural line
Lappmark line
Sameby borders
defining year-round
grazing areas

Könkämä
Saari vuoma
Lainiovuoma
Talma
Vittangi
Rantasvuoma
Laevas
Muonio
Norrkaitum
Mellanbyn
Sörkaitum
Tären Dö
Satta Järvi
Gällivare
Korju
Sirkas
Mettä-Korsotjärvi
Ängesä
Jåkkåkaska
Serri
Kalix
Tuorpon
Lehitäjä
Luokta-Mavas
Semisjaur -Njarg
Staïkke
Udtja
Svaipa
Västra Kikke-jaure
Östra kikkejaure
Maskaure
Gran
Ran
Umbyn
Mausjaure
Vapsten
Malå
Vilhelmina Norra
Frostviken norra
Vilhelmina Södra
Frostviken mellersta
Raitevare
Hotagem
Offer-dal
Tjikl
Såsjö
Handöls-dalen
Tåssåsen
Mittå-dalen
Tännäs
Idre

The reindeer grazing lands of Sweden are divided into approximately fifty herding territories. These territories, called *Samebys*, define zones whose use is conferred on (the reindeer of) certain specific Saami herders. Thus the Samebys define social as well as
territorial entities.

4

an age-old circumpolar culture long since splintered by the advance of the Indo-European and Slav peoples. The basic world view of the ancient Saami, their concepts of spirit and the people's relation to the spirits show a considerable resemblance to the religion of the early American Indians. The ritual bear hunt of the Saami has striking similarities to that of the Ainu in far-off Japan. There may once have been a unified Arctic culture in a world radically different from what it is today.

The Saami have often been characterized as a short people, having disproportionately short legs, broad faces, pointed chins, concave nose profiles, dark hair and eyes, and sparse hair growth. Nonetheless, there are many tall, blond, and blue-eyed Saami. Unfortunately, descriptions of Saami racial characteristics have frequently been tainted by a vulgar Darwinistic ideology. It seems as if many researchers from the mid-1800s to the mid-1900s sought to isolate unique characteristics of their own "civilized race" by making crude comparisons with other peoples. Certain physical traits among the Saami do indeed indicate long periods of genetic isolation. Anthropologists have discovered an unusual distribution of blood types and other definable physiological characteristics within the Saami population.

The Saami language itself provides evidence of long isolated development in the north. There are about 150 words for snow and an equal number for reindeer. Since early historical times, however, the Saami have mingled and intermarried with Swedes, Norwegians, Finns, and Karelians. What has preserved them as an ethnic entity is, besides their language, their unique way of life.

The Roman historian Tacitus made the first written reference to the Saami in A.D.98, but it is plain that his description is based on vague stories. Later accounts, such as that of Paulus Diaconus from the mid-700s, mixed fact with fancy and described the wild Saami, or Fenni as they were often called, as leaping on wooden shoes rather than walking. Other reports told of their sliding along the ground like snakes, therefore obviously servants of the devil. Eventually it became clear that the Saami were able to jump and slide over the ground because of a strange kind of shoe that we have come to know as the ski. They were described as the most primitive savages, who lived in mud huts and were more animal than human. Slightly more enlightened reports claimed them to be a race of white pygmies.

In the past, the Saami were shamanic and believed that everything—human beings, animals, rivers, mountains, trees, and rocks—was inhabited by a spirit. Not all could speak, but all could hear and all could think. Many of these spirits had the ability to occupy (or materialize into) any form. They could, therefore, be both associated with their habitations and considered completely free to move about, seize another form, or possess the body of a person. There were lesser and greater spirits of all degrees, and some of the most powerful were worshipped by all Saami. These were, for example, the Sun, the Thunder, the Goddess of Childbirth, and the God of the Underworld. Anything in nature that stood out as unusual or unique was revered as a prominent spirit. Curiously shaped rocks were often thought to be the dwelling place of a spirit. Such rocks were given the name *seitas* and were worshiped with sacrifices. Many Saami had their seitas hidden in mountain caves.

The Lapland tundra is no longer traversed solely by the Saami and their reindeer. For the past one thousand years the Saami have been in frequent contact with the peoples around them. Much of this contact, however, was not desirable from the Saami viewpoint. Armed bands, Birkarls, licensed by the kingdoms to the south, imposed ruthless taxation on the Saami. A wealth of furs and other wilderness produce was extracted from Lapland. The Scandinavian nations later took over the role of the Birkarls and embarked on a determined program of colonization. The Swedish king, for example, claiming that Lapland belonged to him and God, offered all pioneers to the north great enticements. Swedes who moved north were given title to land and exemption from taxes for fifteen years.

In a country where living was at best a struggle for survival, these encroachments had a massive effect. The heavy taxation levied in furs and skins gradually brought about a depletion of wildlife. This, later accompanied by competition from pioneers, forced significant numbers of Saami more and more toward an economy based mainly on reindeer herding.

The long ski trail left in the snow still speaks of an age-old adaptation as essential to the life of a reindeer herder now as hundreds of years ago. But, should we follow this track, it might well lead us to another trail, a broader one cut by a modern snowmobile, which the Saami call a "scooter," and overhead we might find a great span of cables carrying power from the numerous hydroelectric dams to the towns and cities, railroads and mines.

In fact, the Saami now hold a minority status in their own home territory, and the reindeer herders have been pulled into the market economy, where the reindeer no longer directly satisfies all needs. Of course, the advancements of technology have not been without benefit to the reindeer-herding Saami. Although scooters first came to the tundra in the 1960s, they are already necessary to modern herding, as are helicopters and walkie-talkies. Modern technology has simplified and decidedly eased the hardships of reindeer herding. At the same time the price of modernity is heavy. The future of the Saami way of life is severely threatened by mining, lumbering, and the continual building of new dams to convert the water into the energy so insatiably demanded by the industries to the south. Moreover, severe problems have been caused by radioactive fallout. Saami culture and reindeer herding is pressed to the brink of existence.

In the heart of Swedish Lapland lies the Jokkmokk district with a small town by the same name. It is a Saami name meaning "bend in the river," in this case the Little Lule River. This river and the Big Lule River, which it joins, carry the melted snow water from some of Sweden's most untouched mountain areas. The Jokkmokk district encompasses Sweden's largest national parks and is a focal point for Saami culture.

Besides reindeer herders, the population of Jokkmokk is composed of water power workers, lumberjacks, railroad hands, and people from almost every walk of life, but it is with the reindeer herders that I am concerned here. Even within these limits the spectrum of reindeer-herding method is extremely broad. Each reindeer-herding group has its own system. Even the families within a group have somewhat varying methods. What I present is a personal account of my time with the Tuorpon Saami in the Jokkmokk district. I wish to describe how I experienced the full year's herding cycle and what it is like for a stranger to follow along in the corrals and on the migrations. The life is different from what it was only twenty years ago. In another twenty years the changes may be even greater. At times it is painful for me to see the life I have come to love so well vanish so quickly. But to remain static is also to die. The trick to survival through these changes is to maintain a continuity, an identity—to move toward the realization of self-determination. Although I occasionally regret the impact of modern times on the life I have come to know in Lapland, I feel the tremendous strength of the Saami people and their culture. This strength has recently been demonstrated not least in connection with the nuclear power disaster in Chernobyl. The demise of the Saami has been predicted for hundreds of years, but they and their culture will endure.

1

A Start with Henrik

I met Henrik Kuhmunen for the first time at the Jokkmokk Lion's Club Fair, of all places. It was late spring in the mountains and early summer in the lowlands. The schools were still in session, vacations had not begun and the Saami had not yet left for their mountain homes. These early summer days when the mind has wandered far out ahead of the feet, when winter coats and gloves can be put away, and when the mosquitoes have not quite arrived, is the best time of the year. Jokkmokk is in festive mood, everyone is outside with face turned upward to the warm sun, and every year at this time the Lion's Club organizes a small fair. There is a hotdog stand and a raffle ticket booth, an auction of used furniture, and a sale of old clothes and books. Gunborg Märak and her troop of young folk dancers caper on the village green in a whirl of brightly colored costumes and smiles. The small fairground is thronged with people who are there to mingle, watch, or maybe find a bargain. I knew that this gathering contained many Saami, but apparently most of them had given up their brightly colored traditional dress and were now indistinguishable from the rest of us in ordinary factory-made clothing.

Against this crowd, Henrik Kuhmunen stood out like a scarecrow. He wore a faded blue Saami costume decorated with strips of red and yellow and a matching hat with a huge topknot of red yarn. This was the traditional dress of the Karesuando district, I later learned. Even in his odd hat he was not very tall. His posture was

9

stooped, and he walked with an elastic gait. He was an old man and it looked to me as if he had spent his whole life walking, and learned to do it with the least effort. Incongruously he had a prominent potbelly, and there was a slight clatter when the knives hanging from his belt knocked against each other. One had a hooked sheath made from reindeer antler in the usual Saami fashion. The other was much larger with the sheath made of wood. His belt was fully six inches wide and completely covered with metal eyelets, which could accommodate a wealth of paraphernalia to it wherever he so wished. His boots were made of tanned reindeer skin with curled toes, originally so that the foot could not slip out of the simple Saami ski binding and now a matter of general Saami style. His trousers were stuffed into his boots and held in place by beautiful hand-woven shoe-bands wrapped around the leg in a tight seal to prevent the incursion of snow. The effect was as if Daniel Boone had wandered out of the woods into Radio City Music Hall in New York.

Henrik had obviously not come to buy or bargain, but simply to meet old friends and enjoy the carnival atmosphere. Although to me he looked like a living anachronism, he attracted little attention. Soon he was sitting on the grass with his legs tucked under him, watching the bicycles, chairs, and tables go to the highest bidder.

I was eager to get into the high country but had scrambled my way through enough mountains in the past to realize that this was not a matter for haste. At this time of year, I had been told, the highlands were impassable. Rivers and streams were flooded with melting snow water. Those spots which might still have snow, or ice bridges, were deceptive and deadly. Even on skis, movement was almost impossible. Late spring ice should not be trusted too far. I was told if I should go under to try to crawl out on the side of the hole I had come from. The ice is usually strongest there—at least you know it held you to that point. One added benefit of the simple Saami ski binding and curl-toed shoe is that the skis are easily kicked off underwater. Most Saami over thirty, I was to learn, have fallen through the ice at least once during a late spring season, and there have been many who surfaced, drowned, several weeks later. Sometimes with the help of a seer, one who can see under the ice or who has the power of prophecy, the dead can be recovered for proper burial. Such people are still employed in

Lapland. Their skill in predicting where a body will rise with the summer thaw is phenomenal. The frequency of their use attests to the esteem they enjoy. I had no intention of contributing to their prestige, at least in that way. But here beside me, watching the auction, was a man who had obviously just returned from the mountains. His clothes smelled of birchwood smoke, and his hands were still blackened from handling the coffee pot.

"Have you just come down from the mountains?" I asked him, introducing myself as a foreigner who was interested in hearing how conditions were for travel.

"Water, water," he said, "lots of water." Then he reached inside his large blue tunic or *kolt,* pulled out a handkerchief from the neck slit, and blew his nose. "It's cold in the mountains," he said. "It's given me a bad nose."

"I've got a terrible nose myself," I said. "Where I come from it's even warmer than it is here today, and I guess I'm not used to it." He looked understandingly at my nose as he wiped his, and then leaned over and pulled out a large bottle from inside his tunic. It was a bottle of cognac, and it was this bottle, carried inside the tunic and held up by the wide belt, which had given me the impression that he had a large belly. "It's medicine," he told me, "good for the nose." We took a hasty swig before he stuffed it back into his kolt and looked cautiously about. "My wife doesn't believe in medicine," he added. "She says it just makes me worse." I was a bit surprised to hear that he was married because the topknot on his hat was pointed forward and according to what I had read of Saami traditions, this means its wearer is single. Either he was prepared to flirt with unsuspecting women, or he simply did not care. Henrik certainly did not fit the stereotype of a tight-lipped Saami. When he saw my camera, he suggested I take a picture of him, and wanted to know what I thought about Nixon. "As for me, I think Nixon is better than the Swedes," he said. "At least Nixon lets me fish wherever I want." Then he laughed.

I told him I was bound for Staloluokta as soon as conditions permitted, to join the Tuorpon Saami. My good friends, the Märaks, with whom I was staying, were settled Saami, and therefore would not be moving with the active reindeer herders to the summer land in the mountains. But Johan Märak had extensive acquaintances among the nomadic herdsmen, and he had taken me to meet Isak Parfa, spokesperson of the Tuorpon group. So now Isak was expecting me to turn up in Stalo sometime near the end of June.

Henrik, it turned out, was a member of the Sirkas group, from north of Tuorpon but also within the Jokkmokk district. He knew the entire area well, and he shook his head. "Too much water," he said. "Maybe in two or three weeks," and when he saw my face fall, "maybe in one week. I'm leaving for Tjaktjajaure soon," he continued, "to fish, and later we'll move to Sitojaure and maybe come to Staloluokta for the calf-markings. I want to build a new *goahttieh* in Sitojaure, me and my boys." (A goahttieh is a traditional Saami house.) "You can come too," he said suddenly. "Bring some nails, help fish, and when the water has run off you can walk from Sito to Stalo."

I had no idea where Sito was and doubted if the walk from Sito to Stalo would be so simple for a newcomer, even though I had hiked a lot in the States, but the chance to get up into the mountains at all filled me with excitement. "Just come over in about a week," he said. "Märak knows where I live."

For the next few days I ran about town collecting the supplies I would need for a summer in the mountains. From Johan I learned that Isak Parfa ran a small store in Stalo where it would be possible to buy fish and bread; I would only need to bring enough food for a few weeks with me. I picked up some nails, a coffee pot, rain gear, and of course a bottle of cognac for my nose. Most equipment I already had acquired for previous mountain forays. And so it was with an all too heavy and bulging pack that I set off to meet the Kuhmunens at their winter home on the edge of town.

The house, a fully modern though modest structure, was in total disarray. Bundles of odds and ends wrapped in plastic littered the floor. The sparse furniture in the kitchen was loaded with clothes; string, rope, and boxes were scattered among it all. Henrik sat on the floor making a new handle for a hammer and was not readily distinguishable from all the clothing and packing. Susanna, his wife, was barely able to give a brief greeting before she had to rescue me from the onslaught of three dogs.

The Saami herding dog is like a Pomeranian or a Finnish spitz in type, usually black or reddish with a tail that curls toward the back.

Actually it is a mixture of all sorts of races—such as Russian laika, Karelian bear dog, Samoyed spitz—and is chosen for good herding characteristics rather than pedigree. These dogs are not large, standing about 18–20 inches at the withers, but they are inordinately sturdy and formidable when aggressive.

The Kuhmunen's dogs made a terrific noise at my entrance, and although (Susanna assured me) not in the least vicious, they had to play their roles as protectors before they would allow me to come any closer. She swatted and yelled and pushed, until finally all three lay in the far corner, growling. Whenever they worked themselves up to a higher pitch, Susanna shouted some awful Saami threat that they seemed to understand, causing them to roll their eyes and look most uncomfortable. Henrik rose from among the crates, brushed away the sawdust, cleared off a part of the bench, and we sat down to some coffee, the hospitality drink of Lapland. He was clothed as before in traditional dress, but Susanna wore a plain long cotton frock instead of a tunic. "Do you think we'll ever get away?" she said, gazing over the piles of supplies. The hurry subsided for a while and the Kuhmunens prodded me for descriptions of palm trees and sandy beaches as the dogs began to sneak closer and lay their heads in my lap, hoping I might slip them some sugar.

Susanna was short, rather plump, and gray haired. She had a kind face and a mind full of curiosity. Obviously she controlled the house, and Henrik left most of the talking to her. He would chime in every once in a while asking about something we had already discussed, and there would be a short burst of Saami between the two. "His Swedish is no good," she said. "He spends most of his time in the woods, but I stay more in town because Thomas goes to school. He, she nodded toward Henrik, doesn't believe that people swim in the ocean." And again the Swedish was interrupted by an animated squabble in Saami. Henrik stared into his coffee and Susanna, insisting on being his interpreter, explained that he was afraid of the big fish in the ocean. We were now chewing on strips of smoked and dried reindeer meat that each of us cut from the bone as it was passed around. Henrik wanted to know how big these fish could get. He curled up on the bench, took off his hat, used the red topknot as a pillow against the arm rest, and dozed off.

There was something that struck me as slightly strange and at the same time humorous in seeing Henrik and Susanna at home in their modern kitchen. They did not belong there. Henrik had appeared more at ease on the floor than in his chair. In fact, they seemed to be camping out in their own house. One could see the goahttieh life in their every mannerism.

"I'm glad you're here to help with the härks," Susanna said. "We must take them with us." *Härks* are relatively tame, castrated reindeer and were once used in the migrations to carry the household supplies and pull the sleds. Nowadays, however, it is not so common to find them still at work. The scooter and seaplane have made them for the most part obsolete. Yet, Henrik was attached to his old härks and kept them separated from the rest of his herd. For a Saami, tame härks are the most valuable of all reindeer. During the winter Henrik liked to keep his safe in an enclosure where they could be watched and protected from wolverines and lynxes. He still found jobs for them to do. Even if not employed to pull sleds, a tame härk can be most useful as a lead reindeer. A calm härk led firmly on a harness at the front of a herd will cause all the reindeer to follow.

Susanna saw that Henrik had failed to mention the härks, and in an apologetic tone explained that I would have to help load them into the back of the trailer. I was glad of the chance to help in any way, I declared, but she scowled a little at Henrik, who was still dozing on the bench. "He never knows what he's doing," she whispered. "Do you know what that crazy old man did once? He bought a car when they first came up here even though he couldn't drive it, and to make it last longer he put tar all over it, he even tarred the engine."

At this juncture Thomas appeared, a boy of about twelve, and I was surprised to learn that he was their son, not a grandson. "We have a big family." Susanna told me, "It used to be good to have big families but now it makes everything more difficult. Besides this one there's Henrik Jr., John, Lars, Per, and Paulus. We have a daughter too, but she's married down south. Lars and Paulus are already fishing in Tjaktjajaure, Per has a job at the dam, and Henrik Jr. and John are in the mountains."

Two neighbors who had previously volunteered to drive us into the mountains as far as the road went also appeared. There would be a three-mile walk to the Kuhmunen's mountain place from the end of the dirt road. Henrik hitched up the make-shift trailer with sides made of large boards fastened together with rope, and we were on our way. The house cleared miraculously. Susanna and Thomas rode off ahead in the other car with bags, boxes, and dogs piled high in all the windows.

Soon Jokkmokk lay far behind and we were speeding through woodland country dotted by small clearings and farm houses. Many were abandoned, but some showed signs of life and at one of these our car swung off the road. Here, with friends, Henrik had lodged his härks. Henrik grabbed a lasso from the back of the car and disappeared through a wire fence gate into the woods to return a short while later leading a reindeer. After tying him to the car door handle, Henrik took another lasso and returned with the second härk. The friends inside the house emerged, and after a brief chat we all turned to the task of getting the härks into the trailer. Härks are supposed to be tame, but these were not about to climb into the unsteady cart without a good fight. Henrik talked to them and tried to soothe their spirits, nevertheless the heavy animals had to be lifted kicking into the vehicle.

One hour and many doses of Henrik's medicine later, we reached the end of the road where Susanna and Thomas were waiting beside a good fire. We unloaded the indignant härks, said farewell to the friends who had driven us out, gulped a cup of coffee and warmed ourselves. Once the cars were gone, a new sense of silence descended upon us. No one said much. We listened as the small noises and the awesome silence of the woods washed back over the turmoil of our arrival. Then it was time to move; the light was already fading, though at this time of year it would never die. What we could not carry in one trip we packed together under a covering of plastic. Henrik started out ahead with the härks, and the rest of us spread out along the trail carrying as much as we possibly could. It was a beautiful walk, plagued only by my cumbersome load. It was not particularly heavy, just awkward, and I could never seem to position my boxes properly. Henrik, leading his two reindeer, fit perfectly the requirements of the romantic Saami image, although he managed to make himself look distinctly unromantic as he slouched along with his elastic gait, blowing his nose. The dogs ran back and forth like army scouts carrying messages to and from the front.

A sharp turn off the main trail onto a small path soon brought us to the edge of Tjaktjajaure, a huge lake enclosed by white-topped mountains. The far side of the lake was bathed in a soft, rosy glow, while our side held a faint blue light that reminded me of the early dawn. It was almost midnight. The Kuhmunen's cabin, with a cluster of dome-shaped goahttiehs behind it, stood at the edge of the forest facing the lake. A goahttieh is built with a birch frame, waterproofed by a layer of birchbark, and insulated by a final covering of turf. It looks like a small hill with a window, and if anyone is at home it will emit smoke from a hole at the top. The goahttiehs had probably once been the only living quarters here, but now they were apparently used for storage or to smoke fish from the lake.

The edge of the water was almost 150 yards from the cabin, but plainly this had not always been the case. The dry lake bottom stretched close to the cabin and formed an ugly ring of dead ground all around the lake. The dam operators who controlled the level of the lake were taking no chances of a flood, and had lowered the lake level to prepare for the rush of new mountain water from the spring thaw.

A loud barking broke the stillness of our approach. Dogs streamed toward us from the cabin, mingled with our dogs in greeting, sniffed us quickly, and then dashed back to the cabin to herald our coming. There were a number of tiny sleds, lean-tos, and racks made from birch trees all around. Reindeer antlers hung from tree limbs, canvas protected unknown goods from the rain, and gasoline cans and parts from broken boat motors were scattered out back. There was even an old *pulka,* or sled, which Henrik's härks had undoubtedly pulled in past migrations, leaning against a tree. It resembled a Saami shoe or boat in shape, had no runners but was pulled on its belly. The curved, pointed front guided it over bumpy, snow-covered ground and through bushes. In the flat tundra to the north, there are sleds of a different type: raised, with runners, suited to a different terrain.

Lars met us at the door, a bit bleary-eyed, and helped us in with our loads. He had expected us sometime this week, although he could not have anticipated my arrival. "There's plenty of room," he said, and I was thankful for the direct greeting. He did not appear at all surprised to find a stranger along. There was no big fuss that would have made me feel like an added burden, and I was not called upon to explain myself any more than I chose. Hospitality was a matter of course. I liked Lars immediately. He had a triangular face with high cheek bones, blue-gray eyes, and a narrow nose bone. Most notably, he was rapid in his movements and extremely quick of mind. He asked where was I headed as we sat around the table in the larger of the two rooms. Then he pulled out a map and showed me where we were and all the different routes to Stalo. "No way is good now," he said. "You had better stay here a while."

Lars's wife, Margit, and their two small daughters were asleep in the next room. Paulus, his younger brother, had slept through everything on the bed by the table where we sat. With the midnight sun, sleep is more like a series of fully clothed naps. Schedules disappear entirely. Paulus waited until coffee was ready before waking up. After a hasty cup and a hello, he set out with Susanna to the lake carrying a sack of nylon nets. The arrival of more people demanded more food. If lucky they would even catch a surplus of fish to take into town for sale.

It takes two to put out the nets and strip them of fish (although a good fisher can do it alone if necessary). One person manipulates the nets, the other is at the oars and handles the boat. Lars and Margit formed one fishing team and now that Susanna had come, Paulus joined forces with her. Lars said he would teach me the proper technique at the oars and I could help when needed. Tjaktjajaure was full of char, a troutlike fish with a red belly. "It's the Saami summer food," said Lars, and with that he put on the skillet and fried a delicious meal of smoked char. I contributed a small canteen of cognac to the feast and we were soon in excellent spirits.

I had divided the original cognac bottle into two plastic containers in order to avoid the risk of broken glass in my pack. Later I learned that I had stumbled upon an old Lapland trick. It is impossible to obtain alcohol in the mountains, and so the Saami are known for never leaving a bottle unemptied on the rare occasions when one is available. Travelers who want some left for next time divide their supply and reveal one container at a time. Lars had a generous nature, however, and suggested we save some for Paulus. "It's windy and cold out there on the lake," he said. "Paulus would like nothing better than a quick swig when he comes in. Susanna hates to see him drink; we've got to sneak it to him."

In Susanna's absence, Henrik seized the opportunity to describe the difficulties of obtaining liquor in the old days. When alcohol was scarce and motor transportation nonexistent, people were sent on extremely long hikes into the nearest town to return days later with a pack full of whiskey bottles. If the man hired to run this errand made unusually good time, he might be rewarded by an extra swig. Henrik told of one poor Saami who ran many miles under such a burden, then slipped and fell with a crash on the trail. Slowly something wet began trickling down his spine. With a look of pain and despair, well imitated by Henrik, the carrier turned his face heavenward and prayed that it be blood, not whiskey, which ran down his back.

While listening to Henrik, we took out our binoculars and watched the tiny boat below us on the lake. "They've finished putting out the new nets and are busy checking the old ones," Lars said. "They're taking their time on each one so there must be a lot of fish." As we waited for the boat to turn toward shore, Lars brought out his harmonica and played folk tunes. He knew a number of American songs too and suddenly began speaking English. He was glad to have the chance to practice his school English, he told me, but only while drinking so that he didn't mind his mistakes.

We began to talk about magic, the shamans and magic drums, trolldrums, of the past. Shamanism, the Saami pre-Christian system of belief, has been called the technique of ecstasy, but more than this, it is a technique devoted to the accomplishment of certain practical aims. While in a trance, the shaman seeks to communicate with the spirits in order to solicit their aid in various undertakings. The practices of shamanism concern such things as control of natural forces, where to find game, and the healing of the sick.

Rumors of Saami magic skills had spread throughout Europe in the Middle Ages. It was said that Saami sorcerers could lock ships in invisible chains and hold them motionless in a full wind. A Saami shaman could release his soul to wander while his body remained motionless, prone on the ground, and when the soul returned it could bring tidings from far-off places. With the help of the magic drum, a shaman could fall into a trance and send his soul forth as a bird to fly to higher worlds, or adopt the form of a fish to consult with the spirits of a lower world. His services were often bought, and his wrath greatly feared.

The Saami magic drum, usually oval in shape, was made from a wooden frame covered with a reindeer skin in the shallow "tambourine" form. The hammer used to beat the drum was made from reindeer antler, the head of which branched into a fork. The skin of the drum was decorated with highly symbolic, and often stylized figures drawn with the red juice of chewed alder bark. No two drums, however, had the same arrangement of images. Figures representing the sun, the rainbow, the Wind Man, and many animals could be found.

A shaman was required for practices involving trance, but other rites, like those of divination, could be performed by a layman (though very rarely by a woman). If a hunter, for instance, wanted to determine which animal he should stalk, he would place a brass ring, called an *arpa,* on the drum's surface and from the vibrations caused by his hammer beats cause it to move about over the red figures. If the arpa stopped over the figure of a bear, the hunter knew that the spirits favored this undertaking.

The Saami did not equate shamanism, or communion with the spirits, with bondage to Christianity's devil; yet, somewhat understandably, this was the first conclusion reached by the missionary witnessing a Saami shaman, or *nåjd,* frothing at the mouth imitating an animal, and falling into a trance. Magic drums were burned by the thousands. The shamans did not always fare much better.

The Swedish word *trolltrumma* (from *trolla,* "to enchant") refers to the magical quality of the Saami shaman's main instrument of knowledge and power, the drum; in Saami, *guabbada.* "I have one," Lars said finally, and I was struck with curiosity, for if he meant a trolldrum, there were only seventy-one known to the world and all in museums. "I made it myself," he continued, "just for fun. I'll show it to you." But then the boat turned toward land and we started down to help them clean the catch and carry it over the rocky, dry lake bottom to the cabin. I carried two film cans loaded with cognac for Paulus in my pocket.

The next morning began with bad news. Henrik's härks had found a hole in their enclosure and escaped to the highlands. The härks would undoubtedly try to join the other reindeer and mix with them all summer until the herd separations in the fall when Henrik could once again extract them from the main herd and keep them in a winter enclosure. Hoping to intercept them, Henrik spent the entire day tracking them for miles, but once spring migration fever strikes, reindeer move quickly. Meanwhile the rest of us walked out to the dirt road and carried back the remainder of the supplies we had cachéd there yesterday.

When we returned, Lars produced his magic drum. It was not as large as those I had seen in the Stockholm museum, but was made in the same way and had numerous reddish figures painted on the skin with the juice of alder bark. I was anxious to try it out. Instead of a brass ring, *arpa,* we used a copper coin and it slid around on the skin as it was supposed to when I drummed with a piece of reindeer antler. Bearing in mind its ancient function, I asked the drum to tell me what should be the object of my own hunt. Everyone stood silently watching the coin move from figure to figure along the drum skin. Finally it came to rest on the figure of a woman. I was delighted with this drum. Lars assured me that I would be successful. Paulus took a turn next, and once again the coin came to stop on "woman." Thomas and Lars both had the same result. This occasioned a storm of laughter and protest. Each of us felt that the one-sided response of the spirits strained our belief or desire to believe. Magical predictions can be very tempting when they give just the answer one wants, but too great a coincidence begins to arouse suspicions. Now we were convinced that Lars had experimented carefully with the drum before placing the figure for "woman" in the ideal location, but he steadfastly denied it. Fixing us with a wizard's eye and a wry smile, he cautioned us not to laugh at his drum or the spirits might be vexed and change their minds. We were all cowed into silence at the mere suggestion of endangering our chances with the opposite sex.

Many days slid by, mingled indistinguishably into one endless day under the circling sun. Out of concern for my own comfort, I amassed considerable information about the effects of mosquitoes on reindeer. Mosquitoes, I learned, were "the Saami herders' best helpers," for they impel many free-wandering reindeer to leave the forests for the cool, breezy mountains. A great factor in reindeer movements, on hot days mosquitoes will force the reindeer to seek refuge on high snow patches, and in effect, gather them for the herders. Too few mosquitoes add greatly to the herders' labors when gathering the herd for the calf markings. Too many, however, can plague the reindeer so that they must run endlessly and starve, not being able to graze in peace. Reindeer have been known to go down into mine shafts to evade flies and mosquitos. Forest reindeer herders, who keep their herds year round in the lowlands, build numerous fires to envelop the reindeer in a protective screen of smoke. If reindeer could be so bothered by mosquitoes, I expected the worst.

As time went on, I began to think the reputation of the Lapland mosquito had been exaggerated. Mosquitoes were common, but certainly not in the concentrated numbers I had heard of. The reindeer must be timid animals indeed, I decided, to be troubled by so few mosquitoes. Gradually, however, I began to scratch more frequently. Soon they attacked in such clouds that one was forced to breathe through clenched teeth to avoid making a meal of them. The wet Lapland summer ground was perfect for mosquito breeding. Unless there was a good breeze, to go outside was to suffer. Standard mosquito sprays and lotions were pitifully ineffectual. It was almost as if each repelled mosquito carried away a tiny fraction of the repellent's power, and under such a massive bombardment the protective walls crumbled in no time. Only I continued to swat against such overwhelming odds; the Saami seemed to have an understanding with the mosquitoes. They would not swat and the mosquitoes would not bite. This treaty, I later found, was reinforced by a special mixture of oil and tar, a homemade mosquito repellent few Saami go without. Often it is carried in a small bottle attached to the belt in a leather case. Lars showed me how to mix it, the world looked much brighter, and the smell was not at all bad.

The mosquitoes were still a nuisance even if they did not succeed in drawing blood. The only time we could ever be free from them when outdoors was while fishing far out on the lake. The clouds of furious mosquitoes would follow us a good distance from the shore, but once the motor was running, and the boat flying over the lake

toward the net buoys, they were left far behind. Here their conspic-
uous absence seemed to open up a fresh new world.

Lars would approach the net with the throttle open wide. At the
last second he would make a sharp swerve, cut the motor and let the
stern sweep close by the buoy. After some instruction I learned my
part. I would snag the buoy line with an oar as we swung past and
brake with the other oar to stop our continued motion. Lars made
sure we were always downwind of the net so that the boat would not
drift into it. As Lars, standing in the stern, hauled in the net a bit at a
time, I would gradually back the boat toward the net to ease the strain
on it. It was crucial to keep the net taut to minimize tangling. The man
at the oars must be constantly on the alert to stop the backward glide
should the other man stop hauling in the net to extricate a fish. With
time we became quite an efficient team. Few commands were necessary once I learned to take my orders directly from the drift of the boat
and the slack in the net. On a good day we might pull in as much as
fifty pounds of char. As we came off the lake, the chill left our bones,
but there on the shore were a million swarming mosquitoes to welcome us back.

Securing the boat presented problems. Much depended on the
unknown decisions of the dam operator. If he chose to raise the level
of the lake the boat might suddenly be carried off the land or pulled
under by too short a mooring line. Or, should he choose to lower the
water level, the boat might be stranded high and dry on the rocks a
good distance from the water. In fact, nothing could be left near the
water's edge, because this moved independently of any natural pattern. The water power company had set out high water marks above
which it was supposedly safe to build and to store supplies, but these
marks could not be trusted. We watched the lake from the cabin, and
if the water rose too high we would run down and pull the boats
further up the slope. The Kuhmunens had already lost one boat on
this lake, and Lars told me he had no intention of losing another.

On cold windy days the net froze stiff, like a wire fence, as we
pulled it out of the water. Our hands became numb with cold and a
wet spray stung our faces. Just to keep the boat in one place required
great effort at the oars. Overhead, bad weather battled with the good.
Sunshine speckled one side of the lake while curtains of rain hid the

other. Sea gulls faced the wind like kites on strings, and the water became a patchwork of different colors. Our job would be done in miserable silence.

If the weather was too stormy, it was unsafe to venture out on the lake at all. On such days we sat at the table in the big room or reclined on the beds as the wind shook the walls. Those nearest the stove usually fell asleep. Paulus read American westerns in Swedish, and Thomas fussed with his transistor radio. Susanna talked about the old days. She had moved with her family from Karesuando to the Jokkmokk region when just a little girl. The Norwegian border had been largely closed to Swedish reindeer, and the Saami who had been dependent on Norwegian grazing land were forced to seek pasturage for their reindeer elsewhere. But, the summer grazing land available on the Swedish side of the border could not sustain all the Karesuando Saami. Many families were told to take their herds and move to less crowded pasture lands. Although their ancestors had used the land in Norway from time immemorial, before the creation of the separate states, they were forced south. Susanna recalled that they had no idea what awaited them as they set out by caravan, or *rajd,* to the south in the winter. Cunning Swedish merchants in Karesuando had told them that the south was such a brutal wilderness that they would be unable to purchase coffee or flour there. It was best to buy a big supply now before leaving. And so, the poor härks had unnecessarily drawn pulkas loaded with sacks of flour hundreds of miles over the snow.

Like most northern Saami families who were forced south into Central Lapland, Susanna's family did not find an enthusiastic welcome. It was with difficulty that they could even understand the language of the Jokkmokk Saami. Many amusing stories are told of the first encounters between northern and central Saami. Often the same word in each dialect had two totally different meanings. Frequently compliments were mistaken for insults. But, besides this, Susanna explained that the northern Saami from the Karesuando district brought with them a different style of reindeer herding in stark contrast to the tight, family-oriented "intensive herding" of the Jokkmokk Saami. The so-called extensive herding of the northern Saami was a less individualistic form of reindeer herding in which many families combined their reindeer in huge herds that dwarfed

those of the Jokkmokk Saami. Instead of keeping their reindeer separated and closely watched all year, the northern Saami let their herds
wander virtually unattended all summer. When it was time to mark
the newborn calves or slaughter some reindeer, gatherers would be
sent out to bring the herd together and drive them into a corral. The
Jokkmokk Saami, however, practiced intensive herding. They rarely
left their small herds unattended, and they milked the *vajas,* the
female reindeer, daily all summer. The steady surveillance resulted in
very tame reindeer and a close bond between the herder and each of
his animals.

When the huge "wild" herds from the north swept into the Jokkmokk grazing lands, the small separated groups of reindeer were
swamped, mixed and often carried away in the large herds. The Jokkmokk Saami were furious. How could the northern Saami be such
poor reindeer herders that they could not even control their own herds
and keep them from overrunning those of others? The northern Saami
in turn found it odd that the Jokkmokk Saami had not learned to work
together and should fuss so much when their reindeer were mixed.
Reindeer should be free to roam, they argued, and during those long
periods when the reindeer were left alone, how could anyone be held
responsible for their movements? Each group initially looked upon the
other as hopelessly backward.

The controversy had deep-running currents. What Susanna was
touching upon was a process of change in herding methods that
extended far beyond the confrontation of Jokkmokk Saami and Karesuando Saami. Other compelling factors entered the theater of herding
developments and turned herding toward its modern form. As Susanna spoke, her personal account took on a much broader dimension,
and in her simple description of familial problems I could glimpse the
struggles of all herders.

It is now easy to see that the northern Saami form of extensive
herding was bound to win over the classic intensive form. The transition to extensive methods was but the beginning of a great trend in
reindeer herding resulting from the enormous explosion of modern
communication facilities and the increased demands placed upon
northern resources. The relocation of many northern Saami families
supplied the catalyst.

The effects were long range. Suddenly there was practically an unlimited market for reindeer meat due to mobile slaughter facilities and modern market developments. The money made from the sale of reindeer enabled herders to buy a vast amount of new supplies and foods also brought by the communication network. It became unnecessary to milk the vajas in the old intensive manner, and the reindeer's function lapsed to that of transport and slaughter animal. Of course, one can also claim that with the cessation of milking, the herders were forced to buy new foodstuffs. Gradually the reindeer's function as transport animals also became antiquated through the spread of roads, trains, seaplanes, and scooters. Nowadays the reindeer is regarded almost solely as a meat producer. The modern innovations of reindeer herding today are as new to the northern Saami as to the Jokkmokk Saami, and all have changed from a natural to an essentially money-based economy.

Now that herding does not require such constant care as before, now that the grazing lands are shrinking from displacement by the timber industry, mines, hydroelectric power plants, and tourism, now that fencing, scooters, or other technological wonders ease what work is required, the number of men given full-time employment by reindeer herding diminishes steadily. Young people can usually find more profitable ways to spend their time elsewhere, but despite the tremendous decrease in active herders, there always seem to be too many herders and not enough profit. "We can't afford to put more effort into herding, and we can't afford to quit," said Susanna, summing up the quandary of the modern herder. More effort would not be rewarded by a proportionate rise in earnings, and less effort might completely ruin the family's tight budget.

Like everyone else, herders now center their efforts on the need for ready cash instead of only the natural harvest from the reindeer and the land. Money economy is no longer simply an attractive alternative affording luxuries and new comforts, it is a vital need. And so, the lure of highly paid jobs is hard to resist. As the supportive capacity of herding declines, other jobs gain in importance. It is easy to be drawn away from active herding bit by bit without really knowing it.

The extensive herding today is far more extensive than it was only a few years ago. The long periods when the reindeer are left on their own are being prolonged. What was once an entire way of life has for many Saami become just one of a number of part-time jobs. Ironically, whereas industrialization brought many excellent, well-paying jobs to Lapland, once the power plants were built or the train tracks laid, jobs became scarce again. But the change in the local economy was permanent.

As she spoke of familial herding problems, Susanna showed a remarkably clear perception of the pressures for change. But could perception of the process of change in any way affect the eventual result? Susanna's knowledge did not appear to help her at all. The modern age seemed to rear up like a huge dragon, trampling traditions and cultures underfoot. "Not every family has the same type of economy now," Susanna said. "Many have seen that they must not have so extensive a form of herding if they hope to continue herding at all. Little by little the part-time jobs are becoming more and more scarce. We have given up the Saami life to earn money and now there is no money. It is easy to go from intensive herding to extensive herding or simply to become more extensive, but it is almost impossible to go back. The reindeer become wilder the less they are attended, and the young Saami don't know how to live with them, only how to sell them for slaughter. We all live better now than we did before, we are more comfortable and we don't have to work so hard, but it is as if we have paid for this with our future. There is no future for us as Saami."

Susanna's words were far more than the words of a wise elder who had seen much of a life so different from mine. They were words bearing the simple dignity of the human being beyond the motley web of culture and time. What struck me was not the considerable difference between our lives, the great multiplicity of the human condition, but rather the reverse, the essential likeness we all share as people beneath all our guises. In facing the end, when a culture and way of life slowly wither and die, a glimpse appears of the human beings, beyond bitterness or alienation. And in their plight we can recognize ourselves. As if in death, a culture suddenly becomes self-conscious in a new way. Its members are no longer totally and unquestioningly enveloped by it. Tremendous changes rupture the old shell. We all stand naked to some extent before these changes. Maybe we can hope to find each other more easily under the cold wind.

The more I talked with Susanna, the more I began to realize that my romanticizing of the good old days was often constructed on arguments that, although true, were cultivated by my own attitudes and questions. Certainly, Susanna and many other herders were in many respects adversely affected by the modern transition. Others, however, may have benefited astoundingly as a result of modernization and gradual assimilation. Being incorporated into the Swedish social welfare system has given a comfortable life and a future (though maybe not a Saami future) to many herders who might otherwise have barely survived. It is popular these days to damn the industrial world and idolize the "nature people." When I listened to Susanna without directing the conversation, I found that she was not totally negative about her current life.

"Lars will probably keep some reindeer," Susanna said, "maybe Paulus too, but I don't think Thomas will. He has spent all his life in Jokkmokk at the Swedish school and it is too late for him to be a Saami. To have reindeer is not enough any more. Henrik and I could not continue without our pensions from the government. Per, our third son, has some reindeer but he must work most of the time for the water company at the dam project in Ritsemjokk."

I thought it sadly ironic that so many Saami today are forced into jobs that actively work against the herding life on which they are so strongly dependent and traditionally bound. Few things have harmed the Saami as much as the hydroelectric power industry that builds the big dams like the one on Tjaktjajaure. Not only do the dams create huge artificial reservoirs that flood the most valuable grazing areas—those by the old lake shore—they also force the herders to bring their herd along new and often difficult migration routes. In some lakes, though not all, the natural habitat of the fish has been altered so drastically that they barely survive and fishing is a waste of time. To build a huge dam, full of heavy turbines and complex machinery, a road is needed and after the dam is completed, the road remains, paving the way for easy consumption of the surrounding forests by the timber industry, another serious threat to the grazing lands.

As we sat in the cabin on stormy days or relaxed after work around the table for a cup of coffee, the story of the Kuhmunens' life was gradually pieced together. Once, Lars drew some Xs on my trail map. "These mark where we used to live," he said. All eight Xs were on the blue, indicating that the goahttiehs were underwater. "The first time," said Susanna, "they didn't even tell us about it. The water just rose higher and higher and soon we had to move. The second time we were all called to a big meeting and told that we would be reimbursed for our lost summer homes. We were even given a lawyer to present our case in court, but long before the hearing they had already begun building the dam. Out of our eight lost goahttiehs, we received payment for only one." It was little wonder that no one had bothered to complain to the water company over the loss of a boat.

One fine sunny day, of which there were many at this time of year, Lars and I sat on the front step while he demonstrated the art of engraving designs on reindeer antler. "You must hold the knife at a tilt like this," Lars said. "Press hard into the antler but be careful not to slip." A large scar along the thumb of his left hand showed what happened if one did slip. "Try straight lines first, it takes lots of practice. Carry a piece of scrap antler in your pocket and practice whenever you have nothing to do." Lars could make the most beautiful and intricate patterns with ease. After he had cut the grooves into the antler with his knife, he would lick his finger, push it into his sooty pipe bowl and rub the black charcoal into the engraved surface. The grooves would trap the charcoal and the excess would be wiped away to reveal fascinating geometric patterns in black on the white antler. This is the kind of decorative work one so often sees on Saami reindeer antler knife sheaths and inlaid wooden cups. There are even different design patterns characteristic of different regions. I did not have my pipe to hand, but found I had enough dirt on my fingers to make my wiggly scratches appear with a quick thumb rub.

As we each worked away on our piece of reindeer antler, Lars said abruptly, "Someone is coming today." He spoke with more authority than a guess. "Who?" I asked, assuming someone was expected. "I don't know," he replied. "I just have a feeling, but you'll see, I'm usually right." Sure enough, five hours later a man appeared on foot from the north. It was an old neighbor and friend of Henrik. Coffee was brewed and a plate of char and potatoes put before our new visitor, who proceeded to eat as do most Saami, by using his knife to cut the food and the thumb opposite to hold it. The edge of the knife is deftly turned away and the food is taken into the mouth from the back of the blade. Even a soft slice of bread is cut a bit at a time into bite-size pieces—cut and popped into the mouth in one motion. No one said much, but little by little the old man began to convey the news from the north. News is the traveler's prize possession and should be spent slowly. The conversation was of course in Saami, so I was able to grasp little more than the major topics. Later, when he had finished eating and we all sat relaxed and silent, I asked him about the conditions in the mountains. When he learned I was bound for Stalo, he told me to take the route over Kuorpak to Sito. From there I should take the boat to Akka and walk down the trail to Stalo from the north. The heavy rains had cleared much of the remaining snow, but our visitor cautioned me that the southern route to Stalo was probably still blocked.

The next day the travel fever was upon me. Lars marked the route on my map and gave me all kinds of advice. He knew the country so well that his directions resembled a detailed road map with street numbers and stoplights. Here was the best place to ford a stream and here was the lowest gap to pass through the mountains. Later I was to find that the quality of instruction I received was in inverse proportion to what it was considered I knew. A three-day hike might be described with the admonition to "keep to the right of the marsh." Many is the time I wished I had appeared as ignorant as I proved to be.

Once I reached Sitojaure, I would encounter a trail and there would be no problem, but before that there was a long stretch of overland hiking. All things considered, I should reach Stalo in about a week, weather permitting. Susanna gave me some smoked char for the hike, and Henrik showed me how to make Saami tobacco out of birchbark when he saw that my pipe tobacco can was empty. "A man must have a smoke when he's walking in the mountains," Henrik proclaimed. And indeed the birchbark tobacco was not at all bad, although it could not compare with the real thing. "It's all we had during the war," Henrik said. "Everything was scarce." "Those were hard times," agreed Susanna. "Lots of people starved in the mountains or froze. We were always helping Norwegian refugees. One winter when we reached our goahttieh in Vaisa we found some Norwegians who were so hungry they had eaten up our reindeer hides."

Lars meanwhile had attached some fishing line to a coffee can, added a weight and a lure, presented it to me, and said that with this I should never have to go hungry in the mountains. Almost all the lakes, no matter how small, had char. He demonstrated how to cast the line and coil it up on the can. The can was like a big reel and when turned the right way would release the string like a regular spinner reel. With a little practice it was easy to cast almost as far as one could with a good pole. "The extra beauty of this rig," said Lars, "is that it can be hidden in your pack. The park officials who scour the skies in helicopters for illegal fishing will never suspect you." As a reindeer-herding Saami, Lars could fish openly, whereas I was subject to rigid restrictions.

When I thanked them and started from the cabin, they cautioned me to be careful and not to step on any bears. "If I get in any trouble or break a leg," I said, "I'll just take out my coffee can and start to fish. The helicopter will swoop down on me immediately to check my license and I'll be saved." "Don't be so sure," laughed Lars. "They might just throw you in jail before they fix your leg." I turned for a last glimpse of the Kuhmunens, the cabin and the lake. Then it was all gone behind a screen of delicate birch leaves. Saami do not believe in fussy good-byes. In their lives, full of frequent comings and goings, the word "good-bye" adopts a more serious meaning. "Good-bye" means "I don't think we will meet again." I was sure we would.

2

On to Virihaure

Thoughts are known to outstrip the fastest runner, but I was only walking and had left my mind far behind in Tjaktjajaure. I chuckled again over Henrik's funny stories and wondered how the fishing would go for Lars. Surely he would miss me at the oars, I boasted to myself. But I was enjoying a glorious and gentle day. A light breeze sifted through the birches and made their leaves flutter and sparkle. The high tundra was one enormous sunny meadow. I wanted to lie down in every part of it, roll through all the grass, or make my body big enough to sprawl across all that I saw. On such a day as this my thoughts could not bear to be dwelling elsewhere for long. Memories and conversations were dropped, and my soul was harmonious again as it played through the mountains and forests. Yet with the joy of movement and adventure came also a feeling of solitude that developed into uneasiness. I loved this country, but I did not know all its moods and secrets, and like most beginners, I felt a bit intimidated as I gazed out over the vast mountains I must cross. Eventually, however, I found the rhythm of the trail and began to sweat in earnest under my pack; a hardness crept into me, and I was ready at last to struggle through whatever land and water could offer and enjoy it all.

After a few hours of walking, it gradually became plain what my first trial would be. A painful blister was developing on my right foot. Hiking over the wet Lapland tundra requires knee-high rubber boots, and these boots are notorious for causing blisters. The Saami use shoe grass instead of socks. This special grass molds itself to the foot, makes a soft cushion and absorbs all sweat. Blisters never form. I swore with every step that I would use some grass the first chance I got, and cursed my heavy pack for all its unnecessary contents.

At Kuorpak I turned to follow a stream through a small wooded valley. On one side of the valley, just above the trees, was a huge corral enclosed by a wire fence. Kuorpak was a favorite gathering place for autumn reindeer slaughters and winter herd separations. In scattered clearings along the stream stood bare tent poles, skeletons around circular stone hearths. These hearths would hold fires and the tent poles support canvas homes during the few days of work at the corral each year. Farther down the stream and up the other side of the valley stood the crumbled ruins of four old turf goattiehs. A few families had undoubtedly stopped here for a time during their seasonal migrations to and from the lowlands. In the old days a family might have many different stopping points and many different homes suited to the variety of seasons along the migration route. Modern transportation facilities—train, car, seaplane, snow "scooter"—as well as the growth of ever looser, collective (extensive) herding patterns have eliminated this need. Technology has given people more independence, and they need no longer adapt so totally to the natural cycle. Most reindeer herding families in the Jokkmokk district today have no more than two or sometimes three main homes: one winter home in the lowlands, one summer home in the mountains, and occasionally one in between at the spring-autumn camp. The crumbling old structures I now confronted had become obsolete. I could not help imagining the life and the noise that had once surrounded these goattiehs, now just broken and sagging domes of wood and turf. Only the blackened hearth stones appeared untouched by time. Perhaps, I speculated fancifully, there is a fire spirit living in each hearth, and rather than building a new fire each time, we are instead waking the spirit and conjuring him up again. We coax him forth with offerings of wood. What stories from long ago we could learn from the spirits of these hearths. But no fire had warmed these stones for many years; their spirits slept with the past.

From the top of this hill where the old goattiehs stood rotting, I had a wide view and could survey the route I would take to Sitojaure.

The birch forest died away as the valley sloped into the high tundra land. I wanted to cross to the other side of the valley and should have realized that although the distance would be longer, I would make much better time and see more if I swung around the woods in a horseshoe path keeping to the high tundra. Instead, unacquainted with the land as I was, I plunged back into the trees for the straightest route. I had also to learn what type of ground looks marshy but will hold a person and what looks marshy but is worse than it looks. No sooner had I left the hill than I was knee-deep in mud and water. The mosquitoes, which had been scarce on the wind-swept heights, were plentiful in the birch woods. To pause was to be consumed by the swarm, and the trees were so low that I had to claw my way through them, giving the mosquitoes ample opportunity to strike. It seemed as if the mosquitoes had established a profitable evolutionary relationship with the trees based on the advantages of snagging stupid hikers. It was a trap. Thoroughly discouraged, I abandoned my initial plan and simply did my best to fight my way out of the woods.

Still this folly was not without its reward. There right before me in an open, treeless mire of water and green moss, where only a fool like me would blunder, stood a huge moose cow with her two calves. The mother moose and I froze simultaneously, staring at each other. The two small calves, which could not have been more than a few months old, did not seem to mind my presence at all. Their bodies were so small and their legs so long that they reminded me of flamingos as they walked. The large cow lumbered slowly to the fringe of trees and was gone from sight, although I knew her to be close. I was surprised to see how such a huge ungainly creature could hide herself so perfectly behind a few light trees. The calves continued to pick their way over the marsh with their peculiar birdlike walk and regarded me curiously from time to time before drifting calmly from view. When I began to move again after a few minutes, it was as if something from the quiet scene had subtly affected me. I was no longer fighting my way through the tangled branches or sloshing angrily over soggy ground. I wanted to preserve the silence and be part of it.

Eventually I reached the treeless tundra, where I could see far and wide and where I could move fast and easily. Though hungry and tired I had never considered stopping in the confining and mosquito-ridden forest. Now as I sat on a rock, just to gaze at the view, I told myself, the unusually long pause this view inspired forced me to admit that I was in terrible physical condition, and gazing was not the only reason for sitting. I also had a yearning for a cool drink. There is no need to carry water in this land. Always there is either some cold, clear running water close at hand or else a convenient patch of snow. Beware of gulping cold water on the move, Lars had told me, for soon you'll be drinking like a horse at every pool and stream, and you will become weaker and weaker. The Saami way, I was to discover, was to cook coffee at every stream, that is, when there was no need to hurry. Probably every hiker has heard of the ills of drinking large quantities of cold water when on the trail, but every one has surely ignored the caution and had to relearn its validity time after time. At this point, I convinced myself that a cold drink as opposed to a hot cup of coffee was largely just a matter of custom and Lars's warning just a rationale brewed from the grounds of tradition. At least a little swig of mountain fresh water could not hurt. After all, wild animals cannot cook coffee and they seem to keep themselves in fine fettle. The water was delicious. I gathered some dried wood, built a small fire and fried a smoked char. Soon I was downing cup after cup of mountain water along with the char. When moving again, I became extremely thirsty, weak and in no time could hear Lars saying he told me so. A hiker who needs a full head of steam to move far through difficult terrain, should not continually douse his boilers with cold water.

Before long I was sitting to gaze at the landscape again. The sky was becoming darker, and black clouds swept in from the west with amazing speed. The air below was still and oddly thin, while up above the heavens streaked by and the clouds grumbled. The storm gates were about to open. It was obvious that I would get no farther today. It was best to find a good spot, set up the tent and huddle until it was over. The first drops hit me before I could unpack the tent. I had to race against the storm. Later I would come to know the character of every knot, and the placement of every pin involved in the erection of my portable house, but at that time I had formed no routine at all and fumbled about frantically. A ceiling of water crashed down just as I crawled into the tent. Thunder followed closely on lightning. My frying pan glowed with a strange light outside, where I had left it. The wind descended and threatened to carry the tent away in full sail. At such a time, one is little more than an exposed oyster on the half shell.

A Saami in my shoes, I imagined, would have seen the storm coming long before I did. He or she might have gathered some wood to keep it dry and would probably have thought to fill pots with water in order to enjoy coffee, cooked over a camp burner just under the rain roof by the doorway. He or she would relax in comfort and most likely snooze. I was not comfortable and I could not relax. I did not lack physical comforts, but I was totally ignorant of weather, which throughout life I had done little more than watch occasionally from a window. I did not know what to expect or how to react.

I could understand the desire of so many people nowadays "to return to Nature," to be self-sufficient and live off the land. Granted one would learn a lot; yet, I could not sympathize with anyone who refused to use a steel ax if available. I would not be opposed to using any modern appliance myself if in so doing I was not destroying the kind of life I wanted. I could see how this would call for difficult value judgments. For example, if everyone did as I did, would there be a chance of living as I wanted? And what if someone else wanted a different life which my life-style excluded? Then again, would it be fair if everyone could be satisfied today with the result that our children could not tomorrow? I am sure we have all pondered such matters repeatedly. I cannot pretend to have worked out any revolutionary insights. I shall probably be grappling with such questions all my life, and I feel this is as it should be.

When stuck for a long time in a tent alone, issues such as these are easy to find. I admired the Saami to whom storms and snows were matters of course and who knew how to deal with them. The older Saami certainly suffered great hardships, and today have taken advantage of imported technology to lead more comfortable lives. Yet without nylon tents, rubber boots, and aluminum poles, they were able so to adapt to this often harsh environment that what we might think a hardship could be faced with enjoyment and with no feeling of insecurity or discomfort. We would never have survived long enough to experience what they considered hardship.

The storm raged all night but had spent itself by early morning. The sun shone weakly and the grass looked tired and bent. The birds gave a feeble morning chorus, but their song held little courage after such a beating. The world heaved a sigh of relief. I was soon packed and on my way.

I reached Sitojaure by late afternoon. Sito is one of Sirkas Sameby's summer villages and beautifully situated by a large lake right at the foot of the high mountains. The long revolving sunset framed the white mountains with red and purple. Of the nine or ten goattiehs by the lake shore, only a few were yet occupied for the summer. The first person I met was not a stranger at all—John Andersson, brother to Johan Märak. We had met earlier in Jokkmokk and were both surprised at seeing each other here. John worked for the Swedish Tourist Organization and was busy repairing the Sitojaure boat supplied for traffic across the lake. He was also there to open the small tourist cabin. Today, however, John informed me was not a work day. It was Midsummer, the longest day of the year and a national holiday. "Today is the day to celebrate," he announced. "We should be in town. There will be lots of pretty girls and lots to drink, all day feasting and dancing too." He admitted that he could not dance but it was fun just to watch the girls.

Like most Saami in Sweden today, John was dressed in modern clothes, synthetic materials and rubber boots. It is not that the new clothes are better than the old, but that the old clothes require a great deal of time and plenty of skill to make. Not many Saami can still sew the reindeer-skin summer shoes with waterproof seams, once standard footwear. But knowledge of survival techniques in the mountains are not about to be forgotten by a man like John, who spends most of his life there alone. When he saw the condition of my foot, he immediately offered me some shoe grass from his pack plus a torrent of accompanying advice. I should heat the soles of my feet by the fire and whip them with birch branches to make them tough. I should pack the shoe grass in a special way that resembled a bird nest before inserting my foot, and I should be sure to spread it out to dry each evening. John had a most friendly face and at times a special serious squint that pursed his mouth in preparation for a volley of words. He overflowed with helpfulness and always seemed to have a positive attitude. Expressions of "fantastic" peppered his conversation.

After a short but profound rest I was sitting in the hikers' cabin, contemplating my foot. All at once the door burst open and a Saami I had never seen before asked me if I was "Choo." "Choo," I soon discovered, is Saami for "Hugh." "I'm Lasse Åstot and John told me you were here," he said. "We want you to come help us celebrate Midsummer in my goattieh." I grabbed the remainder of my cognac certain that the occasion demanded a toast. Nothing suited me better than the thought of lightening my heart and pack at once. Lasse led me down a disorienting path in the pale light until we came to a large goattieh with a cozy orange light in the window. John lay inside on a moose hide and waved me in. "Now that you have rested you must join us." He had a freshly cooked pot of coffee and handed me a large wooden cup. When he saw the cognac he laughed with delight. "Fantastic, now we can have a real toast. How in the world did you manage to get so far with all that?" "We will show you an old Saami toast," said Lasse. John produced a copper coin and put it into my empty coffee cup. Lasse poured in a little coffee and John began filling it up with cognac. "When you can read the date on the coin I'll stop," he said. This took a good deal of cognac. Lasse and John filled their cups and we "skoaled" to the midnight sun. (I have encountered drinks mixed in this amusing fashion in a number of counties, but while its derivation might be contested by ethnographers, I doubt Lasse was even aware of the debate. The old Saami did not have to invent the custom to practice it, and we enjoyed carrying it further.)

John and Lasse spoke of people they had known, strange characters, and strange happenings. John was a master storyteller, narrating not only ancient myths and sayings but unusual things that had happened to him, his father, or friends. I forgot who I was and where I was as I listened. What had once been a clear boundary between reality and fiction became vague and confused. How could John have seen something that I could not believe in? I have always been partial to the skeptical slogan of seeing before believing. I began to wonder, however, if this seemingly faithful test of reality might in fact close me off from those powers and perceptions I refused to credit. Believing might be a prerequisite for seeing. Although I myself have never experienced any supernatural powers, my Saami friends have often astounded me with their telepathy and dream predictions. Seeing these powers in others confounds my reason.

This midsummer evening John surrounded us with mystery and wonder; all questions, excuses, and explanations fell away. I remain a stubborn disbeliever in ghosts, but some of John's ghost stories will never leave me alone. I remember well one story in particular, although I cannot hope to tell it the same way John did.

It was in December, not really so long ago, when families used to move together by *rajd,* or caravan, in pulkas down to the winter land. An old Jokkmokk Saami was leading the way down a long slope when suddenly the härk pulling his pulka began acting crazy. It refused to go ahead, and bucked in fright almost turning the pulkas over. The man jumped out and calmed his härk, but soon the incident happened again. The härk had always been one of the best and the man realized that something he could not see was scaring it. Maybe someone had been murdered here, or perhaps the *gadniha,* people of the underworld, for some reason did not want him to pass this way. He grabbed the härk, lifted up the harness strap and peered out under it. This enabled him to see the supernatural. There ahead was a tiny baby clawing its way over the snow with incredible strength, naked and wailing. It was an *äparis.*

These spirits were unwanted children, usually born out of wedlock, and killed by their mothers. It was a horrible thing to do and was commonly done in secrecy. The murdered baby would die without baptism and without a name. Because of this, its soul could not rest. It would wander endlessly crying and terrifying folk until someone gave it a name. An äparis can be so frightening and terrible that it is best to run away. If one can manage to cross some open water there is safety, for the äparis cannot follow, but some Saami have memorized parts of the baptismal ritual and are able to "put down" an äparis and give it a name without fear.

The old man was terrified. He could not "meet" an äparis and he was angry too, because the äparis had frightened his härk and threatened to put the entire caravan in a frenzy. "Go away," he shouted, "go away. I haven't bothered you. I haven't caused your pain. Why don't you go take a just revenge on the one who did this to you and leave us alone?" Suddenly the äparis was gone, the härk calmed down and the man continued on his way. He could hear the tinkling bells of the other härks behind pulling the rest of his family in a long line. Then he heard the dogs barking and people shouting. Everything had been thrown into confusion behind him. He turned and hurried back. His oldest daughter lay dead in her pulka, a shoe band around her neck.

Despite such sobering tales, John, Lasse, and I had an exhaustingly cheerful time. When I finally trudged off to sleep, I was told to pick seven different kinds of wild flowers, put them under my pillow and not utter a word until I awoke. If I carried out these instructions, I would dream of the one I was to marry, at least according to Swedish custom. John and Lasse both admitted to have had fantastic Midsummer dreams by this method, but neither of them had managed to marry any of their apparitions, or anyone else for that matter.

My start was understandably late, and I hiked along with a grumpy gait. I had not spoken to anyone since I had started picking the seven varieties of wild flowers, and even now I did not feel like starting. As soon as I left the village there was no one to talk to, luckily, and I could try to recall the visions of my dreams. I could not remember anything at all, something which I decided meant only that I would not be married before next Midsummer. In fact, I considered myself fortunate not to have dreamed of John's ghosts.

Two days later I reached Ritsemjokk, once a charming Saami village and now the site of a huge electrical power plant. Across the water, Akka, the great mountain cluster, dominated the view and stood as a cornerstone for the three great national parks, Sarek, Padjelanta, and Stora Sjöfallet, the first two of which contain much of the Jokkmokk Saami summer grazing land. It was on the lands now submerged under the Akka reservoir that the Kuhmunens had once lived. The northern end of the tourist trail that ran by Staloluokta started at Akka. The area is crisscrossed by Saami trails, but though these may exist plainly in the minds of the Saami, they are not marked in any way on the ground, and for a greenhorn such as I it would be foolish to attempt anything but the well-marked tourist trail, or the "turnpike," as it is called by the Saami at the height of the hiking season. Although I was very glad that the tourist season had not yet begun, this meant that the boat service across the lake to Änonjalme, the encampment near the base of Akka, had not begun either. The only way across at this time of year was by private boat.

Luck was with me; some workers from the power plant were about to cast off from shore with bread and guns to lure sea gulls to their death. They had nothing against steering a course to the other side of the lake with an extra passenger. Largely because of the massive exploitation of the mountain zones by man, the sea gull population has exploded in the mountain lakes. They are most unwelcome, for they help propagate various parasites, some of which are detrimental to the fish and others which can moreover by harmful to the fisherman. Certain parasites reside in the fish's intestines and prevent it from becoming fat. If a sea gull should eat any intestines from an infected fish that a fisherman had failed to bury after cleaning his catch, the gull will spread the parasite to other lakes. Should someone be careless in cooking and ingest parasites from the fish, some of these parasites can develop into binicky worms in the person's intestines. Saami fishing in even the most remote mountain lakes are now plagued by gulls and the binicky worm problem. To control the problem by shooting the gulls was a solution I considered both unjust and ineffective, so I was glad to see that their association with man had taught the gulls some tricks of their own. They kept their distance until the boat had moved out of range and then they dove on the bread. In the end, all we accomplished was to feed the birds.

In Änonjalme I knocked on a goattieh door hoping to obtain some smoked fish. It might be a few days before I reached the next Saami village and would have another chance to buy fresh food, and I was not at all looking forward to the packaged freeze-dried meals I carried with me. The door of this goattieh, I noticed, was unusually wide.

"Come on in, with your pack too," said a large, hearty, middle-aged Saami woman. "That's why I've put up such a wide door. Hikers these days have such broad packs." Her name was Sara Harnesk. She threw another stick on the fire and put on the coffee pot. As we drank she complained about the poor fishing. "It's all because of the dam, raising and lowering the water as if this lake were a coffee cup, never full and never empty for long. The eggs the fish lay near the shore one day are on a mountain side the next." The dam she spoke of was only one of eleven built along the same lake-river chain for hydroelectric power.

Sara's anger rose as she talked, and she had an amazing way of making the fire flare, spraying sparks as she punctuated her words with a poker. I listened and watched, spellbound.

I noticed that the sticks she threw on the fire were of almost uniform size and many had carvings, names of people and places. I glanced at the wood pile and found it totally made up of such sticks; obviously they were walking sticks. "This is the end of the trail," Sara said when she saw my curiosity. "That's one good thing about all these campers. They leave me their sticks, and I don't have to collect firewood." As she leaned back and gave a great loud laugh, I saw her suddenly as a mythical being, sitting at the end of the trail and burning the walking sticks of men, and in their smoke learning of the long ways they had come. Her face told me she understood my musings, and her laughter held far more than simple humor.

The man who had given me the ride across the lake appeared at the door and greeted Sara rather sheepishly. She did not want to speak to him at first, but soon their quarrel was in the open. Last summer the power plant worker had come over in his boat and ordered twenty flat breads, *glödkakor,* from Sara. She had baked all day but the man had never returned for his order. The bread had gone stale and after two weeks she had had to throw it out. "So now you come back one year later and expect me to have your bread for you," Sara said angrily. Actually the man did have hopes of buying some fresh bread from her, but she was difficult to placate. "There was no possible way I could have collected the bread last summer," he said, "you know yourself it stormed constantly all those two weeks and nobody could cross the lake." A compromise was finally agreed upon, but Sara could not resist calling after him as he left, "Do you know why there are so many sea gulls this year? It's because they were given your twenty flat cakes last year."

Staloluokta was three or at most four days on the trail from Änonjalme, but so many days of continuous good weather is too much for the mountains to apportion all at once. It was already late when I left Sara's, but I discovered I liked walking at "night" much more than during the day. In the evening the sun is low, the colors are fantastic, the air is cool, and there are few mosquitoes. If needed, there are conveniently located hikers' cabins along the trail, thanks to the Swedish Tourist Organization and the Bureau of Crown Land Management. By early morning I had come a good distance and was ready to rest when I saw below me on the shore of a lake a number of goattiehs. Here was an opportunity to hear some news, buy some fish, and maybe have a cup of coffee.

One goattieh emitted a healthy column of smoke. I looked forward to relaxing by the fire and hearing of the trail ahead, but I was not in the least prepared for what met me when the door opened. Instantly I was hit with a blast of heat, and there before me on a bench sat an old man, totally nude. A large wood stove with a layer of rocks on top sustained a furious blaze. I had unwittingly walked into a *bastu,* or sauna bath. The man poured water from a nearby bucket over the hot rocks, and then with a loud hiss billows of steam filled the goattieh. This was an unheard-of luxury, the dream of all tired hikers, and on his invitation, I was soon stripped and sitting beside him on the bench. After a long, hot stint in the bastu, we ran outside and directly into the lake. "Damn." I was out of the water as fast as I had entered it. When I recovered from the shock of the cold I noticed that there were still large pieces of ice floating in the lake. I have never had much bravery in facing cold water, but now that it was over, I felt wonderfully invigorated. My sauna companion produced a delicious cup of coffee with artful timing, and we sat inside his "real" goattieh and chatted as the storm clouds once again came together overhead. I should rest the day here, he cautioned, because all hell was about to break loose. Already the fog was so thick on the mountains ahead of me that there was no way I could see where I was going. And so I spent the day with this kindly host and slept through most of the storm on the reindeer hide he provided. The fire glowed inside as the rain poured outside, and I gloried in the fact that this night I was in a snug goattieh instead of my tent. There is nothing like a tent to make one appreciate a goattieh.

Toward early morning the next day it looked as if the sky would clear. The tops of the mountains peeked shyly from between shifting clouds of fog. "This time of year it never looks much better than that," said my host. I thanked him warmly and hurried on my way to get over the pass before the weather could take a turn for the worse. The higher up I climbed, the more I encountered a winter landscape. The view from the heights was remarkable. Snow blanketed the upper slopes, and the streams had not yet dug themselves free of their snow tunnels. I could hear the water roaring underneath and see in spots a brief cascade of spray where it had gnawed its way through the snow. Farther below, a number of lakes were still encumbered with huge, floating plates of ice. The mountain tops served as seats for the clouds, which would stream out like banners clutching the peaks when the wind intensified in the way seaweed catches on pilings and waves with the current. Reindeer tracks ran to and fro like long, thin, dotted lines over the snow. At times I could see small reindeer flocks with the tiny calves, no more than two months old, running beside their mothers.

When I reached the village of Arasluokta at the foot of these mountains on an arm of the huge lake Virihaure, I learned that I had left the Sirkas Sameby's summer land behind and entered the Jåkkå-kaska Sameby's region. Arasluokta was the Jåkkåkaska Saami main summer village just as Staloluokta was the summer headquarters of most Tuorpon Saami. Although most of my ensuing time would be spent with Tuorpon, I was soon to learn the necessity of a broad acquaintance with the nearby villages and their surroundings. No Sameby functions in complete isolation from its neighbors. In order to understand the herding practices of one Sameby, the often complex relationships with its neighboring Samebys cannot be ignored. At this point it may be helpful to know how the Samebys in this area are situated.

In the latter part of the nineteenth century, an "Agricultural Line" was drawn lengthwise through northern Sweden. The region "above," or west of the line was to be closed to farming settlement and pre-served for Saami reindeer herding. The government of the time was as concerned with stopping settlers from becoming "Saamified" as it was with preventing herders from becoming settled. With special permis-sion, however, there is some small-scale herding east of the line, and when needed, herders may bring their reindeer across the line all the way down to the Baltic coast depending upon season and traditional usage. Nor can the Agricultural Line be said to have stopped all settlement to the west. The line was nonetheless historically signifi-

Mountain Samebys in
the Jokkmokk Region

0 km 10   20   30   40

═══ Mountain Sameby borders defining
       year-round grazing areas

cant. The map demonstrates its influence. Almost all land that the
Samebys can utilize year round are apportioned west of the Agricultural Line.

The northernmost Swedish province, Norrland, is subdivided
into districts, which are in turn subdivided into municipalities. Some
of these municipalities—for example, Kiruna, Gällivare, Jokkmokk,
and Arjeplog, which are west of the Agricultural Line—are named
after a major town or city within its environs. The herding of the
Saami is administered under the Department of Agriculture in Sweden
with local offices in the major herding districts. Of course, it is always
difficult to fit the herding of the Saami onto a jurisdictional grid
designed with many other things in mind. Reindeer and herders have a

notorious and healthy disrespect for borders of any kind. Sameby grazing territories, those land entities which the Saami can use for herding, hunting and fishing (within certain limits) encompass much of the northern municipalities. Jokkmokk Municipality contains the *mountain* Samebys Sirkas, Jåkkåkaska, and Tuorpon, as well as the smaller *forest* Samebys Serri and Udtja. Such divisions are of most immediate importance to reindeer herding.

Tuorpon and Luokta-Mavas, the Sameby just south of Tuorpon, let their herds mingle freely in the summer land. A long fence separates major portions of Sirkas and Jåkkåkaska lands and another divides Jåkkåkaska from Tuorpon. Nonetheless, regardless of fencing, a considerable amount of scattering does occur across Sameby borders. Hard snows can destroy a section of fencing or build a drift over it. Alternatively, the reindeer might take a route over the high peaks where no fence can stop them. It is not at all uncommon to find Sirkas reindeer in the Jåkkåkaska grazing lands or Jåkkåkaska reindeer in the Tuorpon area. The mixing of herds demands cooperation between the Samebys. Communication between them is a necessity.

News is always at a premium in the mountains, however, whether it concerns herding events or not. The "Saami telegraph" was apparently open to other concerns. Shortly after my arrival in Arasluokta, I learned from the Jåkkåkaska Saami that Isak Parfa and his family had just recently come to Staloluokta. This bit of information meant that the supply store would be open; and since Staloluokta was only a short hop away on another arm of the same lake, I realized there was no longer any need to hoard my supplies. Best to enjoy immediately what today is a luxury and tomorrow will be commonplace.

The next morning after a short hike cutting between the water and the mountain, Stuora Titir, I spied the goattiehs of Staloluokta spread out along the shore of Lake Virihaure. The ridge at the far end of the village was occupied by a large tourist cabin built for hikers by the Bureau of Crown Land Management, and nearby stood an incredibly beautiful goattieh church built by Saami from the village. Everywhere people were busily moving about as they cleaned and renovated their summer quarters. Birch branches had to be cut for the goattieh floors, and nets had to be laid out in the lake. In the midst of all this activity, I now searched for a familiar face. The only person I had even met in "Stalo," as I learned to call the village, was Isak Parfa.

The Parfa dog, Beppo, signaled my arrival loudly. When I entered the Parfa goattieh, Isak's wife, Anna, was baking bread over a fire on a flat stone. Baking over an open flame is hot work, and I came to understand that Saami women do not take too kindly to strangers who interrupt them during this job. It is polite to say that the bread will be spoiled if too many eyes watch. Anna was at the height of efficiency, and my business was rapidly kneaded in with the dough. Anna wore a scarf around her forehead to absorb sweat and hold back her hair. She had on a faded apron and was surrounded by her baking implements as she knelt by the fire. Anna was not one to beat around the bush with a lot of useless phrases. When she spoke it was plain that here was a woman who said just what she thought. And what she thought often made people somewhat uncomfortable, to her amusement. "So, here comes the first tourist after my cakes, already! I can't even get one batch made for myself alone." And while I was explaining that my primary purpose was not to buy cakes (although they certainly smelled good), she had already put a tray with fresh, hot buttered bread and coffee before me. Anna would roll the dough flat into a round shape, poke it with a fork to prevent puffing, and then slide it onto the baking stone. When baked on one side, the bread was removed, the other side turned toward the fire, and the whole piece propped up against a hearth stone, close down beside the embers until browned (hence the Swedish name *glödkaka,* meaning "ember cake"). It looked terribly easy.

When I had finished this wonderful snack, Anna had finished pumping me for information about people and weather on the trail. I left her to her baking and, with the help of her instructions, found Isak. Isak had not been sure when and if I would appear in Stalo, but he made a quick inquiry down the hill and ushered me to a goattieh I could use for the summer. This was a delightful goattieh (and one to which after five summers of occupancy I have become quite attached). It had been built by Isak's brother, Nils-Tomas, but was hardly ever used by him. A pile of small birch trees that Nils-Tomas had towed from the other side of he lake on his scooter sled in the spring lay nearby. I could saw up the firewood I needed. I set about arranging the hearth stones and collecting fresh birch branches for the floor.

Suddenly, as I looked up from my labors, there stood before me a little girl eating fresh strawberries with whipped cream. After having hiked three days while eating only freeze-dried mush, I was intrigued to see this dish in a remote wilderness village. "Lundqvist brought them," she said as she scampered away. The strawberries, however, remained a mystery until Lundqvist's seaplane landed another day with a supply of food, engine parts, and mail. The Saami sold him almost all of the fish they did not eat themselves. Lundqvist, who serviced all the nearby Saami groups, freighted their fish by the crate full down to his deep freeze, at Lusbybryggan, in the lowlands for further distribution to the cities in the south.

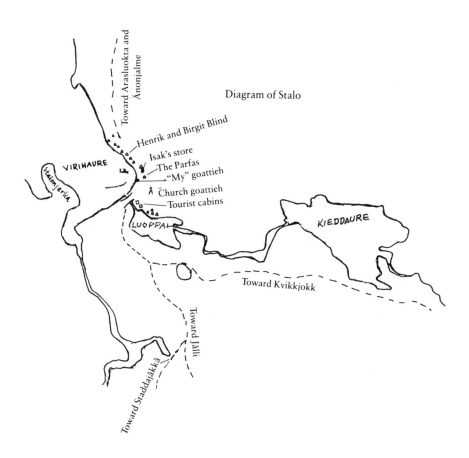

I placed an order with Lundqvist for flour, syrup, and yeast, and the next day I began making dough. In no time I was covered with a sticky mess. I even had dough in my beard. The baking fared no better, and Anna laughed uproariously when I emerged, smeared with dough, holding a few ugly little cakes that were burnt completely black. I continued baking, to Anna's secret amusement, and whenever she was out of bread she took great joy in sending all hungry hikers who had heard of her wonderful bread over to my goattieh. Some hikers were desperate enough to want to buy even my cakes; most tactfully withdrew their interest. Her sense of humor, however, just made me all the more stubborn, and in time even my bread evoked no laughter.

Finally in Stalo I found a true resting place and made my own home. Like most turf goattiehs, mine had a window at the back opposite the door. The hearth, or *arran,* was in the center, directly under *riehpen,* the smoke hole. Between the hearth and the window

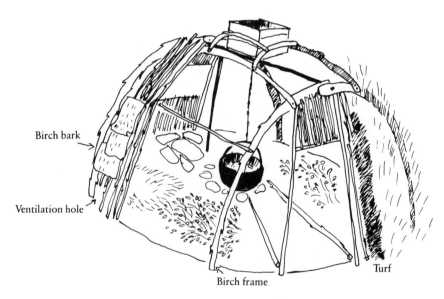

Birch bark

Ventilation hole

Birch frame

Turf

Goattieh Interior

was the kitchen area, the *boassjo,* and from the hearth in the opposite direction to the door was the narrow entranceway, *uksa,* bordered on each side by a large birch log called *biermes.* Wood for the fire was stacked here in the entranceway. A single birch beam crossed high above the hearth and dangled a long sooty chain with a hook on the end down into the fire. This hook could be raised and lowered to any height convenient for suspending kettles over the flames. The same beam was perfect for drying clothes or smoking fish, but in this case a part of the beam not directly over the fire was used. Food should be cold smoked and not cooked in the heat from the smoke fire unless it is to be eaten immediately.

The two sides of the goattieh, *luojddo,* were by far the largest partitions and served as living and sleeping room. Both sides were carpeted with a generous amount of birch branches and these in turn covered with moose or reindeer hides. My nearest neighbor, Johan Parfa, brother to Isak and Nils-Tomas, had shown me how to slap the branches down by the handful in a well-ordered pattern to lay the floor. He lent me a number of hides, and I soon had the largest, most springy mattress in the world. At night I would lie back in a forest of green leaves and smell the air of the outdoors.

Only the kitchen and the entranceway were not covered by branches. A number of flat rocks formed the kitchen floor. The coffee kettle, pots, and pans stood here as well as a bucket for fresh water and one for garbage and dirty water. It is a taboo among the Saami to step over the kitchen in crossing from one side of the goattieh to the other. The boassjo was a sacred area to the pre-Christian Saami, and the old tradition is still very much respected. One must always pass from one side to the other side of a goattieh by crossing over the entranceway by the door instead. At first I disregarded the custom when alone in my goattieh, but I soon found the rule a wise one. In stepping over the kitchen it is all too easy to kick sand and dirt into the food and water.

Anyone who has spent some time in a goattieh is used to having all his food spiced with reindeer hair shed from the hides on the floor. Trying to pick these hairs from the food is like trying to swat every mosquito. Reindeer hair has been known to find its way into a tooth paste tube. Nils-Tomas had read an anthropologist's estimate that a

Saami consumes a reindeer hide worth of hair per year. The report went on to claim this as the cause for the remarkable health of the Saami. I felt the conclusion as shaky as the estimate, but it is certainly true that everyone living in a goattieh eats a lot of reindeer hair. Fortunately, however, each reindeer hair is hollow, causing it to be an especially fine insulator, very brittle, and somehow therefore, not at all irritating to the mouth.

Just under the window and behind the kitchen floor stones stood a tiny cupboard for food supplies or valuables, anything needing protection from the small rodents, *sorks,* or rats as we called them, though really they were only field mice. Around the bottom edge of the goattieh wall at regularly spaced intervals were six vent holes which aired the goattieh and kept the smoke rising through the smoke hole instead of choking the interior. These vents could easily be blocked should the wind blow too hard, but they were usually open, and it was through these that the sorks would creep when all were asleep. Frequently they do not have the courtesy to wait until their hosts are asleep. Actually, sorks rarely do any damage if one takes precautions, but they could be terribly irritating. I have become so angered at night when disturbed by their constant scampering that I have heaved shoes and frying pans at them into the darkness to achieve temporary respect.

In a goattieh one is always sitting or lying on the floor. No furniture is needed. Everything is simple and practical. The dining room, living room, and bedroom are one. Everything is within easy reach. I soon learned to roll around, build a fire, cook, and eat without ever getting up. The same fire which cooked dinner, supplies heat and light as well. I have never lived more comfortably. I could scoop delicious cool water from a spring only a few steps away. A small outhouse and a garbage pit where I emptied my waste bucket were ideally located. There was no dusting of furniture or waxing of floors, fixing the sink or paying the electricity bill. The goattieh life is an outdoor life. If it rains it makes a difference, and if it is cold it makes a difference; one is always in touch with the weather. I could lie on my back and watch the sky through the smoke hole, or if it stormed I would conduct my own campaign to meet it. As the rain clouds gathered I would chop a good wood supply, bring it inside, and pile it in the entranceway where it would stay dry. Over the smoke hole, I built a wire bird cage–like contraption, which I had seen on top of the other goattiehs, and by draping a piece of canvas over it and leaving a hole at the side, for the smoke to escape, I could continue to have a blaze inside no matter how hard it rained.

Of course, there were some petty annoyances too. If the wind suddenly shifted during a rain storm at night, the smoke would not continue to rise through the hole in the canvas covering as before. Instead it might be forced back down into the goattieh and fill it completely. I would have to struggle out of my sleeping bag, into coat and boots and run out in the rain up the small ladder to the roof in order to orient the canvas in a new direction. Many times I remember grumbling to myself on the roof in the cold rain and looking up along the line of goattiehs to see my neighbors equally sour and hastily garbed fussing with canvas and plastic.

Mosquitoes were also a problem. The hot air and smoke from the fire would clear the interior of mosquitoes, but once the fire and I slumbered, the persistent devils were back. I quickly adopted yet another Saami invention, the *rakkas*. The rakkas is simply a bottomless tent strung up inside the goattieh without poles. A person can crawl under it and tuck in the sides all around so as to be completely enclosed. Not only is the rakkas a perfect mosquito screen, it also affords additional warmth as well as some privacy. Like beds, there are double as well as the single rakkas.

Everyone faced the same predicament each morning—how to leave the comfort of the blankets or sleeping bag to brave the chill until a fire could be built and coffee brewed. It did not take me long "to become as lazy as a Saami," according to Johan Parfa. I would gather firewood and birch bark together the night before, fill the coffee kettle with water and have everything ready in easy reach of my rakkas. Birch bark is the secret to starting fires, and I would throw some into the hearth, cover it with wood, hang the kettle on the chain and fling in a match. Once the goattieh was warm and the water hot, I would get up.

Saami coffee is not percolated or filtered. To use the Saami expression, it is "cooked." The coffee is added directly to the water. After the water has boiled, or just as it is brought to a boil, the grounds sink to the bottom. Or, one can hurry the sinking process of the grounds by tossing in a touch of cold water and "shocking the grounds down," as the Saami showed me. It makes an excellent, strong cup of coffee which most Saami drink "on the cube." That is, by putting a sugar cube in the mouth and drinking over it. Cooking the coffee is by far the best and fastest method when hiking in the mountains. The coffee bag, made of reindeer skin and sewn with reindeer tendons, is an essential of every Saami pack. Unlike jars and plastic containers, when the contents of the bag diminish, so does the amount of room it takes in the pack.

Besides the practical aspects of goattieh life, there is a simple social code of goattieh conduct. The mother is ruler of the goattieh domain. Her place is always farthest in, on the right-hand side, seen from the entrance, by the kitchen and hearth. This is her most natural place, since she is responsible for the food. Should any guests arrive, she automatically puts on the coffee. The family's side is basically the right-hand one. Guests should always seat themselves on the left-hand side, and strangers should sit close to the door. The rules are, of course, loose and free with good friends. After some time, when I got to know my neighbors better, the "house mother" would invite me to move in toward the hearth. If the visit is to be short, however, it is common to sit on a *bierme,* or entranceway log, keeping muddy boots on the dirt floor. Should the coffee and company induce one to stay, it is a simple matter to kick off the boots and flop back on a reindeer hide.

Saami are always dropping in on each other. There is no need for invitation or reason other than a friendly chat or a cup of coffee. Often little is said at all. Many, met with this reception, have concluded that the Saami are sullen and uncommunicative. Certainly no Saami will assume a charming front or become intimate with a stranger. Far too often they are met by the tourist who has flown up to the camp in a seaplane, who loudly claims to love nature, and who considers that this justifies some kind of automatic intimacy between him and the local villagers. It is only with time and through daily contact that true character becomes known. To have an unknown foreigner spend the entire summer with them in their mountain village naturally raised many questions. Questions such as what I was doing and why I was

The mighty hydroelectric power dams have altered the surrounding nature in many ways, not least the living conditions of the Saami.

The goattieh with the broad door in Änonjalma. The dry sea bottom bears witness to regulation of the water level by the hydroelectric power company.

Tusse on the roof where he kept watch when Nils-Tomas and Johan were out on the lake.

Karin bakes bread on a stone in the goattieh.

A rakkas is not only a perfect mosquito net.

One never knows how long the wait will be for the reindeer herd to be corralled. Much coffee will be consumed.

Lundqvist's little seaplane. He would fly the gatherers to the best starting locations for them to bring together the animals for calf marking.

A pause on the way to Jålli.

Once lassoed, the calf must be flipped down and straddled for marking.

One holds a piece of the cut-away ear in the mouth while the hands are working. Later such a piece serves as a receipt, telling the herder how many calves he has marked.

Some of them take a last searching farewell of the deer, looking at the ears to see if any have escaped marking.

The author lying on a reindeer hide in the goattieh.

Many of the Saami were dressed in their traditional clothes during the church holiday.

My goattieh in Stalo (farthest to the right) was situated closest to the spot on the shore where the seaplanes landed. Jeknaffo and Jålli in the background.

The wise old härks stood calmly in the middle of the corral. They understood that the calf marking had nothing to do with them.

It is tiring work to pull full-grown deer in the separation corral. It helps if someone scares the deer from behind.

There are other methods to separate the deer if one is big and strong and knows the proper holds.

"Lillselet" means the "little, quiet water between two falls."

Our home during the moose hunt.

here I could hardly answer to myself, but these were not the questions asked. The real question was, what kind of a person was I. Of course, I was being judged, but judged by meaningful values. The uneasiness of a stranger melted away as I made more and more friends. I tried to be both independent in my own needs and as helpful as I could be to the needs of others. I smile now to think of these friends as cold or withdrawn.

The instruction I had received from Lars Kuhmunen stood me in good stead. Some mornings Johan or Nils-Tomas needed a hand at the oars to check the nets. They waited until they spied morning smoke from my goattieh and then we hurried out to bring in breakfast. Much can be told from smoke: who is at home, who sleeps late, when it is dinner time, or if it is a heavy smoke, who is baking bread.

I often found myself wondering as I rowed between nets through a dismal morning rain what made working in Stalo so much fun. There was always work to be done and lots of it, but no one was ever so tired by personal chores that he or she could not give a friend a helping hand. In fact, one hardly had to ask for help. Wherever there was work to be done, people joined in without a pause in conversation. It was the most natural way of associating with each other. Many times I had begun splitting logs for my woodpile only to be joined presently by one or two others who had stopped off on their way to the nets. They sawed and whacked away with an extra ax in the most casual manner as we chatted about news on the radio or the arrival of a pretty tourist girl. And I, who had before regarded work as a necessary evil, found myself strolling among the goattiehs ready to help lift, haul, or chop anything that needed it. It was not at all a question of working in order to get something in return. The helping and the working was fun in itself.

How terribly hurtful it would be if money were to destroy these feelings. None of us in Stalo would consider helping a friend for money. It is this helping and caring that to a great extent makes friends. To give money seems to deny friendship and give it no chance to grow. It was sheer labor, divorced of these qualities, which I had looked upon as a necessary evil. It is not often in our big cities with our alienated financial way of dealing with each other that one can encounter the joy of shared free labor I found here in Stalo.

I would have to snap out of my thoughts to change course a bit where Johan pointed with his nose. His hands were frequently so full of net and fish that he could only spare his nose and a quick jerk of the head to signal me. Not everyone had as good a fishing spot as the Parfas, but no one else would think to spread his nets in "their" fishing waters. No agreement had ever been formalized, but each household had its own general fishing territory well respected by the others. Because of the relatively poor fishing in Virihaure this year, a number of families were taking their nets to other lakes for better luck. One may well wonder how large fiberglass boats ever reached Stalo in the first place. Like all heavy articles, they had to be transported in early spring when the snow is hard packed and they could be pulled by scooters on sleds.

Isak had freighted up a tiny boat no bigger than a tub and this enabled him to fish in a number of small lakes round about. The only problem was to pull the boat overland, and this problem was considerable even though he had bought the smallest boat possible. I helped him pull his boat to Keddijaure, the lake just above Virihaure, and although it was not far, our path led through tangled fields of bushes and up the sides of two waterfalls. "Here is where Stalo used to be," said Isak when we had crossed the first ridge. "It is because of the seaplane that everyone has moved down to the lake. They want to be near the boats and the nets, but only twenty years ago hardly anyone fished with nets at all. Saami didn't eat so much fish and we never used to sell it; we never could before. Except for the fishing, this is a better place to live. It is protected; down by the lake the wind can blow free a long way." Isak pointed to a small clearing in the brush, "Over there is where the corral used to be and when the first plane landed on Virihaure, we were in the middle of a herd separation. The corral was full of reindeer, but everyone dropped his lasso and ran down to the lake to look."

I could see old goattieh sites from time to time. Only the hearth stones remained in the center of a shallow ring where the turf covering of the old goattieh had reunited with the ground. The birch framework had simply been torn down and put together again in the new location by the shore. The tent goattiehs used earlier by the native Jokkmokk Saami left even less of a trace. Isak showed me the site of his childhood goattieh, "And that one over there is where Guttorm Labba lived when Johan Märak worked for him as herder." I had never quite believed the stories Johan told of Guttorm Labba, so I sounded Isak out a little and learned that the tales were absolutely true. Guttorm had been able to cook a pancake inside his goattieh, flip it up and out through the smoke hole and then run through the door and catch it in the skillet.

Since the first plane landed at Stalo more than twenty years ago, air traffic has steadily increased. Not only did Lundqvist come with mail and supplies, but two small competing private airlines, Norrlandsflyg and Lapplandsflyg, also landed on the lake bringing tourists into the mountains. Norrlandsflyg had two ancient planes, built in the 1930s with engines made in Detroit, and though not as maneuverable and quick as the Lapplandsflyg Cessnas, they could carry much more. Martin, one of the pilots for Norrlandsflyg, was a favorite because like Lundqvist he did not charge for overweight and no extra for dogs. If ever I needed to cash a check or exchange American currency, Martin flew my check down and returned with Swedish crowns.

Although the Saami themselves usually traveled with Lundqvist, the arrivals of the other planes were also moments of interest during the day. The newcomers would bring with them the freshest news and we were always curious to see what they looked like. Sometimes friends would fly up or Martin would surprise us with a beer. Johan or Karin Parfa always accompanied their four-year-old son, Per-Jonas, to meet the plane. Martin had brought Per-Jonas an ice cream cone one day and from thenceforth he had always become excited when he heard the engines drone overhead. No one could tell which plane was coming as well as little Per-Jonas from just the far-off sound of the motor.

When the fog rolled in across the lake it could stay for many days and no engines would be heard overhead. Campers who had planned to fly out were left stranded. Often they had programmed their food supply down to the last day and with the added delay their stores ran out. They would walk from goattieh to goattieh asking to buy fresh fish or bread, and Isak's supply store did a flourishing business. I baked only for my own stomach, and so to get some peace, I drew a fish and a bread loaf crossed out with a big X on a sign and tacked it to the door. This international message did stop many knocks, but the

Saami found it so amusing they would disguise their voices and bellow "Glödkaka" from outside before coming in to visit.

In a small, tight village like this, it is understandable that everyone knew what everyone else was up to. If we could not fuss and gossip about each other, it would have been a dull life indeed. On beautiful clear days, distances seemed to shrink; far-off sights appeared close at hand (a phenomenon for which the Saami have a word, *sjärat*). We would lie outside on the grassy hills, often with a pair of binoculars to spot boats, planes, and people, or to watch the flocks of reindeer far off on high snow patches where it was cool and they could be free from mosquitoes and flies. The reindeer could stand there for hours nearly motionless. They looked like a swarm of bees hanging to the hive. These restful days were ideal for making the "goattieh round."

Of those goattiehs along the lake shore, mine was the southernmost, and if I strolled northward along the line of goattiehs, it would not be long before I was visiting and drinking coffee with neighbors. Among my best friends in Stalo were Henrik and Birgit Blind; usually when making the rounds I never progressed farther than their goattieh.

Henrik was about thirty-seven years old and by all standards the best reindeer herder in Stalo. He never said much, but he could never keep still. He always found work to do. When inside the goattieh he would whittle with extreme concentration on a stick, forming wonderful designs and sculptures only to toss them into the fire and storm out to a new job. Sometimes I thought he took a perverse pleasure in working himself to the limit. He was known to fish all day, run off on a three-day mission to inspect his reindeer, and upon return expend his remaining energy on the woodpile. One Sunday, Henrik had simply been unable to resist hammering a few boards on the storage hut he was building and by mistake gave the wrong nail, his thumb nail, a mighty blow. The neighbors shook their heads and said that is what comes of working on Sunday, but Henrik's attitude was, "I'd rather be at work and think of God than in church and think of work." Most of all I admired Henrik for his skill with reindeer, the confidence with which he did everything combined with surprising humility and sudden boyish humor.

Birgit is not a full-blooded Saami. She came from one of the old Swedish pioneer families of the North, but it was hard to imagine that she had not been born in a goattieh. In fact, her ancestors had been among those settlers who had become Saamified and who had mixed with the Saami considerably. Saami women as a whole are strong characters, but beside Birgit many seemed pale. At first she had had a good deal of trouble gaining acceptance from the others in the village. It was feared that she would force Henrik to give up the Saami life. Such fears were soon dispelled. No one could possibly do more than Birgit both to adapt herself and also help Henrik in every way. She learned a man's work and a woman's work, and what is more, had good sense and never restrained her opinion. She gained everyone's respect. Like Henrik she was strong and impulsive, but unlike him, she loved to talk and to read. Birgit had the only books in Stalo, and after reading nothing more than the directions on soup cans, it was a pleasure to borrow a thriller from her "library." "It's so easy to read here in Stalo," Birgit commented one day. "You don't even need a bookmark, just find the page with the last squashed mosquito."

In the goattieh just south of the Blind goattieh lived Henrik's parents, Anders and Anna, as well as Henrik's brother, Nils-Anders, his sister Siri-Mari, and, a niece, Marianne. It is common that all unmarried children stay with the parents, help with the herding and in time take over the herd. Henrik, Anders, and Nils-Anders formed a team. They worked together and if for some reason separated could mark each other's reindeer. If there was gathering to be done, Henrik and Nils-Anders would take turns. This teamwork, however, did not end with the immediate family. The three families living just north of Henrik and Birgit also worked with "the Blind group."

The name Blind is as common to a Saami in Sweden as Smith is to an American, and in Stalo there were many Blinds, sometimes only remotely related to each other. (It seemed that everyone was related to everyone else at least to *some* degree.) Nonetheless, if one used the term Blinds, it was generally understood that one meant the Henrik and Anders group, for this group I discovered formed a reindeer-herding entity (or *sita*) separate from the rest of the herders of Tuorpon.

Stalo was split into an extensive herding group and a relatively intensive herding group, although the latter could not consider itself intensive by the standards of the old nomadic herders of the past who lived in tents with their herds all the year round. Henrik, Anders, Nils-Anders, and the three neighboring families formed the more intensive group and the remaining Stalo herders, in conjunction with the other Tuorpon herders from Nuortvalle, formed the extensive group. Of course, conditions were always changing. Not so long before, the Nuortvalle herders had been among the most intensive in all of Sweden, and there was always talk of reintensification.

The other members of Stalo's intensive group were Karin and Olle-Björn Blind and their boys, Lars-Anders and Nils-Gustav; the Labba family, Per, Ella, and their son, Per-Henrik; and Ol'Henrik Blind, cousin to Henrik. Except for Ol'Henrik whose ill health limited his participation, these families based their living almost entirely on their reindeer. Rather than let them fall prey to wolverines, wolves, and lynx, these herders kept their reindeer together, watched over them, and migrated with them to and from the mountains.

Although the Blind group's intensiveness could not match that of the classic form of the old native Jokkmokk Saami, its members were determined to keep a tight control on their reindeer and ensure that the extensive trend would not lure them into an inactivity that might eventually endanger their existence as herders. Herders are always in danger of becoming trapped in an extensive spiral whereby the less work one devotes to the herding task, the more reindeer one loses, with the result that one cannot afford to devote more time to a losing business proposition, and so on. Yet the Blinds' efforts stood against the flow of the times and sometimes against the desires of Stalo's other herders. How, for example, should the funds in the communal treasury be spent, to the advantage of the extensive or the more intensive herders?

The placement of a new corral may be of benefit to one group but not the other. Or, there might be differences of opinion concerning the utilization of certain grazing areas. In such instances the Sameby as a whole might hold a meeting and the issue be put to a vote. A herder is not necessarily limited to one vote. A herder with many reindeer has more votes than another herder with a small herd. Generally the system functions well despite the problems and conflicts that are bound to arise. Usually the various groups are far too dependent on each other to permit any serious quarrels. However, there have been cases of bitter feuding between the groups within some Samebys, especially when the total reindeer population grows to press grazing capacity and the distribution of resources becomes an inflamed issue. Tuorpon's herd size was far from the limit imposed by the Swedish herding authorities. Comradeship ran high; the Tuorpon members were strongly tied to each other with the bonds of work, friendship, and blood.

If I could tear myself away from the company of Henrik and Birgit and continue northward along the lake shore, I would reach the Labba's goattieh. Ella Labba was a most interesting woman. She was known for her healing hand, a power she had received as a little girl after recovering from a terrible illness. If anyone in Stalo was in pain or felt ill, he or she would visit Ella. She fascinated me with stories of old Saami cures. Not so long ago it was very common to swallow a few drops of liquid mercury when feeling ill. One would always talk to the mercury and tell it which part of the body to go to. Sometimes a special reindeer tendon was tied around the wrist to ward off muscle strains. One cure she told me about I will never forget, and believe that even modern doctors will find it infallible. Although it may not fully cure a toothache, patients invariably admit to an easing of pain. A live toad is placed in the patient's mouth for a minute, and when removed the curer asks simply, "Feel better?" before releasing the toad.

By the time I reached the northernmost goattieh I would be shaking from caffeine, a condition known in these parts as "the coffee shivers."

 3

Calf Marking

I n the evenings under the midnight sun we might meet on a level plot
and engage in a wild soccer game. We played under international
rules, with one addition: if anyone was knifed, he would be given a
free kick (this rule, I think, was added to see if any newly arrived hiker
were foolish enough to believe it). The early summer days were spent
settling in and renewing social contacts. Herders who might live separated by many miles in the winter may be neighbors in the summer and
vice versa. Building, fixing, baking, and fishing were the order of the
day. Every so often, however, a small number of men with dogs would
set out to gather the reindeer from the mountains for a calf-marking,
and all of us were ready to drop everything suddenly and head toward
the corral.

Some Samebys pay a salary to the men who do the work of
gathering. The older men who are not up to the task are thereby able
to compensate the young for their services. Old people without young
family members to help them are thus able to remain active herders
longer. This practice varies from Sameby to Sameby, it being relatively
undeveloped in Tuorpon as each family is usually able to put at least
one able-bodied man into the field for the collective herding tasks.

The major events of the summer are the calf-markings. Indeed,
this is the reason why the Saami move to their summer homes.
Although most of the summer may be spent fishing, repairing the
goattieh, or chopping wood, it is the sudden days of intense activity

during the calf-markings that are the reason for it all. Out of the many weeks spent at Stalo the calf-markings may constitute a lesser tally of days, but these are the most important days. It is then that the herders harvest their crop. The calves must be marked while they still run with their mothers, otherwise it is impossible to say who owns them. It is in every reindeer herder's best interests to mark all his calves in the summer while they are on the open tundra and can be easily gathered. Above the dense woods the reindeer can be spotted miles away, frequently with the aid of binoculars. July is the main calf-marking month. In the winter the animals may be impossible to find, and a one-year-old calf may well be independent of its mother. Calves not marked by September are often lost to the owner. The only thing that can be done with an unmarked reindeer is to auction it off and put the money it brings in the Sameby's communal treasury. Altogether there were four calf-markings my first summer in Stalo.

One never knows how long the wait for the arrival of the herd at the corral will be. It may be several hours or several days, but however long, it is best to be prepared for the worst. As a general rule, if the weather looks good, it will probably become miserable, and if it looks bad, it will usually stay that way. It is unwise to approach a calf-marking without food, rain gear, and a tent.

Saami conversations begin and end with the word "maybe." Few people are so loathe to organize a schedule or set a date and a time. One would think a life that demands as much teamwork as reindeer herding would necessitate concrete plans. Those who intend to gather the herd must agree on a day to start. The neighboring villages must be notified that a calf-marking is underway. The Jåkkåkaska Saami in Arasluokta would, for instance, want to be on hand at the Tuorpon corral. The reindeer are mixed in the summer grazing land, and those gathered by the Tuorpon Saami might well belong to Saami from many different villages. Relaxed and vague commitments, however, are the rule, and surprisingly enough, all that is necessary.

If the Saami are noncommittal in these matters, it is because the reindeer and the weather make them so. There is much that is a mystery in the reindeer's behavior. Why do they always run against the wind? (The Saami often refer to them as "wind noses.") This habit can make herding them into a corral something like tacking a sailboat into harbor. Why, once in the corral, do they always run in a counter-clockwise circle? The theories have been many, but unconvincing.

"The reindeer decide," is the continual reply all Saami use when faced by the anxious tourist trying to set the hour for the calf-marking. The trained eye can see an approaching calf-marking hanging in the air in the form of heavy smoke from the goattiehs. There is usually a flurry of baking before a marking so that the men have fresh bread with them as they set out. Someone is always busily fiddling with a walkie-talkie trying to pick up a signal from the gatherers.

Although no date or time can be fixed, the teamwork of the Saami is uncanny in its precision. A Saami will look up at the sky, see that the weather is unstable, and decide to postpone the gathering. Without consulting them, he can be sure his comrades have decided the same thing. Or, when the weather clears, he sets out knowing that the others are either just ahead or behind. By reading the weather and trusting each other to reach the same decision, Saami can dispense with more formal agreements. It has often been said that they can read minds; at times I was forced to agree.

I remember once in early July, Isak Parfa, Olof-Johannes, and I were speeding in a rowboat with a powerful outboard motor over Lake Virihaure toward a corral on the other side. There was to be a calf-marking in Alleluokta. "We must keep our eyes open for Nils-Henrik," Isak said. How Nils-Henrik could know we were bound for Alleluokta that day was beyond me. He had spent the week fishing in another lake far away, no one had spoken to him during that time. The decision to go had been made only that morning. What is more, the lake where he had been fishing was miles out of our present course. Still, Isak said we should keep our eyes open. Half an hour later we spotted a thin column of smoke on a hill over the water. We turned toward land and met Nils-Henrik on the shore. He had walked fifteen miles to intercept us; he clambered aboard like a man catching the morning bus to work.

At Alleluokta we had to wait two days for the herd. Nils-Henrik and I were sleeping soundly in my tent, called the "Hilton" by the Saami because of its size, when we were awakened by excited shouting. "They've come, they're here!" called a voice, and we shot out of our sleeping bags. Nils-Henrik grabbed the coffee kettle and ran down to the lake for water. I hurriedly got a fire going, and as the coffee cooked we pulled on our boots. In our haste to prepare ourselves for the corral we had hardly looked around. Hoarse laughter made us pause. Ella Labba ran down the hill clutching her side, hardly able to keep from rolling on the ground. I looked at my watch, we had been asleep for only one hour. Nils-Henrik scanned the hills with his binoculars. The herd was many hours away resting on a snow patch. It took hours of trying to go back to sleep before we could fully appreciate Ella's sense of humor, and it was fortunate in this instance that Ella could not read our minds. The calf-marking was otherwise smooth.

Most of the Tuorpon calf-markings occurred at the Jålli corral on the Stalo side of the lake, eight miles from the village. If the herd was widely scattered, Lundqvist would fly the gatherers and their dogs, a few at a time, to the best starting locations. He could land wherever there was enough water, and by distributing them behind the reindeer flocks, he saved the gatherers time and effort. They had only to move toward the corral, driving the reindeer before them in a gradually tightening noose. Continually walking, the gatherer stops only occasionally to use his binoculars or to seek contact with his comrades by walkie-talkie. He must frequently climb high up to establish radio contact or to gain a better view for spotting reindeer. Each man sweeps a huge area; the reindeer run miles ahead of him and bunch in growing numbers as the net closes. Only at the end of the drive do the men come together and for the first time get a close look at the reindeer they have collected. It is a job that can go on for days in rain and fog. There is little rest until the reindeer are secure in the corral.

One foggy day in July, doors began slamming and everyone in Stalo began hurrying to stuff their packs and cover their goattieh smoke holes. Logs were leaned against the doors outside, indicating to all that no one was at home. It was time to start the trek toward Jålli. A faint walkie-talkie signal picked up in Stalo indicated that the gatherers were nearing the corral. Boats from Arasluokta arrived with the Jåkkåkaska Saami. Within a few minutes the way to Jålli was marked by a line of bobbing heads.

I was throwing food into my pack when there was a soft knock on the door. Little Per-Jonas Parfa came in with a lasso over his shoulder, a walking stick, and a tiny knife in his belt. "I'm going with you to

Calf Marking

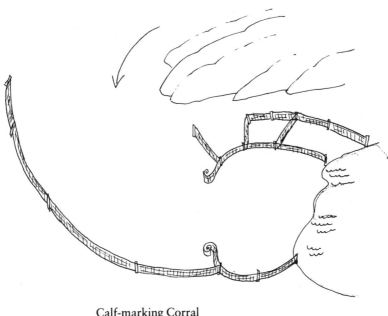

Calf-marking Corral

Jålli," he said and tried to look as manly as his four years allowed. Johan, his father, was one of the gatherers. He had even taken Tusse, Per-Jonas's puppy, with him to train as a herding dog. "Hurry up," Per-Jonas said, "we must help Pappa and Tusse." He knew very well that Karin, his mother, would not let him go, and so he hoped to sneak off with me. It was hard for him to stay at home with all the excitement streaming toward the corral.

I told him that we must climb the hill near the church goattieh to spy for the herd. If we could not see any reindeer they were still far from the corral and there was no use going. Per-Jonas swung proudly along the trail but had to be lifted over the biggest rocks. To everyone we met he shouted, "we're going to Jålli." When we reached the top of the hill Per-Jonas was already tired out. Of course, it was impossible to see any reindeer; the corral was miles away behind many mountains. "We must go home," I said, but Per-Jonas had me fooled. No sooner had he put his eyes to my binoculars than he shouted, "there's

Pappa and there's Tusse!" "Do you see any reindeer?" I asked. "Lots and lots of reindeer," he cried. Fortunately he was exhausted and when Karin found us, he did not complain too much at being carried back down the hill. "Papa waved to me," he told her.

Dusk was falling as I approached the Jålli corral. I could see a row of small campfires glowing in the distance. The men before me carried bundles of dwarf birch they had thoughtfully pulled from the ground to feed the flames before we had climbed high above the treeline. Logs that had once been fence posts for the old corral (freighted here by horse) helped keep us warm through the cold night. We drifted between the fires drinking coffee and chatting with friends.

The corral, expertly situated thanks to generations of experience, was built at the focal point where two valleys merged. It was possible to herd the reindeer along the high valley sides that all led toward the corral, the critical point in the drive coming only at the very end when the reindeer, who prefer heights, must be driven down off the slopes directly above the corral. A lake was used as one side of the corral, and long fences, trap arms, radiated from the central enclosure to direct or funnel the reindeer toward the center. In the old days of intensive herding, when the reindeer were tamer and the herds smaller, it was common to drive them out on a peninsula. There was no strong, wire fencing in those days—and before the advent of helicopters and snow scooters the transportation of heavy rolls of wire into the mountains was practically impossible anyway—and so a few dogs were stationed across the peninsula neck, and one dog at the tip to keep the reindeer from running into the water.

In the past, fixed corrals were not so necessary. The reindeer could simply be driven to different sides of a snow patch or an open meadow and contained there by the herders. The herders carried staffs that could be used to prod the reindeer to a certain side, while the dogs maintained the outer boundary. Or, a quick blow to the antlers (especially sensitive at this time of year) would usually be enough to make even the most obstinate reindeer obey. Fixed corrals became an important feature of the new, collective herding, so important, in fact, that before wire fencing became available the first calf-marking corrals were built painstakingly of trees, bushes, or rocks.

Silence spread quickly as a shout, and everyone below the corral sensed that it was time to quiet down and crouch behind a ridge. The reindeer herd was approaching. The least sudden sound or movement could send the timid animals scampering back uphill. The reindeer must also have felt the tension, for they paused briefly at the entrance to the corral. The wire fence was rolled back on one side to be replaced once the herd had passed. Brightly colored nylon camping tents cluttered the hollow below the corral. Only moments before, children had run and wrestled. The boys had practiced lassoing girls, and we had all talked cheerfully around our smoky fires, drinking coffee or watching the mountains with binoculars for the first sign of the herd's approach.

Five men had been out for three days and nights gathering in the herd step by step, with the help of their dogs driving the reindeer with barks and shouts toward the fence that formed the long trap arm of the corral. The rest of the village—and even members from the neighboring villages who would certainly have reindeer mixed in this herd—were all now waiting quietly in the rain with their lassos coiled over their shoulders. We had bad luck with the weather, I thought; it rained and was very cold—but this is the way it almost always is on Jålli, I learned. Of course, it was necessary to do the marking late at night or early in the morning, when it was cool. Otherwise, it would be impossible to coax the reindeer off the snow patches and windy peaks where they can avoid the insects, which swarm in the heat of the day, but thin out as it cools toward night.

The famous midnight sun did indeed provide us with a sufficient amount of light, but I felt it gave no more warmth than the moon. Whereas the cold at least served a purpose, I found it difficult to grant the constant rain any redeeming features. We waited a number of hours crouched behind the ridge. The herd twice turned back, breaking through the ranks of the Saami herdsmen and their dogs. At last, they were close. We could hear the soft snapping tendons of many thousand reindeer legs and suddenly the rushing thunder as they all plunged across the line in a panic. We peeked cautiously over the ridge as they swept toward us, and we could feel the ground vibrate. The fence was rolled across in seconds, closing the corral. The spell of silence broken, we felt free to speak again. The men and dogs whom we had watched as tiny spots in our binoculars now came together from their different directions, hungry and tired. They were soon sitting with their families around the fire, drinking the hot coffee they would need for the work ahead.

Only the newborn calves did not look tattered and shabby from the shedding of the winter fur. The larger reindeer lost tufts of hair by the handfuls in the summer, making them especially vulnerable to mosquitoes and flies. The warble fly, *Oestrus tarandi,* digs its way into the reindeer's back and deposits its larva under the skin. Another fly, the reindeer fly, *Cephenomyia trompe,* tries to spray its eggs into the nasal passages of the reindeer where they hatch. The reindeer's breathing canals may become so clogged and swollen that the reindeer dies. It is lucky for the reindeer that winter never fully leaves the mountains. Not only are the snow patches cool and windy, they alter the direction of the polarized light from the sun, and insects who often orient themselves by this light become totally confused when encountering it reflected from snow patches.

While the men ate and rested a little, the reindeer were left alone in the corral to calm down. The calves need time to reunite with their mothers. It is important, once the work begins, that the calf run with its mother, since one owns the calf only if one owns its mother. A great din of bleats and grunts rises in an even chorus from the enclosure. One of the interesting facts about reindeer is that a mother can identify her calf by its grunt, and vice versa, even at great distances. When all the calves have found their mothers again, it is time to begin the calf-marking.

In ones and twos, the men crawl under the fence with their lassos. A small knife hangs from each belt, and it is with these specialized knives that the mark is cut in a calf's ear. Each Saami has his own pattern of notches and slits that he cuts into the ears to mark the calf as his. A Saami can cut his mark without thinking about it, and he can recognize his mark upon furry ears instantly, the way a man turns when he hears his name. Marks are often inherited, and as a family grows, new marks may be created by adding more notches or slits to the basic family pattern. Often one ear is the "personal ear" and one the "family ear," in a manner similar to first and last names. A herder who is too old to continue may sell his mark to another herder who then takes over all reindeer with that mark. It is possible for one herder to have a number of marks, but according to law he should phase out all supposedly "extra" marks and keep just one. To avoid confusion, marks nowadays are all registered and checked so that no two Saami in the same area have identical or overly similar marks. Moreover, it is important that one mark not be able to "take" another, that is, it should not be able to be changed easily to become someone else's mark. Henrik Blind had needed to change his mark three times in order that it not be confused with the marks of other northern Saami immigrating to the Jokkmokk district.

The dogs who have worked so long and well are tied outside the fence. They bark and protest against this insult as the work begins. The lassos are uncoiled, stretched taut from a fence post to iron out any twists, and are soon flying in all directions. A herder's eyes are on the reindeer as he coils his rope for a new throw. He is looking for his mark in the tightly packed crowd of circling reindeer. Suddenly he spies a mother bearing his mark with a young calf beside her, and he rushes off to position himself for a throw. As he runs, his eyes never leave his reindeer. If he has a comrade helping him, usually a family member with a similar mark, they will approach from two sides, corner the calf against the corral fence, and force it to run between them. So important is this teamwork that some right-handed Saami have trained themselves to throw left-handed in order to have a better angle when working opposite a right-handed thrower. The Saami assumed that I, coming from the land of the cowboy, would be a lasso expert, but not only is the Saami lasso technique, using a piece of reindeer antler in place of a slipknot, totally different from that of the American cowboy, I had never touched a cowboy lasso.

A calf soon learns that it is the target, and its mother tries to protect the calf by running between it and the Saami. Or sometimes they find refuge in the thick of the herd, where the hundreds of swirling bodies can block the reach of the rope and where even the most keen-eyed Saami can easily lose sight of his mark.

Anonymity is brief, however. A call from a friend at the other end of the corral may signal the Saami that one of his calves has been spotted. The owner will run across the center of the corral aiming to cut the calf off in its counter-clockwise run. The reindeer are forced to stop and turn, and just then, when the calf is closest, the herder's lasso shoots forth with amazing speed and accuracy. To catch a running calf from between the much larger bodies of full-grown reindeer is no mean feat. I have seen lasso casts that I still find hard to believe, the rope curving uncannily under the other reindeer before tightening around the two back legs of the running calf.

Once caught, the calf is thrown carefully to the ground and straddled by the Saami. The mark is cut in seconds with the sureness of long habit. While the owner's hands are busy making his mark, he holds one of the newly excised pieces of ear between his teeth. When the calf is released, he scampers off grunting loudly for his mother like a child in need of sympathy. The piece of ear is stuffed in a pocket and serves as a kind of ticket stub that the owner uses to keep count of the number of calves he has marked, and as the summer ends and the calf-marking season is over, one will often see in Saami goattiehs these ear pieces strung on a string and hanging from a nail like a strange necklace. The calf-marking goes on until about two o'clock the next morning. The corral has become one huge mud puddle.

Still, there are many unmarked calves, and lassos trail behind people like long tails that crisscross in the mud. I have my own lasso and do my best to help whenever I have the chance. At first I am sure I was no help at all. I could not read any marks or tell one calf from another. I had to wait until a Saami had missed his throw before I knew which calf to aim for, and this meant I had to station myself downstream in the circling herd from a Saami who looked ready to throw. Usually he would not miss, but if I ever did get a chance to throw, I almost always missed. Of course, lassoing just any reindeer is no problem; the hard part is lassoing the one you aimed at. My first throw tangled in the antlers of a large bull reindeer who in a moment had jerked the entire rope out of my hands and run off with it dragging behind. Being disarmed in this manner was naturally a bit embarrassing, but I found that I was not alone in my predicament. An empty-handed Saami rushed by and asked me if I had seen a lasso crossing this way. We were soon able to catch our ropes and disentangle them from the antlers.

After a year's practice, I began to master the technique and even to be able to distinguish the different calves. I've never had more fun in my life than when trying to catch these reindeer. It seems impossible to be at a calf-marking and not be infected by its spirit. And though I still missed frequently, every lucky catch looked like the dead-sure shot of an expert, and I would proudly turn the calf over to its owner to be marked.

Those who have finished marking their calves turn to the next phase of the roundup, that of castrating the bulls. Bulls that are not castrated undergo many bodily changes during the mating season beginning in September. The uncastrated bulls, or *sarvs,* are at peak weight during the mating season, but afterward lose weight dramatically. It is not worthwhile to slaughter a sarv in the winter. The castrated bulls, härks or so-called ox-reindeer (a term often applied to those castrates destined simply for slaughter rather than use as lead, sled or pack deer), on the other hand, avoid all the mating season effects. Although they never weigh quite as much as a sarv in his prime, they carry much more meat during the winter. It is therefore wise for a herder to castrate a goodly number of bulls before the rutting season begins, to have a supply of winter meat. Moreover, härks are not "loners" to the extent sarvs are prone to be. There are sarvs that stray far afield from the other reindeer and are missed in all the gathering operations, a total loss to their owners. Castration increases the chances of finding the reindeer with the herd.

In the past castrating was commonly done with the teeth. The glands were chewed and crushed. A knife was sometimes used to extricate the glands if castration was performed in the early spring when the sarvs are sexually dormant and the glands are small, hard, and cannot be properly chewed. Castration by chewing in the summer and autumn could only be performed by Saami with a good set of teeth and a perfect bite. It was also a matter of skill, for the type of reindeer resulting—and there can be a good deal of flexibility in this—depended entirely on the way the job was done. One could, for instance, crush all of the gland to make the reindeer entirely sexless, or only part of the gland. Those who understood the art could look at a härk and tell who had castrated it. Today this method is illegal, but it has not vanished completely. The new method, using tongs to crush the gland ducts, is often unsuccessful and completely lacks the flexibility of the older method. But as most castration nowadays is directed toward making härks for slaughter only—the tame sled härks and pack härks being basically a thing of the past—tongs have for the most part replaced teeth.

Like most people, I grimaced when first hearing of the old castration technique—no doubt the same attitude of distaste that, along with concern for making the operation less painful, initiated the prohibition of the teeth method. Seeing this reaction, the Saami commonly adopt a toothy grin when explaining the old system. Even when legal, the operation was often performed under a jacket to spare the nerves of unaccustomed strangers. All generally agree that castration by tong is far less painful. The reindeer I saw castrated in this way were obviously pained, but not to the extent I had imagined, and their recovery was swift. With the old method it was obvious that pain was considerable. An occasional illegal teeth castration might still be performed for a special reason, but modern herding hardly requires it. Because the tong method is fast and less painful for the reindeer, use of the tong is mastered by all herders.

Wrestling one of these large sarvs to the ground is not at all as simple as marking a calf. Two, maybe even three men are needed to twist the antlers of the sarv, turn him on his side, and hold him down. The actual castration takes half a minute. Before releasing the newly made härk, a few shallow knife cuts might be made along the fur on one side of the reindeer, forming stripes to indicate that he has been castrated.

The last phase of the roundup is usually the auction of the unidentifiable reindeer, the mavericks or "whole ears," as they are sometimes called. If a reindeer has not been marked by the time it has stopped following its mother, there is no way one can determine ownership.

Isak, being the elected spokesman for Tuorpon, was the auctioneer. He stood holding the reindeer, and those interested formed a loose circle around him as he began the bidding. All the discourse concerning the reindeer was conducted in Saami, and therefore I was at first surprised to hear that Swedish only was used for the bidding. I asked Per-Henrik about this after the sale; the answer was simple: to say 212 in Saami is "Guokta tjuot guokta låge nan," literally, two hundred two and ten. It seems the herders found the shorter, Swedish counting method better suited to rapid bidding.

Once sold, the new owner takes possession of his reindeer and marks it on the spot.

The herders from the other villages are allowed to bid on the "whole ears," but it is considered very bad manners if they drive up prices too high or prevent the struggling youth of the host village from increasing their stock in this way. It is a different matter entirely if the total herd size of the Sameby has reached the limit allowed by the Swedish herding authorities, the so-called rational herd size specified for each village. Then the host village might be pleased to sell its "whole ears" to outsiders.

Gradually the action within the corral died down. The reindeer were tired and walked more than they ran. We sat more than we walked. Almost all the calves had been marked, the castrations finished, the auction over, and most of the lassos were once more coiled and hanging across shoulders. Some Saami had already crawled out under the fence and were drinking coffee down by the tents. Others took a last searching farewell of the reindeer, squinting at all the ears to see if any had been overlooked. When all the lassos were idle and everyone satisfied, the fence was rolled back. One of the old lead härks with a bell around his neck was caught and led out of the corral. The others at first seemed suspicious of their regained freedom and made no move to leave, but with their leader out in front and some urging from behind, they soon swarmed out together.

Seconds later they were sweeping over the mountains; soon they appeared far away like a swarm of ants, and then disappeared. The clicking, clanging, grunting mass of commotion was gone. Only a few scattered calves, temporarily orphaned in the surge to freedom, scampered worriedly in all directions. Their small frightened complaints sounded most pitiful in the returned quiet after the passing of the herd, but their distress was short-lived. The missing mothers soon returned to answer their bleats and, reunited, they hurried away two by two.

We all returned to our tents for coffee and to talk with friends and relations from the other villages. Friends who have not seen each other all winter may first meet in the calf-marking corral. They stand and talk briefly until one rushes off in midsentence with throwing arm cocked in pursuit of a calf. Now, around the fires, we were more relaxed. I was cold, wet, hungry, and exhausted, and for me the remedy for all ills seemed to be a short sleep.

I must have slept about an hour; when I awoke my tent was the last one left below the corral, and I was alone on the mountain. The only proof that I had not dreamed it was the still smoldering fires and the thousands of reindeer tracks in the soft mud of the corral. In a few hours I would be comfortably stretched out on a reindeer hide, drying my clothes and my shoe grass by the hearth inside my goattieh. The thought of this hurried me home to Staloluokta.

4

At Home
in Staloluokta

L ying warm on a reindeer hide in a goattieh with the fire blazing as
  the wind screeches by outside searching for someone to freeze—
this is the fulfillment of all the dreams spawned by a noisy, hectic
world. A goattieh is only a small bubble on the ground, but it is cozy
and protective. Unlike the raw strength of a huge stone mansion, the
round goattieh matches its surroundings and never isolates itself from
the world outdoors. An apartment in the city is like a space capsule
with a regulated environment; the goattieh is like a raft on a river, and
living in a goattieh is a constant adventure. I am thrilled by the wind
and laugh like a tiny mouse, happy to be in its hole. My thoughts drift
with the smoke through the riehpen and out into the night. The midnight sun no longer paints the sky with fantastic colors. It is late in
July. The fire flares and crackles, sending a spray of sparks streaking
upward, mixing with the smoke and turning into stars overhead.

Few things fascinate as does a live fire. It holds the eye and the
most profound philosophies burn, glow, and die with its logs. There
is a soft knock on the door and Isak stretches himself out by the
hearth across from me. The silence is hardly broken, and we share
something more important than words. When I first came to Stalo, I
found this difficult to get used to. I felt a pressing need to say something, to fill the long silence, to make my guest feel welcome. My
efforts as a considerate host were usually met with a calm, "You
don't say." And after a brief address on the topic of how unusually

cold it was for this time of year, silence would settle once again. Finally I learned to relax.

The longer I lived in Stalo the more I shared with my neighbors and the more natural conversation became. We all knew each other well, and in a feeling of true companionship, each person was expected to behave just the way he or she was. In fact, behavior that was truly idiosyncratic, if normal for a particular individual, would be accepted from this person as a matter of course without comment.

Among the Saami there was never any great fuss over a visitor's comings or goings. I had been raised in a society where neighbors rarely visited each other and then usually by invitation only. A stranger cannot help but consider it abrupt if someone suddenly rises and leaves without a word, but once my uneasiness was overcome, I grew to appreciate this straightforward behavior. Here in Stalo everyone held open house. Visitors streamed in and out of the goattiehs, and after the usual cup of coffee it was not considered at all impolite if the "goattieh mother" simply continued with her work weaving shoe bands or preparing a stew. Nor was it the least unusual for the visitor to stay until the stew was ready and join in the family's dinner.

Isak and I interrupted our thoughts to indulge in a cup of coffee. We cut strips of dried, salted reindeer meat to add to our cups, both cooking the meat slightly and flavoring the drink. It gives a fine salty taste to the coffee, maybe, I suggested, one of the reasons Saami have acquired a taste for salt in coffee—a trait more famous than the fact warrants, but not without some truth. Many have questioned the origins of the habit. To enrich mineral-free melted snow water is another attempt at an answer. Isak put on his most serious expression and proposed that the old folks had first started using salt because they had no sugar. Good thinking I agreed. Certainly in modern times sugar has almost totally replaced whatever salt use there was with coffee.

We sipped our coffee thoughtfully with new understanding, and I threw another log on the fire, making sure to turn it so that the root end was toward the back kitchen and the direction of growth toward the door. Not that this mattered to the fire, but I had learned that it could matter a good deal to my guests. If the wood was placed upon the fire backwards, I was warned, my child would have a very difficult birth. He would be born backwards. I was, at the moment, in no danger of acquiring a child, not to speak of a wife, and so claimed myself immune to such worries. But whether or not anyone believed in the superstition, and I doubt anyone did, the truth of the matter was that putting wood on a goattieh fire "backwards" was just plain irritating to a Saami. Once I had been cued on this point it was impossible not to be meticulous in its observance. Even with a fire that is out on the open plain, the least one can do is lay all the wood in the same direction.

Coffee finished, Isak and I once again stretched out on our backs and watched the shadows play upon the birch framework of the goattieh dome. The secret of the entire construction is the arch, used by the Saami centuries before the Romans. Two large, naturally curved birch trees hinged together over the doorway form one arch, and another pair of curved birches formed a second arch over the kitchen.

The great Saamiologist Ernst Manker has hypothesized that the prototype for these arches comes from the North Sea coast, where the early Saami hunted whales and may have built small goattieh-like homes with arches made from pairs of whale rib bones. The four large curved birch trees that compose the two great goattieh arches are not easy to find. They must be sought on steep slopes where the drift and accumulation of snow force the trees to grow partially sideways.

Isak and I had still hardly spoken to each other, but the screaming of the wind outside called forth a memory from him. It was wonderfully eerie to hear his voice rise from the dark floor shadow without seeing him. "That's the way an *äparis* can sound," he said, referring to the souls of the unbaptized murdered babies John had told me about on Midsummer Eve. "It screams and cries but sometimes you can be tricked. A comrade and I were once skiing through the woods when we heard a terrible wailing. My friend fell to his knees, asked God to protect us and began to mumble the baptismal rites. But I just kept going toward the noise and soon found the äparis. The screaming emanated from two birch trees that had grown so close that they rubbed against each other and screeched in a hard wind. Foxes in the autumn can make the same kind of awful cry. Lapland is full of baptized trees and foxes."

I learned much from Isak. He told me of the thieves' cave, Shlappa, on the other side of the lake where long, long ago a crew of thieving hunters had lived and eaten the reindeer of the Saami whenever hungry. They were well armed and could not be approached. When they were all out on a hunting foray, a number of Saami hurried across to the cave and dug gunpowder down into their firewood. When the thieves returned and began to cook their kill, the wood began to jump and explode. The thieves ran from their fortress at full speed, sure that it was haunted. The fire in my goattieh was now just a heap of embers, an eye glowing in the dark. Isak left as quietly as he had come.

Alone once more, I lay on my back and again contemplated the internal structure of the goattieh in the fire's last light. The patchwork of the birch logs fascinated me. The straight logs fit ingeniously to form a rounded surface, and I have never tired of studying their arrangement. Slowly the deep shadows between the logs grew to swallow the room and my own eyes must have closed with that of the fire.

I awoke to the sound of an airplane engine overhead. I must have slept late; it was Lundqvist. I dressed hurriedly and checked my provisions in case I had to place an order. Lundqvist came with mail and supplies in return for which he had the sole license to transport the area's catch of fish. "Lunken's" arrival was one of the few fixed events of the day, weather permitting, and everyone dropped whatever he or she was doing to meet the plane. Even in my pre-coffee condition I realized that Nils-Tomas and Johan Parfa must have already checked the nets. Or else they were still out on the lake, in which case I could pick up their mail. I bounded outside into the brightness of a new day and found a plastic bag containing two fish hanging from my door handle, a most pleasant indicator of a successfully completed fishing run.

First Lunken gave us our food packages, collected our order slips for next time, and lastly sat himself on a gas tank to dole out mail. To my surprise I was handed a large food package although I had no memory of having ordered anything. Maybe something left over from last time, I figured, and concentrated on the mail. Most of the mail consisted of newspapers. "It's odd," said Siri-Mari, "but here in the mountains we get the newspaper daily, while down in the lowlands in our modern winter home beside a road, we get the paper only twice a week." I received a card addressed simply "The American, Staloluokta" from a hiker thanking me for a rain-free night in the goattieh. The fact that no one else thought this in the least unusual made me appreciate it all the more.

Lunken had just begun to wade from shore in his hipboots pushing his seaplane free from the sand, when little Per-Jonas called out, "Lunken, it's Saturday today." No one else knew for sure what day it was, but a quick glance at a newspaper proved Per-Jonas correct, and Lunken had to wade back and bring out the lollipops he distributed to children wherever he landed on Saturdays. The rest of us stood around grinning wishing we were kids.

We soon discovered that our food boxes were full of strawberries, though none of us had ordered any. I had two liters of strawberries and a carton of whipping cream. We all loved strawberries, but two liters per person was a bit much. Lunken, however, was already in the air. He could be sure that a mouth full of strawberries could not grumble over the bill. "It's happened before," said Siri-Mari, "he must have just received a huge strawberry shipment and didn't want them to go bad."

I breakfasted on fresh mountain char followed by a surfeit of strawberries and whipped cream. To have such delicacies in the mountains, where life is in many ways so Spartan, greatly enhanced their flavor. The new day stretched before me completely free and open to the slightest whim. There was no such thing as a normal day in Stalo. There was much I could busy myself with, but I could just as well ignore all chores. Mornings brought workdays or holidays depending on mood. A coffee break from a half-finished job could easily degenerate into a soccer game, and plans for the next herd gathering could just as easily be discussed during a "time-out" in the game.

I was not unemployed for long. Outside I found Nil-Tomas Parfa digging bricks of peat to spread as a final covering over the new goattieh he was building. I lent him a hand carrying and packing the heavy peat blocks around the birch framework. Someday I hope to build my own goattieh, and helping Nils-Tomas was the best way to learn.

Laying the peat was practically the finishing touch. Before that we had needed to debark the approximately three hundred birch trees so that they would dry and become hard. One of the main problems was to find four large curved birches paired evenly into two arches, a problem of symmetry that I suppose, thanks to the whale, never troubled the early Saami. Actually I never believed the whale rib bone explanation for the origin of the arch. The Saami professor Israel Ruong presents a far more reasonable theory tracing the gradual evolution of the arch from the basic three-legged stand. Arches make the goattieh spacious and able to bear the weight of heavy snow. Once we had raised the framework, we had to spread a layer of birchbark over the outside for waterproofing before adding the peat. Even cutting peat blocks with a shovel, I learned, has an art to it. By cutting with the shovel at a slant, the edges of the peat cakes become slanted and when packed around the dome-shaped goattieh, fit its curve more exactly.

After a few hours of hard work, Karin Parfa called us in for a lunch break. The usual fare was dried meat, glödkaka, and fish, but today she had a special treat for dessert. I was worried that her treat would prove to be strawberries, but fortunately it was *jobmo,* a dish made from cooked and mashed mountain sorrel leaves. Jobmo is known as the "vegetable of the Saami." The taste is slightly acid, so it is frequently eaten with sugar and milk like a dessert. It can be quite refreshing, certainly nutritious, and is almost the only form of green I have ever seen Saami eat even when given access to the vegetable counters of a large supermarket in the lowlands. One of the few other green plants eaten in the mountains is *kvanne,* or the *Angelica* plant, known as "Saami candy." It is a tall plant with a celery-like stalk and cauliflower-shaped flowery heads. In the spring and summer before the flowers have bloomed or the stalk dried out, it can be peeled and eaten like a piece of sugar cane though quite different in taste. Kvanne has a sharp, bitter almost mint flavor. The jobmo was not at all bad, although I failed to understand why these few plant specimens should rate in the Saami diet as dessert or candy. The jobmo made my teeth feel strangely dry and rough.

Nilas Blind joined us for a cup of coffee as we relaxed after a good meal, and as usual in Stalo, the work day was forgotten and the coffee break prolonged indefinitely. Nilas was well worth listening to. The older people in the village spanned a life of change hard to imagine. There are few places in the world where changes have come so rapidly. Nilas often took upon himself the role of my educator. Time and again he cautioned me that in order to understand modern reindeer herding, the group structure of the Sameby, the pressures and directions of change, it is not enough to grasp the situation in a single instance. It is necessary to know something of the past as well, and who was better fitted than Nilas to inform me of the old days. I was the eager listener, Nils-Tomas the artful prompter, and Nilas the source of the most fantastic and vivid narratives of a bygone age.

Still in the early part of this century, Nilas and many of the other Tuorpon Saami moved all the way to the summer land by *drag rajd,* sled caravan, in the early spring and stayed so long into the winter that they could return by the same means. Later on another pattern was adopted. The stay in Stalo was shortened. The caravans reached the highlands later and left earlier. Nilas migrated part of the way by *klövje rajd,* pack caravan, when the ground was bare, and the reindeer carried their loads like pack animals without sleds. He told of the terrible hardships during wolf attacks when the herd had to be guarded constantly. Wolves were commonly hunted down on skis and killed. A wolf could change a rich Saami to a pauper in one night. He spoke of the Norwegian coast when the herds had to swim the sound. It could be a treacherous swim. Although the reindeer's fur, composed of thousands of hollow hairs, makes it buoyant, swimming the sound could be dangerous, especially for those young calves born on the mainland. Should the herd panic while in the water, it might turn and swim around and around in one huge circle of struggling bodies, creating such a whirlpool that reindeer can be sucked under and drowned.

All the while he spoke, Nilas whittled thoughtfully on an arran stick, or hearth poker. It is a common practice and I believe one of the main reasons that everyone has these sticks. They are everybody's whittling property and frequently achieve artistic brilliance. It always hurt me to see these works of art, the results of hours of collective concentration, carelessly tossed into the flames once considered finished, with nothing left to carve.

No matter how hard they might work, Nilas did not give modern herders much credit. Now and again I saw a slow smile creep across Nils-Tomas's face. "Modern herding," Nilas was saying, "the collective Sameby form, is no real reindeer herding at all, just some form of hobby. The youth of today, he snorted, aren't at all close to their reindeer. They mark them and slaughter them, that's all. We milked our reindeer back then. Before we moved anywhere we had to guard our tame härks day and night to make sure they didn't stray. Without them it would be impossible to move. Now we just tell Lunken how many liters of milk to bring, and when the time has come to move, we fly."

It is true that herding has changed drastically since Nilas first moved from Karesuando to Jokkmokk in 1923 soon after the governments of Norway and Sweden agreed to limit the reindeer traffic between them. Herders now have a much broader economic base, and reindeer are no longer the be-all and end-all of the herder's life. The process of change produced a series of herding methods of differing duration following the rapid developments of communication and settlement in the north. For example, there was a period before the advent of seaplane traffic when the vajas were no longer milked and goats supplied the village with dairy products. Goats roamed everywhere in Stalo, and the goattiehs were often surrounded by small fences to keep the goats from grazing on the turf roofs. Stalo's history is an exciting and complex story. In only a few places in the world today can we still see the current development of a cash economy out of a subsistence economy and the pros and cons of modern technology as it meets a wilderness life-style.

Nils-Tomas did not always agree with Nilas as to the virtues of the past, but on one point they were of one mind. The trend toward what Nilas termed "hobby herding," made possible by and fostering the extensive trend, continues to increase. Fencing, snow scooters, helicopters, and walkie-talkies all enable fewer men with less effort to accomplish the same result. Too many herders have drifted to other jobs. This modernization combined with the ever-diminishing grazing lands as more and more roads slice through the country and more and more forests are cut for the timber industry brings herding to the brink of doom.

The older herding generation is often unfairly hard on its replacement. To say that herding today is no more than a hobby for the modern herder is a gross exaggeration. Yes, there are those herders who do no herding work and keep a few reindeer in order to maintain their Sameby membership with its accompanying hunting and fishing rights, but there are many more small herders who are struggling desperately to survive and who work diligently with their small herds. There is a point, however, where it becomes counterproductive for a small herder to spend more time herding. The time he invests in his herd, if it is small, might not give him as much return for his efforts as the same time invested in some other form of work.

The small herders of the past, of course, had the same problem, and usually had no other recourse than to become fishing Saami and leave herding. With the new, collective, Sameby form of herding, and the ability to find part-time employment and other sources of income in the wake of Swedish settlement and expansion, however, small herders can hang on longer. Moreover, with the decreasing grazing lands and the rising subsistence minimum in reindeer—that is, where two hundred head were enough for a family in the past and five hundred head are now required to meet the same standard—big herders are reduced to small herders. The number of active herders has declined drastically in the past thirty years, and of those active today, herding accounts on the average for little more than half of their subsistence. Nilas gave Tuorpon Sameby little more than twenty years life expectancy.

Conversation lapsed after this pessimistic prediction and Nilas whittled on in silence. He had carved the top of the stick into a perfect little foot with shoe. When it was finally finished Nilas rose to go and, as I had foreseen, flung the stick into the fire. It was not just the coffee, our conversation, or the hour that decided the length of Nilas's visit, but equally important, the completion of his wooden creation.

It was in this way, by doing, seeing, and listening, that I gathered a picture of the lives of the people in Stalo. Information, stories of the past, or explanations of complex reindeer herding practices can never be demanded. Small pieces and scattered fragments from hundreds of conversations over thousands of cups of coffee, after numerous calf-markings and during all kinds of shared labor can only gradually be put together. It is only by joining in the way of life that one could encounter and grasp the meaning of things in context as they occurred.

My reindeer-herding lesson for the day was apparently not to end with Nilas. No sooner had I returned to my own goattieh than I was visited by Nikke Labba, a friend from the Luokta-Mavas Sameby directly south of Tuorpon. The Mavas reindeer shared parts of the same summer grazing land with Tuorpon and therefore it was necessary for a few representatives from Mavas to spend the summer at Stalo and participate in the Tuorpon calf-markings. Mavas would always have two or three members in Stalo each summer to mark their calves and any belonging to a fellow Mavas member. To these visiting ambassadors—Nikke, Martin Sjaggo and Per-Johan Palopää—Stalo was not a true home but a foreign station, and instead of permanent turf goattiehs, they quartered themselves in more transient tent goattiehs. These they could disassemble when the last calf-marking was over and they could leave for home.

When it was rainy and damp inside his tent goattieh, Nikke would sometimes stroll over to dry out by my fire. In truly bad weather, it is often hopeless to try to get fully dry in a tent goattieh. A turf goattieh can hold a much larger fire without filling so thickly with smoke. Of course, it was not only bad weather that brought Nikke. Today was a fine day and Nikke was out making the "goattieh round." As usual he pulled out his pipe, propped himself comfortably against the wall, and puffed with a wide smile on his face. It took a long time before he said anything other than "yes" or "no," but his expression indicated that he could tell me a thousand interesting things if only he felt like it, and today he finally did.

"You can learn a lot about reindeer herding here," said Nikke at last, "but you've still got to find yourself a tjappa niejdda before you can start on your own." A *tjappa niejdda* means a "pretty Saami girl." It would be illegal for me, a non-Saami, to become a reindeer herder unless I married someone with that right. By this time many a friend had promised to find me a tjappa niejdda, but if the truth be told they had enough trouble looking after their own interests. "Maybe I can start in Alaska or Canada," I replied. "There have already been Saami herding there and in Greenland too." "It's difficult on your own," said

Nikke, and to my astonishment added, "Myself, I worked as a herder for two years in the Highlands of Scotland."

Nikke slowly unfolded the tale of Mikael Utsi, the Jokkmokk Saami (of Karesuando origin) who had married a British anthropologist and immigrated to Scotland with a reindeer herd. "It's a good idea to learn something about herding in different places," Nikke assured me, "Mavas is another example. We're very close to Tuorpon, but our grazing land is distributed so differently that the entire year's cycle differs from that of Tuorpon on many points. For instance, most of us in Mavas have as many as four homes, whereas most Tuorpon Saami have only one summer and one winter home. The Jokkmokk mountain Samebys—Tuorpon, Jåkkåkaska, and Sirkas—all have an abundance of summer grazing land and a good deal in the winter as well. Both grazing areas are good enough to sustain the herds for a long while. Mavas, on the other hand, has sparse winter, autumn, and early spring grazing land."

To summarize Nikke's discourse: if Mavas were to let its reindeer roam at will, they would eat too much of the precious moss in one area leaving little or nothing for the next time. For Mavas to be able to feed its herds, the reindeer must be driven from place to place at frequent intervals to conserve the seasonal distribution of food. Whereas Mavas must drive its herds gradually step by step from the summer land down to their winter land so that the winter grazing will last, Tuorpon (at least the Nuortvalle part) can make a much quicker transition from summer to winter land."

Nikke, like Nilas, had instructed me on a critical point. It is most valuable to compare the herding practices of different areas, from different environments. In this way the main determinants stand out. Where two Samebys differ in herding technique, there one can find the truest measure of environmental dictates. Environments change considerably from year to year and from place to place within even a small region. That is why there is no general formula for the reindeer-herding cycle. Each Sameby, and each group and family within each Sameby does things differently. Each year presents new variations demanding different adjustments.

When Nikke had made his point he lapsed into silence, took a stick from the fire and with some difficulty relit his pipe. In Saami one doesn't smoke a pipe, one "drinks" it. To smoke a pipe for a Saami would mean to hang it up with the fish on a rack above the fire. A smoked pipe would be similar to a smoked ham. It looked to me as if Nikke had drunk from the same pipe for years without thinking of cleaning it. The bowl was so caked with charcoal, there was hardly any room for fresh tobacco. I produced a pipe cleaner, something Nikke did claim to have seen before, and some cleaning fluid, which he had never heard of. In moments the draw was restored, and Nikke left happily in a cloud of smoke. He had not had such a good drink in ten years.

As I once again fell to contemplating the goattieh framework I marveled at how much I had learnt in one short day, a day without order or plan. If anything, this was what was typical of a day in Stalo. Even if you did nothing yourself, things happened to you. Stalo seemed to contain an inexhaustible store of surprises, and my days there were filled with learning, adventure, companionship, and humor.

My goattieh in Stalo, or "Choo's goattieh," as the Saami called it, was nearest to the spot on the lake shore where the seaplane landed, and was thus often crowded with friends who preferred a warm fire to the rain or cold while awaiting the plane. Fortunately my goattieh was well situated to alleviate the noise made by the planes when taking off. Pelle Gunnare claimed that his goattieh rang like a bell when the seaplane lifted. "As if someone put a bucket over my head and beat it with a hammer." We all agreed that the tourist flights should be limited, and yet at the same time we were most grateful for their existence. Should anyone fall ill or break a leg, a plane or helicopter could be called within minutes for an ambulance flight. Because I was alone in a goattieh capable of housing many more, I would often invite friends in need of temporary lodging to stay with me. I was never at a loss for good company.

One such guest was old Johannes Orpus from Parka. He had not been to Stalo for more than ten years. This summer, however, it fell to his lot to look after the family's interests during the calf-markings in Stalo. Like Nilas, Johannes was originally from Karesuando but had moved south into the Jokkmokk district with his entire herd when he married. His wife's family was also from Karesuando but had been forced south much earlier when the use of Norwegian grazing by Swedish Saami began to be tightly restricted. Inga Orpus was one of the few who could still sew the old-style leather summer shoes with watertight seams. Nowadays high rubber boots are standard and only Johannes continued with the old hook-toed leather model.

The soles of these shoes are cut from cowhide; the rest is of reindeer hide and sewn with tendon thread, a laborious task. Before the Saami "took to the air," Inga once told me, Johannes could wear out three such pairs of shoes in one summer. It was easy to understand how rubber boots gained immediate popularity.

In the evening as we sat watching the fire, I arranging logs and Johannes thoughtfully smoking his pipe, he drew forth what appeared to be two huge wrinkled prunes. "For you," he said. They turned out to be a pair of Inga's Saami shoes which Johannes had left in Stalo ten years ago. They were folded, rolled and dried out, but had never been worn. I was thrilled. But before I could wear them Johannes said he would soak them in water to loosen them up.

The next morning I was most anxious to try out my new shoes. As I threw out the old coffee grounds and cooked fresh morning coffee, I peered in all the kitchen pots hoping to find my new shoes soaking. They were nowhere to be found. Johannes had said he would take care of them and so I did not want to ask, but I could not help being curious. After a fine breakfast of fried char we stretched out on our reindeer hides, Johannes with pipe in mouth. The conversation drifted back to the pros and cons of rubber boots when Johannes calmly sat up, poked an arran stick down into the murky garbage pail, and pulled up one of the shoes. He squeezed it a few times and poked it back down amid the grease, coffee grounds, and floating fish bones with the comment, "not ready yet," while I tried hard not to laugh. It took another day in the garbage pail before Johannes pronounced the shoes ready. When I tried them out I came to realize why Johannes persisted in using them inspite of the advent of rubber boots and what a sacrifice it was for him to part with this pair. These shoes came to know my feet as no premolded rubber boot could.

With the end of summer and beginning of autumn, conversations change color; calves and fish yield priority to the coming moose and bear hunt. The hunting season does not begin until September, but already in early August before the villagers disperse, hunting companions can be heard planning strategy or reliving past glories. The work of separating the herds lay closer at hand, but then again, this is work, a matter of routine, and not at all as exciting as the hunt. Hunters of course are always full of stories.

A standard Lapland bear yarn tells of the hunter who took his friends out hunting in order to impress them with his prowess. "Stay here in the cabin," he said, "while I go out and bring in the food." Not far from the cabin the brave hunter ran into a huge bear. The man shook so that he could not fire a shot, and he was soon running with all his might, the bear close behind. The hunter burst into the cabin startling his companions and swung behind the door. The angry bear charged after him through the open door, crashing into tables and chairs. "You cook this one," yelled the man to his terrified friends as he ducked outside slamming the door, "while I go back out and try to find another."

Ivar Läntha, a visitor, told us one evening of a time when he was only five years old and began to notice a lot of whispering and scurrying around the house. Soon there was a huge black cauldron out front with a delicious smell steaming forth. Ivar was given a "marrow bone" almost as tall as he was—that is, one of the eight leg and thigh bones cooked for their marrow content—and ate it with great appetite. His father had shot a huge bull moose out of season, and to still his son's queries, he told Ivar that he had shot a rabbit. A few hours later the game warden happened to cross the lake and met Ivar playing by the shore. "Do you know what?" said Ivar full of pride. "My Dad has shot a rabbit," and stretching his hands out as far as he could, "it had marrow bones this big!" The warden wore a suspicious frown and said finally, "Ivar, my boy, I don't want to hear you talking about that rabbit anymore." The family heaved a sigh of relief when the warden departed, apparently ignorant of the illegal kill. "Why didn't he believe me when I told him how big this rabbit was?" asked Ivar later at dinner. His father promptly lost his appetite and worried for days that the police would arrive, but nothing ever happened.

I had no desire to shoot a moose, but was excited by the prospect of being along on the hunt. For me, shooting a moose would have been nothing but a test of marksmanship, a matter of pride, and no good reason I decided for taking life. As a meat eater I would not shy away from helping with the work this involved, but preferred to leave the shooting to those who would not look upon it as a thrilling novelty but instead a necessary part of living. There is much more to the hunt than just shooting. There is the slaughter, transport home of the meat, butchering, and dividing among the hunting team. Besides the work directly connected with the moose, there is a special atmosphere about the hunt, a comradeship among the hunters and a treasure of story and tradition. My plans for leaving Stalo and returning to the United States were wavering. Maybe I would stop off in Jokkmokk a while to be along on the moose hunt before continuing homeward. As the summer grew old a decision was called for, and I proved easy prey to the enticements offered by my friends from the Parka village, Sigge Pavval and his goattieh companion Martin Sjaggo.

With the calf-markings over, and a few weeks before the herd separations, Sigge and Martin dreamed of a quick vacation. I sat with them in their tent goattieh drinking coffee as they planned a hike across the Norwegian border to friends in Sulitjelma, a small mining town, when suddenly Johan Parfa brought fresh news from the walkie-talkie. There was to be a calf-marking at Rovi early tomorrow morning. The Rovi corral lies midway between Stalo and Parka. Although the reindeer had been nearer to the corral at Jålli, they had been driven to the Rovi corral in order to bring them further east toward the winter land. With the reindeer already in Rovi there was certainly no time for a vacation. After the marking in Rovi, Sigge and Martin could continue directly home to Parka.

"There in Parka you can learn how to gather," said Sigge. "Here in Stalo the gatherers are flown out by Lundqvist and the Sameby's treasury has to pay the bill, so you can't go along. But in Parka we head out on foot. You can come along with me when we gather for separation at the Parka corral. You must learn what it is like to gather." Sigge and Martin's visions of Norway evaporated and two hours later they packed themselves and their dogs into the crowded seaplane bound for Rovi. As Sigge and Martin flew by overhead, all that remained of their summer home was a circle of stones, a floor of birch branches and a still smoldering fire.

I just could not abandon the opportunity to join Sigge on a gathering expedition. I had to see the corral from the gatherer's perspective. I could meet Sigge in Parka to gather and then join Johan Märak for the moose hunt. My return to the United States was postponed indefinitely. I had been drawn into the Saami year. Each new experience added more meaning to past experiences. A Saami is aware of the demands of each season at all times. Much of the work done in summer is preparation for the winter. The reindeer slaughtered and buried in the snow during the autumn migration will be eaten four or five months later during the spring migration. It became clear to me that one can never grasp a single piece of the Saami way of life unless one sees it in the context of the full year's cycle.

There was one last thing I insisted upon doing before leaving Stalo and heading toward Parka. I must make the pilgrimage to Stalo Rock, which I had heard so much about. Staloluokta is named after the large but stupid troll of Saami mythology, Stalo. This Stalo troll liked nothing better than to eat naughty Saami children. Many stories are told about him, mainly how he was outwitted by the clever Saami. Some of these stories resemble that of Odysseus and the Cyclops. Experts have claimed the Stalo troll to be a reflection of contact with the Norsemen. The word "stalo" apparently derives from the word "stål" in Swedish or iron (steel) in English, and therefore the Stalo troll has been interpreted as being an iron man or symbol of the Vikings who wore armor. Whether or not he is a truly Saami figure in origin, stories of him are told to this day with characteristic Saami flavor. It is not at all uncommon for parents to call in their children with threats of Stalo lurking in the darkness.

Susanna Kuhmunen told me that as a little girl she had always awakened first and run outside to play. Her parents were by no means as eager to rise at that early hour to keep an eye on her. "You cannot go outside when no one else is awake," they told her, but Susanna was stubborn. Finally one night when she was asleep, her parents went outside and erected a large scarecrow-like Stalo troll in front of the goattieh door. Stalo will scare her so much she'll stay inside they thought. But next morning Susanna was overjoyed. "Look, Mama," she shouted as she ran out. "I'm not the only one awake. Now I have someone to play with."

Not far from Staloluokta, across the swiftly flowing Stalojokk, stood Stalo Rock. "You will know it when you see it," Johan Parfa assured me as I begged a ride across the lake to bypass the high water in Stalojokk. "Make a fire on the shore when you want to be picked up," said Johan as I started up the hill. A little while later I spied a huge rock alone on the tundra far in the distance. There could be no doubt, this was the rock that according to legend was Stalo's goattieh. The legend says that Stalo terrorized the Saami for many years until one brave soul waited for Stalo to go to sleep inside the rock and then walled up the opening.

From afar, one could not help but observe that this rock was unusual. It stood upright in a most unnatural way, but even more strange was the absence of any other large boulders in the vicinity. It stood as foreign to its surroundings as a flag on the moon. How had such a large rock arrived just there? "Stalo placed it there" is the legend's explanation; only he would be strong enough to move it. A closer look revealed that the rock is remarkable in other ways as well. A layer of rare, red moss covers two sides, but what interested me most was a large pile of stones blocking an opening in the rock. This was Stalo's door, and these stones his prison wall. But after all the years, the wall had partially crumbled, and the top part of the cave was exposed. I crawled in as far as I could. Stalo was gone, escaped. He roams the high tundra land once again, lurching against the mountains, tearing up the forests, a danger to all.

When I reached the shore, I started a small fire and the smoke soon signaled those on the other side. Johan sped out in his boat to fetch me. "I ought to mark a trail to the rock," said Johan when he came, "and then charge tourists an enormous fee for a ride across the lake." Back in the village the idea was further embroidered. Nil-Tomas would hide in the rock and make weird wailing noises like the trapped Stalo troll. Johan would sell odd pieces of reindeer antler as amulets against him. Ancient Saami magical charms he would call them. We egged each other on all evening, building for ourselves a bigger and bigger enterprise, and then forgot it all when time came for sleep.

I awoke next morning from an awful pounding on the goattieh door. "Have you got any glödkakas in there? Or fish? I want to buy some fish," screeched an old lady with a throaty dialect from southern

Sweden. All the while she never stopped pounding. My goattieh guest, Nisse Pavval from Parka, called out that we had nothing to sell. I swore and told her to go away. I had been awakened by inconsiderate tourists more than once, but this one drove me crazy. "I know you've got fish in there," she cried. Nisse and I yelled back. I was still in my sleeping bag and groggy, but Nisse had crawled out to start a fire. The pounding continued. "Get your pants on, boys, because I'm coming in," cackled the old woman, and Nisse scrambled for his clothes. I was doubled up laughing. I knew finally who it must be, and sure enough, when the door swung open, in stepped Pastor Johan Märak sputtering like a granny from Skåne.

No one is more welcome in Stalo than Johan Märak. He grew up with everyone in the village, at one time herded reindeer with them, is one of the few Saami preachers, and spoke their language. Nor would Johan wish to be anywhere else than in Stalo. He always managed to arrange for himself at least a week in Stalo during the summer. He would lie in the goattiehs all day with his childhood friends, fish with them, or help them chop wood. Then in the evenings he would wash his face and walk up the hill to the goattieh church, where he held services. Many a visitor from the tourist cabin has been surprised to hear Pastor Märak discoursing in church on Saami pre-Christian religion or simply telling ghost stories all evening. The church goattieh in Stalo was never more crowded than when Johan came.

Johan was not one to condemn the old paganism of the Saami as had the early Christian missionaries. He respected the religion of his forefathers and said that he felt himself on holy ground when standing at an old sacrificial site. The old gods may have been dead, but no Saami would scorn or despise their memory. In fact there is great interest in the past traditions and most of the Saami with whom I discussed the topic were very knowledgeable and had much to tell me about the old *nàjds,* shamans. There are many remnants of the old religion of the Saami in the stories, art, and superstitions of Lapland, but if there can be any measure, the Saami must be considered as having been fully Christianized for quite a while now. I was glad to see that Johan, representing the Church, actively fostered interest in the past religious heritage of the Saami.

Johan brought with him cakes, rolls and coffee to celebrate the big church holiday at Stalo that crowned the end of summer. Many of the Saami wore their *kolts,* traditional dress, for the occasion, and all of us had at least changed to a clean shirt. It was such a clear day that we could see the Norwegian Queen, a face formed by the Norwegian mountains across the lake. For me this was the final calm. I could feel the hiking fever in my legs and my thoughts were on the separations in Parka. I knew that soon I must take to the trail.

The beginning of August heralded the end of the summer season for most of us in Stalo. It seemed to me I had hardly arrived, laid the goattieh floor, and made the goattieh rounds before it was time to pack up and go. But the calf-markings were over in the summer land. The ground was covered with ripening berries. Already winter was in the air, and most of the reindeer were slowly wending their way eastward down to the forests. Only the intensive Blind group kept most of their herd tucked in a large natural pocket between steep mountains and a broad rapid river, the Tuokijokk. Here they remained until autumn migration, which generally occurs in November. Already in October the herders of the Blind group return to the mountains to gather together the reindeer. Then they drive their herd in one large mass across the frozen Tuokijokk and over the snow-covered tundra down to the winter land.

The other herders did not migrate with their reindeer, but let them drift on their own in small, scattered flocks eastward before the snows. During the move, the sarvs tend to split off from the rest of the herd, seeking their own special grazing areas where they undergo the bodily changes occasioned by the mating season.

The mosquitoes disappeared as suddenly as they had come. It would have taken more than an August chill to attract the reindeer into the forests otherwise. We could now enjoy a few brief days freed from our artificial tans, a result of the tar-and-oil mosquito repellant. Soon, however, the *knott* (Lapland black fly) would arrive to fill the gap vacated by the mosquitoes. I will unfortunately have cause to describe the knott in more detail elsewhere.

When I packed my belongings after that first summer in Stalo, I had no idea that next summer would find me there again, and the next and the next. Now that my return is more expected than not, I do not bother to freight down pots, pans, and extra food supplies. Instead, like all Saami, I simply stock them in a *boda,* small wooden storehouse, until next summer, spring, or autumn. But at that time, I did not know I would see Stalo again and certainly not so soon. I had carried all my belongings up to the mountains, but it was impossible to carry them all down. I seemed to have accumulated a pile of things filling a large cardboard box as well as my pack. Martin the pilot saved the situation by freighting the box down in his seaplane, freeing me to plan my own move on foot.

One morning I climbed high over the village for a last look at Stalo. I waved to Martin as he passed overhead in his seaplane, and the plane dipped its wings. Smoke trailed from all the little goattiehs except mine. I watched the tiny people down in the village or fishing out on the lake. I knew each one by the color of his or her hat or jacket. I wondered if they understood how grateful I was to have shared the summer with them.

I decided to avoid the main tourist trail as much as possible and instead of following the Tarra Valley to Kvikkjokk, chose to take the Ruonasvagge valley route. Nils-Tomas had drawn me a notorious Saami map of the best way to go, which proved to make sense only in hindsight, after I had blundered through all other possibilities. "Ruonasvagge means the green valley," Nils-Tomas had told me— good walking country, I thought. I pictured high plateaus of grass and moss. "It's a bit rocky," he had added, and I laughed bitterly at the phrase mile after mile over the most cumbersome rough rocky passes. There was much snow among these rocks. A white, cold, and damp fog blanketed everything. By late afternoon it was impossible to see more than a few feet ahead into the mist. At first I thought I had found a series of stone trail markers, but each one I approached flew away, birds. There was nothing to do but put up the tent and wait. When dawn broke I was sure Biegolmai, the wind god, had repaired his broken shovel. My tent poles broke with a snap and I was enveloped in a mass of fluttering cloth. It rained; it snowed; it hailed, flashed, and thundered.

The wind had at least blown away the fog. There was little I could do but move on, and when the storm finally quieted, I felt exhilarated and silly. My feet seemed to step of their own accord.

They did all the walking while I watched the storm's incredible retreat. When I finally stopped and looked back along the way I had come, I had no recollection of walking at all. More than two hundred years ago the famed Swedish naturalist Carl Linnaeus had traveled this stretch, though in the opposite direction, from Kvikkjokk to Stalo. In human years this was long ago, but to the mountains it is no time at all.

If I stopped my own motion for a while, removed my thoughts from my own hurried life, and simply sat on a stone, then maybe I could sense what time was for the mountains. If only I could see without intruding, then I would see what the mountains saw through all time. All who have wandered in the mountains know the feeling well when suddenly one seems to have awakened. Personal existence is forgotten in a few minutes of eternity and one is a bit startled upon return to find a body and a life to live. As I sat dreaming on the stone, I imagined that Linnaeus came trudging up the trail from Kvikkjokk. He stopped and rested with me on the rock. Each told the other briefly what lay ahead and then the trickling of melted snow water drew us both into silence. Whether together at a precise instant or separated by two centuries, it seemed to make no difference. Our communion rested in the mountains and perpetual snows, stretching to all who had ever come this way and to all who are yet to wander here.

Kvikkjokk was a welcome sight. Though consisting of only a few houses, a charming church, a store and a tourist station, Kvikkjokk means civilization to the weary hiker. Of Kvikkjokk's civilized wonders, cold beer was always the most immediately appreciated. After a few months in the mountains, it would be natural for anyone to celebrate. It is a shame that such periods of understandable exuberance are taken to confirm the bad reputation of the Saami for drink. Alcohol has been a problem in the far north, and is in fact one of the reasons behind the puritanical Laestadian revival, but it is certainly not a problem confined to the Saami.

Kvikkjokk is the hub of a great wheel, the spokes of which are the numerous valleys and lakes leading to and from the high mountains. It is the natural starting and ending point for almost all expeditions into the surrounding highlands. This tiny village has a long and fascinating history. It was here that a famous religious duel occurred between a preacher and a Saami shaman, or nåjd, in the eighteenth century. To demonstrate his powers, the nåjd flew from tree to tree like a squirrel until the preacher made the sign of the cross. The shaman fell to the ground and broke a leg. Soon after he was converted to Christianity.

In the seventeenth century the area was notable for its silver mines, and Saami were forced to work as slaves transporting the ore by reindeer caravan. An inlet in the Kvikkjokk delta land is called "Lappviken" and is where recalcitrant Saami who refused to haul ore were punished. Two holes were chopped in the ice a good distance apart, a rope threaded between them under the ice, and the Saami pulled from one hole to the other until he died or agreed to do as he was bid.

The road from Jokkmokk to Kvikkjokk was finished in the 1950s, a result primarily of the construction of the huge Seitevare power plant. A road was necessary to carry the heavy machinery to the dam site. It is remarkable how a single road can entirely alter the lives of the people it touches. Farms that had been more or less self-sustaining grew to be more and more dependent on goods from outside. Many farmers were given such good jobs working for the water power company that they gave up their livestock and crops. Then, when the dam was finished and the water power company gone to a new site, they were left like a piece of driftwood on the shore. Many have been forced into the cities to find jobs. Roads always begin as agents of transportation and distribution, but almost invariably bind the country people all too strongly to the industrial areas and end by drawing them to concentrated cities. The division of labor, the compartmentalization of people into specific jobs, taught in our history books as one of the building blocks of civilization, has destroyed much of the wilderness culture of Lapland and in many instances replaced it with nothing.

I picked up the box Martin had flown down for me and bought an ice-cream cone for him to fly up to my little friend Per-Jonas Parfa. The ice-cream cone would also be a sign to Nils-Tomas that I had survived Ruonasvagge despite his Saami map and was enjoying the delights of civilization. I had not seen a car for so long that they struck me as amusing to watch and also quite terrifying to ride in. I caught a ride with an elderly Swede named Nevada Larsson, named he said after an American cowboy comic book hero. Larsson is a common name, and therefore Nevada's father had chosen unusual names for his sons. Nevada's brother was named Tex. In a short while we had traveled what would have taken two days to walk.

Nevada told me that when he was a child, before the road existed, the Saami had migrated across the lake in front of his house. It was always a high time when the Saami came by. He remembered that one spring when they began to move back to the high mountains, there was one old man who was too weak and tired to make the trek. When he realized he would have to be left behind, he went out on the lake, cut a hole in the ice and jumped in. The lake had thawed and frozen over again, however, and so when he jumped he did not drop far before hitting another layer of ice. He was stubborn and sat down on the bottom layer with the water to his shoulders and waited until he froze to death. When the others found him they cut him out of the ice and brought him to the Larsson's barn before freighting the body down to the churchyard. All that night the wind had howled and Nevada and Tex were terrified, thinking the old man yoiked his ghostly songs in the barn.

Old Saami in the past had traditionally ended their own lives rather than become a burden. Sometimes they could be quartered in the homes of friendly settlers, but nowadays the old can be cared for in the old folk's homes, run by the municipality. There is such a home now in Jokkmokk. To exchange the mobile free life in the mountains for the confines of a nursing home is a nightmare for many; yet, there they receive good care and comfort. For many Saami, however, used to a totally different life, death is far preferable to a long decline at the nursing home.

At home in Jokkmokk I was mobbed by the Märak children, Gulle, Annika, David, and Nillan. Johan had flown down from Stalo a few days before. Gunborg supplied me with a strong cup of coffee, and we all spilled out summer experiences as fast as we could. Johan laughed at my description of the hike. Ruonasvagge did indeed mean green valley he explained, but the green did not refer to grass. The valley was named after the green lichen on the thousands of rocks.

Sitting there in a chair by a table, I felt I had come through a rabbit hole to a totally new world. I nearly went outside into the bushes to urinate, and it felt very odd to use a toilet indoors. Soon I was floating in the bath. All travels end sooner or later in a hot bathtub.

5

Parka Separations

As I stepped from the 1933, made-in-Detroit, "Norseman" seaplane, I was hit by a cloud of *knott* welcoming me to Parka. The knott resembles the hated North American black fly. It creeps down collars and up shirt sleeves, has a most uncomfortably itchy bite, and unlike the mosquito, is not at all fragile. It often takes more than one swat to squash a knott. By far their worst trait, however, is that they are not in the least concerned for their own lives. A knott that is lucky enough to survive the first swat will not thankfully retreat; instead, it will shrug and take the opportunity to bite again. The mosquito is a tricky ballet dancer, but the knott is an angry bulldog. Fortunately I had not removed my tar oil repellent bottle from my belt.

I was not the only passenger to Parka. The plane was full of Saami, packs, and dogs. Moreover, each of us carried a large box full of food supplies to last us until the work was finished. Parka had no flying grocery delivery as had Stalo. It was most usual for those who came for the August separations to fly up from Kvikkjokk with a heavy load of food and walk down later when there was little left to carry. Those who lived in Parka all summer needed far more thorough provisioning and had therefore freighted up necessities and food by snow scooter in the early spring. Cheese, milk, and other fresh foods were, of course, highly valued in Parka and much of the space in our supply boxes was filled with such luxury items for our friends there—not to forget the latest newspaper.

My home in Parka was a converted horse trailer made of wood that had been pulled up by scooter by Nils-Tomas and Johan Parfa a few years earlier. Before I left Stalo, Johan had said that when I reached Parka I could join him and Per-Henrik Labba in "the tube," as this simple construction was called. The tube lacked smoke hole and arran, and was by no means as large and comfortable as a goattieh, but fully adequate for short spring and autumn visits. Johan and Per-Henrik would fly direct from Stalo to Parka, and since I was the only member of our new household to dip into civilization between visits in the two Saami villages, they had both sent shopping lists with me. Per-Henrik had ordered new crystals for his walkie-talkie. He and Johan were moose-hunting companions and planned to arrange a secret communication channel. Johan had a more troublesome request, a wood stove and eight feet of chimney pipe for the tube. August could be cold in Parka, and our small cooking burners would be insufficient. I managed to send the stove up on an earlier, less full, flight, the chimney pipe strapped to a pontoon, and I hoped that it would be already installed when I arrived a few days later.

Most of my fellow passengers on the seaplane were bound for Tuorpon's *tjelti-goattieh*. This was a goattieh built by the Tuorpon Sameby collectively, to house its members when they streamed in for the heavy work periods. Jåkkåkaska, the Sameby immediately north of Tuorpon, had also constructed a tjelti-goattieh in Parka. These goat-tiehs could become crowded, even though many of those eligible to live there preferred to stay with good friends or relatives among the established, summer-permanent Parka population. This time there were eight people and eight dogs crowded into Tuorpon's tjelti-goattieh, and I was grateful for Johan Parfa's invitation to join him in the tube.

After installing myself, putting my milk cartons in the cold spring below the crest of the hill, and exchanging news and messages, I set off to acquaint myself with my new surroundings. I had not wandered far before bumping into Johannes Orpus, who had given me the shoes, chopping wood outside his goattieh. Now it was his turn to play host. He took me inside, cooked coffee, and Inga, his wife, began frying a pan full of Parka fish. I had anticipated a meeting with Johannes and so when he settled back with his ever-warm pipe I was able to hand him a pouch of tobacco from the "big city."

My experience of calf-markings had taught me that the best way to get a picture of reindeer herding's current situation is to ask or listen to everyone in sight. So little is a matter of fact, and so much a matter of intuition and guesswork that the clearest forecast for markings or separations, vague though it may be, is derived from a mosaic of opinion. Over the fish and coffee I learned that there had been a meeting earlier in the morning. The day for the first gathering and separation may not be set, but the fact that there had been a meeting at all was significant in itself, and I thought it best to find Sigge Pavval in a hurry if I was to accompany him while gathering.

Johannes directed me to the Pavval goattieh: through the corral, down the hill by the side of a tiny lake. My knock was greeted by a chorus of barks, growls, and howls. Sigge's dog, Snutte, gave me a grumpy sniff of recognition when I entered. Sigge, his brother Per-Israel, and their father, Per, were stretched out on the moose hides within. More coffee. "Be ready." said Sigge. "Pack in advance. When we come, we'll be in a hurry. The trail we start off on goes by the tube and we'll meet you there—maybe tomorrow, maybe the next day, no telling when." This was not much to go on, but it is never possible to know more.

Per explained that the fence running through Parka from Kvikk-jokk and separating the summer from the winter grazing land was not constructed until the 1930s. The system of gathering and separating the herds as practiced today in Parka was apparently a relatively recent technique. The Kvikkjokk-Parka fence was not built for the purpose of aiding reindeer herding. The original reason for the fence was to keep the reindeer coming from the mountains out of the low-land farmers' hay fields and crops. The herds were not allowed to pass into the winter area before August 10. And, later in the spring, all the reindeer belonging to the mountain Samebys were to be above the line in the summer area by May 1. Although there are no longer any farmers who care about the old fields today, the law still holds that any mountain reindeer killed by car or train in the winter land after May 1 will not be compensated. The laws often seem to imply that the Saami should know exactly where every head of their herd is grazing in a wilderness of hundreds of square miles.

Now that most reindeer herding is extensive, it is not always so accurate to use the term "herd." Instead, the reindeer drift eastward in small scattered clusters. The fence stops them and enables the gatherers to bring them together, forming a "herd" only briefly to be driven into the corral, separated, and then released to scatter once again in different compartments of the winter land.

It was fascinating to listen to Per. Through his words I saw a changing pattern of life moving so fast that it was difficult to understand or grasp the forces behind these changes. It commonly happens today that we regard less modernized life-styles as age-old or static. Everywhere one turns one hears of the once isolated tribe only now beginning to break from its weighty traditions and dissolve in the industrial world. But this vision cannot be applied to the Saami, at least not during the last 1,100 years. Their way of life is certainly unique, but this does not mean they have lacked contact with the "outside world." When one looks at a picture of an old reindeer caravan, it is common to view it as a remnant from a timeless past. Actually, wholly nomadic, intensive reindeer herding appears to have developed largely as a result of colonial pressure 400 to 500 years ago, and it has evolved continually. Per's generation was undoubtedly not the first to speak of the good old days and then to recount incredible hardships sometimes as if they were fond memories.

On my way back to the tube, I stopped off at the Jåkkåkaska tjelti-goattieh to greet friends I had not seen since the last calf-marking. Among those inside was Petrus Gruvisare, eighty-four years old and still actively herding reindeer. He was one of the few who always wore his kolt, a Jokkmokk kolt. His close relative had been one of the greatest and most respected Saami leaders in the Jokkmokk district, Nils-Antaris Gruvisare from Sirkas Sameby. Like so many of the older Saami, Petrus spoke with a loud, high-pitched voice that could carry across the mountains against a wind though we listened only from across the fire. What's more, he had the habit of removing his false teeth for important or emphatic remarks.

He was telling me about a young female anthropologist who had come to Parka some time ago. The story had gotten him quite worked up. Every time he put *snus* (ground, wet tobacco snuff) under his lip, she would make a note of it. She followed him everywhere with a writing pad taking notes. "I kept walking through marshes and bushes to try to lose her, but she stuck right behind. I didn't have a moment to myself," and here he took out his teeth, "She wouldn't even let me alone long enough to piss." I expressed disbelief, but the others in the goattieh verified his tale of woe. "Petrus had to shout to us for help in Saami and we would try to distract her with some make-shift anthropological tidbit long enough for him to slip away." They had taken revenge, however, for when she expressed the desire to learn the art of milking a reindeer, they had lassoed a large sarv and laughed themselves silly when she tried to milk him.

Someone in the goattieh turned on his walkie-talkie, and amid all the chatter came the sudden information that the gatherers were setting out to bring in the herd for the first separation. When Sigge had said be ready, I had no idea he might mean already that same afternoon. Having not yet even been back to the tube, I was still unpacked and not in the least ready. I dashed out of the goattieh over to the tube and began throwing things into my pack: food, coffee bag, cup, rain gear, binoculars and tent. I was pulling on my hiking boots when Snutte the dog appeared followed by Sigge and three other gatherers with their dogs.

Other groups of gatherers were spreading out in different directions, the strategy being routine to all but me. Our group had its own assignment, to "turn the corner," and seal off the reindeer between the Kvikkjokk-Parka fence and a high mountain ridge. The fence ran parallel to the long ridge, and once over the ridge and behind the reindeer we would all split up, taking different positions to scare the reindeer toward the fence. We would have walkie-talkie contact with the others, and as the reindeer were driven down the slot all the gatherers would converge on the corral.

We went up the ridge in drizzle and cold, swung down to the valley floor behind, then proceeded to the end of the long mountain crest, the "corner" from which we were to swing across to the fence, like a three-mile-long closing gate. We stopped while still on high ground to spy with binoculars. It is interesting to consider what reindeer gathering was like before binoculars. With the extensive herding system as it is today, it would be almost impossible to gather without their help. The reindeer are spread out everywhere. In the past, however, herding was more intensive and the reindeer were always gathered and always guarded. Binoculars were not as necessary or regularly used in herding as they are today. Yet even in very early times, Saami commonly carried with them small, collapsible telescopes. Instruments granting the ability to see great distances have, of course, always been valuable for herders and hunters.

A large flock was heading slowly toward the fence of its own accord. No need to "close the gate" until they are inside, we decided. The time was right for a coffee break. We had maintained a fast pace in the rain and it was just as well to rest until the flock had moved past us. All of us had been wise enough to carry dried birchbark in our packs, so we had no trouble starting a fire despite the light rain. I had remembered birchbark but found to my dismay that in haste I had packed butter without bread. Fortunately the others had plenty to share. Saami trail food is as a rule easy to share because everyone has the same standard rations: coffee, bread and butter, dried reindeer meat, and maybe a smoked fish.

Sigge had always been interested in American Indians. I was hungry and thought it a good opportunity to show him the Indian game, actually a form of Nim I had learned from some Navajo children in Arizona. I persuaded him to stake one of his smoked fish. The game is played with 15 stones in piles of 7, 5, and 3. One can take any number from one to all stones from any single pile in turns, and the object is to avoid taking the last stone. In fact, it is no game at all because if one knows the proper combinations it is easy to win. We played again and again. Sigge lost each time. When he understood that there was a trick to it, he insisted we go through every possibility so that he could learn the winning combinations. I had to promise never to show anyone else in his village the winning patterns. He was rubbing his hands together at the thought of beating everybody for high stakes.

When the flock had moved close enough to the fence we split up. Sigge, Snutte, and I were to take the outermost arc down into the birch forest. The other three men and dogs would block the reindeer's retreat and funnel them down the slot on the "inside" slope of the mountain ridge. Sigge and I set off quickly behind the flock, occasionally emitting a long howl, "aaa wi wi wi wi," to frighten the reindeer in the desired direction.

Snutte proved to be far more interested in hunting field mice than herding reindeer. I have never seen a dog behave so much like a cat. But when leashed and commanded threateningly in Saami to bark, he did his duty and let the reindeer know that a dog was at their rear. The reindeer were always moving far ahead of us and once we entered the birch forest, it was rare that we even caught sight of them. Snutte barked like a machine on cue as we bellowed and stumbled through the woods. Had it not been for Sigge's sense of direction, the reindeer could easily have outmaneuvered us.

When we emerged from the woods after hours of constant scrambling, the reindeer we had helped gather were already far down the slot, being driven by other men. We could see long strings of reindeer high up on the inside slope above the tree line, moving toward the corral. We had closed the reindeer's retreat, but estimated that we had actively driven them only a brief while before those running from us had encountered the other gatherers. It was wonderful to see how these men worked together naturally, without detailed orders and plans. They have done it the same way hundreds of times, know the land thoroughly, know how the reindeer react to their movements, and know that they can count on each other.

From the walkie-talkie we learned that every area had been covered and there was nothing more to do but make our way toward the corral where we would all assemble for the final delicate drive. We met other gatherers along the way, struggling back toward the corral, having performed their part in a group effort which had temporarily swept past them. Altogether we knew there were about fourteen men in action. Some of them we could see far off as moving dots with smaller dots, their dogs, dashing about them. Most of the men I would not even see until the very end, when we converged at the corral. But in a sense we could see the men by their actions. If the reindeer suddenly broke for freedom, we could see how they were checked and turned back in the right direction, and we knew we had a watchful comrade there on the flank whose name we could only guess.

It was late in the evening before we began to ease the reindeer off the slope down to the grazing enclosure below. This was a large corral, where the herd, I estimated at about 1,500 head, would spend the night before being driven into the smaller adjoining separation corral early next morning. Now that the weather was cooler, we could corral the reindeer during the day, and moreover, the disappearance of the midnight sun made working in the late hours impossible. The herd had stopped as it met a wall of gatherers ahead. Another line of gatherers was strung across the crest of the slope above the herd, and as we came up behind we too spread ourselves out in a long row. The reindeer soon realized they were in a gradually tightening box, three sides composed of men, the fourth being the fence with the open corral gate.

This is the most delicate moment, when the herd is forced downhill. As the noose tightens, the herd becomes more and more nervous. For the first time they feel themselves completely surrounded. Now the dogs are hushed and no one shouts as before. A single mistimed bark could make the entire herd panic and instinctively fly uphill, costing us hours of wasted labor. A cornered and frightened herd is hard to contain. Too sudden a movement might cause the reindeer to stampede and crash through the wall of men. The reindeer are tense. They do not like the presence of men and stop repeatedly to look for openings in the walls. The downhill drive to the grazing enclosure is a gentle but firm pressure. We walk silently downhill along the herd's edges, never hurrying and always on guard.

The entrance to the grazing enclosure is masterfully planned. The opening is situated under a rise and the fence runs a good stretch uphill before squaring off. The reindeer, which are always trying to flee uphill, could not see that part of the fence that cut off their uphill flight. They paused thoughtfully at the opening, but as we on the outside tightened our hold even more, they suddenly poured through the gate and dashed madly uphill thinking they had thrown off their oppressors at last. By the time they reached the upper fence, we were busily rolling wire netting across the opening.

We had been walking for many, many hours, and when the gate was up and the job done, we stretched out on the bank and talked to those we had worked beside so long in silence. I was exhausted. The others did not seem at all tired. There could be many more rounds of gathering and separating these next weeks at Parka. Each successive time they had to comb a wider area to bring together a sizable herd. This first sweep was nothing, they said. Often they are out three or four days walking constantly in rain and snow. I was glad to crawl off to sleep in the Parfa tube, especially as the herd would be put into the separation corral and the work begin at 3:00 A.M. next morning.

In the years to come I was to gather many times. No two gathering expeditions are ever exactly the same; there is always more to learn and experience, but there comes a basic understanding of the land, the reindeer, one's companions and the procedure as a whole. And how very much more of this understanding have they who have grown up into it. Reindeer herding is not the kind of work that can be mastered after a few courses. I encountered more than just gathering procedure at Parka. I was made aware of the enormous amount of teamwork herding requires and the great skill and knowledge it demands of each herding member. Even a skilled herder from one area cannot immediately adapt himself to another area. And someone who does not share the specific knowledge of the terrain in the Sameby's territory, knowledge that is best learned from a life time of herding there, will be of little help to his fellows. It is for this reason that the Sameby as a collective whole decides who is to be permitted to join its ranks. There are many more eligible herders than are actually active. By Swedish law, to be eligible for Sameby membership one must be of Saami origin and have a parent or grandparent who has at one time had herding as a steady livelihood. Today there are only about nine hundred active herders in all of Sweden. This figure depends largely on the fact that the government has limited the number of reindeer allowed in each Sameby (to prevent overgrazing). Would-be herders, those who are not born into the Sameby, must wait until the current herders feel there is enough room. Even when there is plenty of room, the members of the Sameby frequently bar admission to someone they do not believe they can work beside. In the main, this is the kind of life one is born into, and one's working companions are almost all friends and relatives.

By the time a strong cup of early morning coffee had cleared my vision, the herd was in the small corral and the work underway. Those calves that had been missed during the calf-markings, and were still "whole-eared," were now marked. Separating the herd before all calves are marked may result in a mother's being separated from her calf, and if the calf is unmarked, there is then no way of knowing who its owner is. This year had been an excellent calving year, and since bad weather had hampered the markings all summer, there was a considerable amount of work to do. The long, light calf-marking lassos were flying in all directions, and the thicker, stronger separation lassos were laid aside until the full-grown reindeer were to be caught and pulled. The wise old härks stood calmly in the center of the corral as the calves ran to and fro in frenzy. They realized that calf-marking was no concern of theirs.

Although the calves now being marked in Parka were only one month older than those marked at the usual summer markings, I was amazed to see how large they had grown. A reindeer's growth is much slower during the cold season. A few calves were noticeably smaller than the others. They had been born late and would have a difficult time surviving the winter should it be severe. Even a slight deviation from the norm can prove fatal in Lapland, where changes are sudden and drastic.

This was the first meeting in the Parka corral this autumn, and everyone was busy greeting friends. These separations have the atmosphere of a country fair. Often the whole family is present to join in the swirl of activity. After the calves are marked there is a coffee break that comes like the lull before a storm. A fence with two narrow gates (sliding doors so that when being opened they do not block the path of reindeer and herders) runs down the middle of the dividing corral with roughly half the herd on each side. All the Arjeplog Saami work on the one side and the Jokkmokk Saami on the other. When the separation is over, all the Arjeplog reindeer will be pulled by their owners through the gate to the other side. The Jokkmokk Saami pull their reindeer across in the opposite direction. Those reindeer who by simple luck entered the corral on the proper side of the gate have saved their owners the considerable effort of pulling them across. Each owner is responsible for his own reindeer, and so some must work far more than others.

It is no easy matter to pull a fighting reindeer. The sarvs have already begun to show signs of the approaching mating season. They have grown heavier. Their necks are thicker and stronger and they are not as timid as is generally the case. It is all too easy to get a reindeer antler in the face or a swift kick in the shins. Fortunately, everyone pitches in and helps each other. The women and children carry small birch branches and help scare the reindeer toward the gate. They swat the reindeer from behind, push, wave arms and legs, and shout. But even this does not always help. Sometimes it takes two men, one on each antler, to make a stubborn reindeer move at all.

Calves can be picked up, tucked under an arm, and carried across. The lighter reindeer can be walked across on their hind legs by lifting the head and forelegs with a wrestler's hammerlock. The older men, who still have keen eyes for spotting their mark and lassoing, appreciate the help of the younger when the time comes to pull. The gates become congested with action. A Saami hurries through the gate, lunges against the frame post, and lets it relieve the strain on his lasso. He braces himself and pulls. His wife scares the reindeer from behind, and it begins a furious zig-zag kicking dance before being pulled through the gate like a fish on a reel. Once on the correct side, it may take two men to hold it still enough to unfasten the lasso from its antlers.

Only a few months ago they had hardly any antlers at all. Now the male reindeer have huge, often three-foot-long antlers with numerous spikes. The vajas too have antlers, only smaller. The reindeer (and the North American caribou, wild reindeer) are the only deer species where both male and female have antlers, but what I find even more amazing is that they grow and shed these huge, heavy crowns yearly. During the main growing season, in the summer, the antlers are filled with blood, comparatively fragile, and covered with a soft furry skin (velvet) and sensitive nerves that make the reindeer guard them with great care. In their hind feet reindeer carry a small gland that stimulates antler growth. In spring and early summer one can often see reindeer standing on three legs rubbing one of their small new antler shoots with a hind foot. The Saami say that the reindeer is "making antlers." Should a reindeer be lame in one back leg and unable to rub the antler on that side, that antler will often be stunted or deformed.

With the coming of autumn and the approach of the mating season, remarkable changes begin. Three of the biggest sarvs in the corral in Parka had already begun to shed the velvet covering of their antlers. It looked as if rags hung from tree branches and the bared antler underneath the skin tatters was red with blood—a striking sight, like a huge wound. Something cruel, sharp, and hard was emerging from something that was once soft and fuzzy. The blood and nerves disappear as the antler dries to a hard dueling weapon.

The härks, however, who have been castrated, no longer follow the regular antler-growing schedule. Their antlers would still be covered with skin long after the mating season was over. We had to be careful in Parka not to pull too hard on an unhardened antler. It was not uncommon for them to break. Reindeer have bled to death through broken antlers and should a bad break occur, it is best to tie off the stump with a piece of string to contain the bleeding.

A dead calf hung limply from the corral fence. In its frightened run to avoid the lasso, it had run into the side of the corral and broken a leg. There was nothing for its owner, Johan Parfa, to do but slaughter it. We would have a calf-meat feast in the Parfa tube when the work was finished. In the days of the big herds, even a fully healthy calf might be slaughtered. The hide of a calf is the softest and finest for the making of winter clothing. But nowadays nylon and wool have replaced most reindeer-skin clothing, and (unless there is a grazing shortage) it is usually more profitable to let calves grow to full size.

As the work progressed and all the Arjeplog reindeer were collected on one side and the Jokkmokk reindeer on the other, the Saami had also shifted sides to look over their assembled herd. Then when all was done a part of the fence was rolled back on each side and the two herds streamed out in different directions, separated by another long fence dividing the winter grazing lands. Johan, Per-Henrik and I were so tired that we could hardly keep awake while waiting for our calf-meat meal to cook. We ate hungrily and crawled into the tube to sleep. It was only early afternoon, but I doubt there was a soul in Parka left awake.

That evening I found Sigge in his goattieh looking slightly thoughtful and confused. After the usual cup of coffee, he laid out fifteen matches he had been puzzling over and asked me once again to demonstrate the winning combinations of the "Indian game," Nim. Apparently Sigge had taken on all bets with great confidence and lost twice in a row to Per-Israel, his younger brother. The trick had backfired, and Sigge was fit to be tied.

The following day was a Friday, a day for recovery, and the next gathering sweep would not begin until after the weekend. While running through the woods with Sigge and Snutte, I had noticed many a wonderfully formed birch tree knur, the kind used for making Saami *kosas*. The kosa is the Saami drinking cup, coffee mug, and sometimes food bowl. The growth of the knur is irregular and because the wood grain never runs straight, the kosa will not split when holding something hot or drying out. If only we had not been in such a hurry chasing reindeer, I would have wanted to cut a knur loose to make my own kosa. But I had had neither saw nor ax with me then—and now that I was equipped with borrowed tools, there was little chance I could relocate the choice pieces I had seen the day before. Still, with luck I could find new knurs, and so I hastened into the birch woods to search.

The knur growth on the birch is a disease that infests some forest areas and not others. The crooked, slow-growing mountain birch is especially susceptible to the knur disease, and I had soon found more material than I could possibly carry. I did not lack for teachers in Parka. Notwithstanding that few Saami are professional craftsmen, nearly every one of them can make his own knife and kosa. Nisse Pavval, half-brother to Sigge and Per-Israel, was quite an accomplished kosa maker. He lent me the tools I needed to scoop out the inside of the knur and gave me my first kosa-making lesson. A freshly cut and roughly formed kosa is always in danger of cracking as it dries. To prevent this from happening, it is cooked in boiling water to withdraw the sap. Afterward it is smeared with fat, oil, or even glue so that it will dry slowly.

My kosa-to-be was happily cooking away in a pot of bubbling water inside the tube when there was a knock on the door. It was the doctor from Jokkmokk. Saami are known to be so loath to go to the doctor that the doctors must at times make the rounds to go to them. We all knew each other, so it was not purely an official call, but he asked about our noses and wondered if anyone needed any pills. The conversation turned toward a comparison of old and new cures. Per-Henrik had often seen the older people swallow pellets of quicksilver if they were feeling ill or had cut themselves. It was supposed to cleanse the blood. The doctor winced. Johan told about a remedy for pain called the *duovle*. A piece of a certain birchbark fungus is placed in the fire until it becomes a red ember. One must be sure to take the duovle growth from the "night side," that is, the north side, of the birch. If someone has a bad back pain, the glowing duovle ember is burnt into his back. The skin burns, it hurts horribly, and it leaves a brandlike scar.

These cures may not seem so effective to the men of modern science, but there is one Saami practice that has gained the respect of all who have come in contact with it—the art of stanching blood. Some individuals through special powers of concentration and unknown influences have the ability to stop the bleeding in severe wounds. Such people are rare, but if they have the power to stanch blood, it may suffice to telephone them, tell them who is hurt, and where the cut lies for the bleeding to stop. The veins seem to become cramped. A few people who have themselves been saved from bleeding to death by the timely help of such a person have told me that it feels as if a cold hand entered the wound and closed it off with a tight grip. Those who stop the bleeding say it requires a tremendous effort on their part.

Nowadays people are less and less inclined to trust or believe in such powers. The number of people able to stanch blood has declined steadily. Someone who does not believe it possible will not recognize or foster the ability. Maybe it demands faith by the victim as well. But one thing is certain, as many a skeptical doctor has been forced to admit: it does work. In time, however, there will be no one left who can stanch blood, and then the past will be looked upon with a smile and everyone will feel too wise to believe in such foolishness.

The doctor emphasized preventive medicine and told us we should try to eat more greens and fruits rather than just meat, fish, and bread. "We eat lots of plants," said Johan, "you can join us for dinner and see for yourself." The doctor eyed the pot a little questioningly. Johan took off the lid and through the cloud of steam a large lump of wood came into view, my kosa-to-be. "It'll be ready soon," said Johan. "More salt," chimed in Per-Henrik. The doctor was quick to remember that he had just eaten.

Dinner was reindeer meat and bread instead of birch wood. After we had eaten we rested on our reindeer hides, leaned against our packs, and told stories. Both Johan and Per-Henrik had seen ghost caravans and ghost reindeer herds. They had appeared suddenly from nowhere and seemed perfectly real. Johan, for example, said he was once surprised to find an extremely large herd where he would normally never expect one. Curious, he skiied toward it. He approached the reinder and was on the point of trying to read one of the earmarks when, all of a sudden, the whole herd was gone. He was startled to find no tracks at all. "If only I had thrown my knife over the herd when I had the chance," he said. "But how was I to know it was a ghost herd?" According to old Saami folk belief, if one manages to throw a piece of steel or maybe a lasso over a ghost herd, or a herd belonging to the people of the underworld, the reindeer will become real.

Winter was just around the corner, so as I listened I automatically braided a shoe band I hoped to have ready before the first snow. Wrapped around the bottom of the trouser leg over the top of the shoe shaft, the shoe band bars any snow from creeping into one's socks. Each Saami district has a characteristic type of shoe band, often different for the two sexes as well. The Jokkmokk band is braided, not woven. Gunborg Märak had taught me the proper technique, but it took many hours to produce a few inches.

Per-Henrik told me about *guottalvis,* the death bird. It is not much larger than a sparrow, but heralds death. The guottalvis tries to take a piece of personal property and fly with it to the churchyard. In flight it emits cries or shouts that sound oddly like the person whose soul it carries in the scrap of clothing or hair. If the death bird reaches the churchyard with its burden, the person is doomed. But, should someone hear the guottalvis in its flight and recognize the voice of the doomed one, he or she can call out the person's name to the bird. The guottalvis will drop his booty and the person is saved.

This, explained Per-Henrik, was why Saami always took care to burn or otherwise destroy their discarded clothes so that the guottalvis would be unable to find the least fragment. They were especially careful with old shoe bands. Of all articles of clothing that can be thought to contain the soul of its owner, the shoe band is probably the most personal and long lasting. After many hours of work on my still-unfinished shoe bands I could well understand that they were thought to be so important. I was glad to hear that old tradition accorded them such respect.

That Sunday we had church services followed by coffee in Johannes and Inga Orpus's goattieh. The Lapmark's preacher Olavi Korhonen had come with cakes and rolls and even a quickly eaten shipment of ice cream for the children in Parka. We were at least forty people crowded into the little goattieh. Olavi held services in four languages: Northern Saami, Lule Saami, Finnish, and Swedish. Church services are almost the only type of occasion when many Saami are gathered in one place, other than when they are working with reindeer in the corral.

Tomorrow, Monday, would bring a new gathering expedition, this time sweeping reindeer from areas even further west. And on Wednesday or Thursday we would probably once again be together separating reindeer in the corral. The process of gathering and separating would continue until all the reindeer around Parka—and at least as far as Rovijaure to the west—had been pulled through the corral and released in the winter land.

When the work was over I left Parka on foot in the company of Per-Henrik, once again bound for Kvikkjokk. There would be a brief pause in the life of the reindeer herder, a vacation until it was time for the sarv slaughters beginning in early September. But in between the separations and the slaughters fell the moose hunt, and although this had nothing to do with reindeer, it was an important part in the lives of all reindeer herders. A full-grown moose can yield one thousand pounds of meat, a decisive factor in any family's economy.

6

Lillselet and the Moose Hunt

An early September morning Johan Märak, his brother John, and I churned slowly over Lake Karatj toward Lillselet to join the rest of our hunting team. Besides hiking in, one could reach Lillselet only by the Karatj lake route—by boat when the lake was open, by scooter once it froze over. And twice each year, with the first brittle ice formation and later at winter's end with the final break up of the ice route, Lillselet would be barred to both boat and scooter traffic. Already we could feel the sharp edge of winter on the wind. Spray from the lake stung our faces and made us squint as if we were facing a bright summer sun. The drone of the motor kept us silent for most of the twelve-mile ride. We could lapse into our own rambling fantasies and admire the fiery fall colors. The birches were no longer camouflaged by the large evergreens. Here and there they blazed forth fully golden like fires in the night and on the high mountain slopes the blaze spread unbroken. In places, long tongues of bright color jutted down into the dark green woods.

Back in Jokkmokk things had been hurried. There was strategy to discuss, provisions to buy, rifles to clean, and walkie-talkies to synchronize. Everyone had talked moose hunt. It seemed as if the end of the herd separations in Parka had emptied the mountains of people. I had bumped into one friend after another in town, all of us on the same errands. At first I had hardly recognized them. I had associated them all too closely with the tundra land and never really considered finding them on the street. What's more, I was used to identifying them by particular hats and jackets so I was caught off guard. In the big city we had all taken the opportunity to change out of our well-worn summer gear. Greetings became a matter of "Where will you hunt?" and last words were invariably wishes of good luck. But now on the long boat ride over Lake Karatj to Lillselet everything had calmed down, and we were back in our mountain clothes with a promise of adventure ahead.

Lillselet was Johan and John's family home, and the home of nearly all their relatives in the closest generations before them. Johan's paternal grandfather had founded the small settlement, and the three families still living there retained their old hunting rights over an enormous territory. Times had changed and the settlement had diminished; the young people were attracted away from home to find jobs around Jokkmokk. Yet, for a few short days during the hunt, Lillselet revived its past as the remaining families once again grew to full force and sent a swarm of men into the woods. The rest of our hunting team, Uncle Gustav, cousins Pelle, Tommy, and Stig, along with in-law Palle, would be waiting for us there. Tomorrow we would split into pairs, Johan and I, John and Stig, Pelle and Palle, Gustav and Tommy, and scatter through the huge evergreen forest and marshlands around Lillselet.

John shouted over the roar of the motor, and pointing this way and that to various cottages along the shoreline, he painted a picture of how things had been in his youth. The lake had been full of activity. All the life and movement that was now concentrated in Jokkmokk and similar towns had once been spread around this lake and others like it. We sped past a cluster of houses empty and boarded, the village of Rakka, where so many of my friends from Stalo had grown up. Almost all the farms around the lake had had horses, cows, and goats. The nomadic Saami used to leave their goats with the settlers (settled Swedes or Saami) over the winter and pick them up on the way to the mountains on spring migration. The herders would often give a so-called slaughter reindeer in payment for the boarding and care of their goats over the long winter months. Each homestead had its own name, a name that frequently was as linked to the people living there as their family name. So there was Harrok Inga to distinguish from

Henrik Kuhmunen in Saami dress of the Karesuando type.

Henrik and Birgit Blind's goattieh. The "bird cage" on the roof holds up the tarpaulin when it is raining while still letting out the smoke.

Lars-Anders caught a calf, which he delivers to its owner for marking.

In mid-May, as the snow retreats into the high mountains, the calves are born.

To wrestle down a big sarv is not at all as easy as marking a calf.

Petrus Gruvvisare, eighty-four years old and still an active herder. He was always dressed in his traditional Jokkmokk Saami tunic.

As the rutting season approaches, remarkable changes affect the sarvs. The bare antlers under the tatters of skin are red with blood. The blood and nerves disappear as the antlers dry into hard dueling weapons.

A smoke break in −20°F—the first cigarette in weeks. The autumn migration has reached the lowlands and inhabited territory.

There are many work-saving methods one can use in the winter corral. One can run, following alongside the reindeer, in a circular arc until reaching the booth gate.

A herder stands motionless, searching for his deer as a forest of horns swirl around him.

Per-Henrik drives the herd westward through the birch woods.

A calf has been lassoed on the hind leg and watches with worry as its ear is notched with its owner's distinctive mark.

Granudd Inga on another farm, and John was often called Lillsel-John by those he had worked and played with up and down the lake.

Now most of the farms were abandoned, though a few of them still served as vacation cottages during the summers. What had happened? It was the usual story of roads and powdered milk. The people around Lake Karatj had owned a horse-drawn mill, but store-bought flour came in with the new road and the mill closed. The same story could be told over and over about all manner of things. As the once self-sufficient community grew increasingly dependent on the towns, people were drained from the country. Lillselet, at the farthest extremity of Lake Karatj, was the only inhabited settlement left that had not been reached by road. Although Lillselet was not devoid of modern comforts, even common appliances struck me as odd gadgets imported to an old world. Little by little the new world was gaining ground: more comforts—but fewer inhabitants. Johan and John's mother, Amanda Andersson, kept her home warm with a wooden stove, though she had recently installed a small diesel generator to provide the electricity needed to run a freezer in anticipation of storing large quantities of moose meat.

Lillselet had once been full of people, especially in the days when timber was cut and floated down the lake. There had been stores and a nomad school for the education of Saami children. The school goattiehs now stood rotting. Nils-Tomas and Johan Parfa had gone to school there, slept in those goattiehs, and wakened with their hair frozen to the wall. Anders Blind's and Per Labba's families had lived next door. The sleds they had used during past migrations lay crumbling and forgotten. Time seemed to sneak about on tiptoe here. Changes in life-style that to the student of anthropology appear momentous and terribly significant had happened with a sleepy ebb that stirred hardly a ripple. I could almost see Amanda gaze serenely at the abandoned homes of her old neighbors, shrug her shoulders and say, "They've been gone a long time on this migration; wonder when they'll come home."

The name Lillselet means the "small, still water between two falls," often separating two lakes, in this case Lake Karatj and Lake Peuraure just to the west. This lake-river chain is one of the few remaining natural undammed water systems in Swedish Lapland.

Besides Amanda, her two brothers Gustav and Arthur Larsson with their wives, Ingrid and Kristina, were the only people still living in Lillselet. On the shore of Lake Peuraure, five miles further west into the mountains at a spot called Levik, lived seventy-six-year-old Sven Larsson, yet another brother. These old people lived a hard life that would break the toughest unaccustomed youngster. The lack of modern accommodation gave to Lillselet a deep peacefulness well worth all the hardship. But these were not ordinary people. I have never met a more colorful crew.

Arthur Larsson was one of those rare men who could stanch blood. He had inherited the gift from his father, Skaite Janne, who had settled twelve miles west of Levik at Skaite on the far end of Lake Peuraure, a day's march from Parka. Arthur was once forced by sickness to Jokkmokk and the nurse there insisted on giving him a blood test. Unnecessary said Arthur, but the nurse knew better. Not a drop, said he, and no matter how many times she stabbed his finger, he would not bleed. She called to another nurse who was equally unsuccessful, and soon he was surrounded by a crowd of white coats. Within this crowd he spotted a friend's daughter, and to her Arthur said he would donate a few drops. When she stabbed him, he bled.

Gustav, Johan's other uncle in Lillselet, was a legendary figure whenever people began recounting tales of hardiness. He could walk the legs off of most men even now at sixty-five. The only thing faster than his legs was his tongue. In normal conversation, every other word was a swear word, and anyone who has had the luck to be in the vicinity when the boat motor or scooter engine refused to start has experienced a remarkable exhibition of vocabulary.

In the early years of this century when tuberculosis was taking such a toll in Lapland, the medical centers sent out X-ray trucks to check as many people as possible, free of charge. The people from Lake Karatj were called down to the road for the check-up, and it turned out that no one knew what an X-ray was, and only Gustav could speak some Swedish. The Saami were confused by the truck, and when it was conveyed to them that they were to strip, they nearly sent the medical team packing. Saami are generally quite modest, seldom enjoying temperatures that would demand otherwise. Gustav was approached in desperation. He was given the task of interpreting and with great seriousness he commenced to have a good time. He first explained the purpose of the X-ray and was then asked to tell each one who stepped into the truck to lean against the machine, raise his chin, and take a deep breath. The X-ray technicians were startled when those who came behind the curtain began bowing, dancing, hopping on one foot, spinning in circles and singing before finally leaning against the machine and taking a deep breath.

Sven Larsson from Levik was every bit as renowned as his brothers. We are both partially bald and this kindled an immediate friendship. I doubt if I shall ever meet another man as strong and stubborn for his size. In his younger days Sven had roamed all over the Virihaure district with a heavy wooden boat upside down across his shoulders. In this fashion he had hiked from lake to lake fishing and hunting. The remains of his boat could still be seen near Stalo, where he had finally left it. Last summer the Saami there had shown it to me with a touch of awe.

Once, at dinner, Sven's comrades at the Suorva damming project began boasting of various feats of strength. Sven remained silent, let them finish, and then bent down and lifted the entire table with a setting for six in his teeth. The conversation was over.

Two dentists had to take turns pulling and drilling whenever Sven needed a tooth extracted. For many years he had not bothered with the dentist and instead had packed his worn molars with plastic padding. He built them up a little at a time, layer by layer, keeping his mouth open for hours to let the plastic dry.

Coming to Lillselet was always a pleasure, and as usual Amanda seemed to know exactly when we would arrive and had coffee ready. No sooner had we sat down at the table than Pelle, Palle, and Stig strode in to make final plans. This team had been hunting together for so long that little had to be said about communications and which pair would cover which area. Only I was new to the system. Where were Tommy and Gustav, I wondered? Already out trying to spy moose from their camp site so as to know where to look tomorrow when the season opened. The rest of us would split up early in the morning, John and Pelle taking their moose dogs with them.

A good moose dog is rarely a good reindeer-herding dog as well. The hunting dog is trained to chase prey, the herding dog to guard, drive the flock, and feel responsible for the reindeer's welfare. Such contrasting natures are almost impossible for one dog to combine. Guided by their dogs' noses, John and Pelle would be able to penetrate thick woods where the human eye would be nearly useless. The rest of us would spread out to the high passes and ridges with the best views. Should one group spot a moose far away, a quick buzz on the walkie-talkie could alert those with a better chance of reaching it.

Early next morning Johan and I sweated under heavy packs as we made our way toward Kavlak mountain where we would pitch camp. Besides an overly generous supply of food, we carried a large tent cloth for the tent goattieh we would construct at camp. The trail ended after a few miles. Johan led on without the least hesitation. He not only knew the location of every hill and swamp, he was able to read small details and understand entire dramas that passed me by completely. A dried mushroom stuck on a pine twig a yard above the forest floor he explained was the work of a squirrel who thoughtfully stored food for winter above the coming snow level.

We came upon an old nine-pointed moose antler in the moss. Here too I was to learn something. Like the reindeer, the moose sheds his colossal antlers each year, but unlike the reindeer, only the bull moose grows antlers. "The other one should be nearby," said Johan, and sure enough after a cursory search we found it as well. I had collected fallen reindeer antlers in order to use them for making knife sheaths and lasso eyepieces, but I had never found that a pair of reindeer antlers had been shed simultaneously. A reindeer with only one antler is a common sight. But moose apparently face another problem when shedding their antlers. Moose antlers weigh so much that when one is shed, the poor moose is completely off balance. It is so tiring for the moose to carry this uneven weight on his head that he hammers and scrapes the remaining antler against a tree until it too falls off.

We crossed marshes in swirling gold and red to climb Kavlak mountain where we would raise our tent. Kavlak afforded us an enormous view over the largest marshland I have ever seen. So immense were these marshes that the Saami called them *ap'pe* which is the same word used for ocean. This ocean of marsh had probably produced as many insects are there are fish in the sea, but by now the hand of

Nature had swatted my main tormentors. The successor to the knott, the *svidon,* an almost invisible gnat with a terribly visible, itchy, and long-lasting bite, had vanished with the autumn chill. Lapland was at last freed from the insect hordes.

Fall in Lapland is glorious and for thousands of years has been the prime hunting season of the Saami. With the arrival of winter, all wildlife lives on minimal sustenance. The reindeer and moose become scrawny, but now in the fall they carry their maximum weight after a summer of plentiful grazing. In the past, before the use of firearms, hunters had perfected ingenious traps, snares, and pit complexes to catch game. Not far from Parka, for example, indeed not far from Kavlak mountain, one could discern an elaborate and expertly planned system of pits dug by the ancient hunters to trap the wild reindeer that they stampeded into them. The technique of driving a herd of reindeer against trap arms of fencing into a corral is strongly reminiscent of this age-old practice.

Erecting the tent was a quick and easy matter, and in no time we were relaxing on a bed of birch branches around a stone hearth. I took the opportunity to ask Johan about the *yoik,* the traditional Saami form of song. I had read a good deal about yoiking, but I had never heard a yoik other than from a record. Saami author Johan Turi has called it an "art of remembering." By putting the "feel" of the subject into his yoik, by trying to imitate its characteristics in sound, the Saami evokes a summer pasture, a lost friend, or a wobbly newborn reindeer calf. While yoiking, a Saami strives to merge with his subject and create an intimate contact with it. Traditionally it is a solo song and, at least in the past, was never performed as entertainment. Many Saami even today have their personal yoik, which evokes their history, background, or personality, and is composed by their friends to honor and recall them. In the old days, a shaman who sought to take the shape of a wolf and attack an enemy's reindeer herd might well have yoiked a wolf yoik and howled in such a way as to cause Christian missionaries to shudder. In the past, any Saami caught yoiking, or singing to the devil, as the Church saw it, could be hanged.

Many Saami still believe that yoiking is sinful, and because Johan was a preacher, I approached the topic cautiously. In time I was to learn that Johan is one of the most prominent Saami yoikers. His example encouraged others to overcome their inhibitions about yoik-ing. Nothing could be better for the soul he assured me. "This is the right place to yoik and to talk of yoiking," said Johan, "under the open sky. Houses do not even have smoke holes, so it is hard to be inspired inside them. The yoik must be able to go out somewhere with your thoughts. When people ask me to yoik I often feel bad, because I cannot be inspired for the asking. Then I sing like a recording so as not to disappoint them."

We rested just long enough to cook coffee and establish the feeling of home before scrambling up to the highest bluff with binoculars and a walkie-talkie. Every large distant boulder on the open plain was a grazing moose until it grazed in one spot too long to be anything but a rock. Once every stone and tree in sight had been a suspect moose, we could readily perceive the slightest change or motion in our field. Unfortunately, the only motion we were to spy turned out to be that of reindeer. Dark-colored reindeer especially, at great distances made the heart jump with initial excitement until common sense stilled the blood. Moose do not usually travel in large numbers or move the same way as do reindeer. However, mistakes are often made. Although it is often illegal to shoot a moose cow on the first day of the hunt, experi-enced hunters frequently become suddenly nearsighted. The worst perfectly honest mistake was reported a few years ago. A wildly enthu-siastic hunter raced into a sport shop and called for more ammunition. He claimed to have shot twenty-four moose, but when skeptics fol-lowed to determine the truth of his boast, they found that he had gunned down an entire reindeer flock.

Every hour and half hour we listened for news from our comrades on the walkie-talkie. Each person had his own number during walkie-talkie communications, both to make things simpler and to preserve a modicum of secrecy around our movements. The walkie-talkie was teeming with hundreds of hunters chatting steadily, and they could hear us as well as we them. Were we to speak openly over the air without the slightest precaution of code, other nearby hunters might be able to deduce the location of our target and reach it first.

Although the moose are lawful prey to hunters for only four days each year (in this area), they are always well aware of their brief peril and hide themselves most effectively. The day before the hunt one might see moose everywhere without exerting oneself in the least. The next day they are gone. Heated quarrels can result if a thoughtless hunter shoots a few practice rounds in the woods and warns the moose population before the hunt. Johan and I spied without luck till nightfall, and from the tangled garble of voices on the walkie-talkie we heard nothing to make us believe our teammates had fared any better. Gustav and Tommy had apparently moved out of radio contact behind a mountain and their silence made them our greatest hope.

Johan stood on the bluff in the dark and soon I could hear the low rumbling tones of the moose yoik. The depth of the voice sang of something heavy and in the slowly rocking rhythm I could feel the moose plodding over a soggy marsh. He trudged past us in the night and lumbered into the dense woods. It was silent again. Our tent goattieh glowed from the fire within like a Chinese lantern hung among the trees. Its soft warmth drew us in. The night had quieted us, as if the limitation of our sight had increased our need to hear all the more. We lay inside and listened. Our thoughts began to wander as our ears grew accustomed to the sounds of the night. When finally Johan spoke it was anything but a troublesome call back to reality.

The richest family in these parts obtained their wealth from the Gadniha, the people of the underworld, many years ago. A young Saami boy lay in a tent goattieh such as this one. It was his turn to stay with the herd. He was roused from his thoughts by the sound of laughing girls. They were skiing toward his tent joking with each other, and though the boy could not recognize their voices, they seemed to know who he was. As they drew nearer he could distinguish three voices. "You're the prettiest," said one, "why don't you go in to him." "No you go, you have the most reindeer and he's sure to want you the most." "Do you want me to be stuck in the human's world? You go to him, you won't find a better husband in the underworld." They taunted and chided, pushing each other toward the door. The boy could see the tent cloth bulge inward as the girls pushed and fell against it. He took out a needle from his sewing case and after much deliberation pricked one of the girls through the tent cloth. A few drops of blood dripped through the cloth inside. "Good-bye," said the other two girls. "Now you must stay with him." When the herder came outside he found the most beautiful girl he had ever seen. She had become human.

After they were married, the new wife told her husband that he must collect her dowry. She bade him stand by a ford in a swift stream where she said her parents used to drive their herd over on migration. Soon he could hear dogs barking, voices shouting and bells ringing, although he could see nothing. Finally he could hear a fast tinkling bell telling him that the lead reindeer was shaking the water off himself. The herd had crossed to his side of the stream and the boy threw his lasso out into the empty air. It was a long cast and all of the Gadniha reindeer contained under the arc of his lasso became real. The Gadniha bride had brought her husband a large dowry and their descendants were extraordinarily rich for many generations.

"The Gadniha are not always so kind," Johan was continuing. He had once been forced to move his tent in the middle of the night because of their disturbances. Should this occur, however, there is undoubtedly a reason. One has possibly camped unwittingly over a Gadniha sacred spot or maybe some terrible deed has been committed there.

An inquisitive owl fluttered outside our tent, finally coming to rest on one of our tent poles. He peered down at us through the smoke hole and cocked his head again and again as if he too wanted to hear a story: An old woman had once learned from her worried neighbors that wolves were in the vicinity and threatened their herd. That evening, to the bewilderment of all, she put on her kolt inside out and skied around the entire herd. In the morning they could see the tracks of a large wolf pack that had approached the herd during the night. As soon as the wolves had reached the ring formed by the old woman's ski trail they had turned back. Not a single wolf spoor crossed the ski track, and the herd within had been saved. The owl must have enjoyed Johan's stories for he came back to his perch next year to hear more.

In Lapland storytelling is still a living art. Many people are noted for their great ability to tell stories, but as with most other active art forms, it has declined to a soft whisper. The decline of storytelling in Lapland, however, is not yet due to a lack of storytellers, but rather to a lack of listeners, a lack of situation and mood. Story atmosphere dies before storytellers disappear.

The next morning a fully dressed and excited Johan was shaking me with one hand and waving a cup of coffee at me with the other. It was terribly early, but this is when chances are best to spot a moose out on the ap'pe, and Johan was trying to tell his slow-to-move partner that he had already been up on the top of Kavlak scouting and had seen three moose close at hand below. He had shouldered his rifle and was about to swing downwind through the trees to a point closest to the moose before he had to break cover and try to sneak over the open marsh. When in the woods he would not be able to see his quarry, and I was to sit atop Kavlak with the other walkie-talkie giving him an up-to-the-minute report on moose movements as he walked.

Johan had a small earpiece for his walkie-talkie so that my reports would not be blared out to the moose and warn them. But even the noise of an idling walkie-talkie can be a warning at close range and a bother when trying to shoot, so Johan turned his off when he finally left the woods and could see the moose himself. Unfortunately, this was just when I was trying to reach him most desperately. His march through the woods may have gone unnoticed by his initial targets, but two pairs of huge moose ears only two hundred yards away from me had been alerted. These two other moose must have been lying in the tall grass, for they materialized out of nowhere. The two close to me would have been a much easier target, for they stood at the edge of the woods where a hunter could hide. But Johan was already crawling over the open marsh toward the first group of moose, and there was a good chance that they would discover him when still at a considerable distance. This is indeed what happened, the huge bull moose closest to Johan froze suddenly and bolted back toward the forest for cover. Johan was too far for a sure shot, but he tried anyway. From Kavlak his shots sounded far away and hardly disturbed the morning peace. The large moose ran for his life and managed to reach the trees in safety. The other two moose in his company melted away with him. Meanwhile the two moose close to me had heard the faint blasts of danger and were loping easily westward in the opposite direction.

All the while I was shouting into my walkie-talkie calling Stig, John, Gustav, Pelle, anyone who could hear and come that there were no fewer than five moose below me. Apparently they could hear me but I could not receive them. I could, however, hear them talking back and forth to each other, and the consensus seemed to be that "Choo" was seeing things or mistaking reindeer for moose. Who ever heard of five moose at once by Kavlak! They had seen nothing all day. When Johan puffed back up the mountain, however, he could confirm my message. Two big moose were loping westward in plain view. Maybe if the others moved fast they could intercept them before nightfall, but the chances were that the moose would change direction and then be long since out of sight.

The next morning brought good news. Although the moose Johan and I had seen had escaped, Tommy and Gustav had enjoyed better luck. Tommy had shot a ten-pointer (one with ten antler points) as soon as it had become light enough to shoot. We were jubilant and hurried down to Lillselet as instructed by walkie-talkie. The moose had been shot a mile to the west of Lake Peuraure and all of us had to gather for the toilsome task of carrying the meat to Lillselet. We made contact with Stig and John, spreading the good news and the request for help. They were already in Lillselet when we arrived. Pelle and Palle appeared soon after and lastly came Tommy and Gustav with slow elephant-like steps, each carrying 130 pounds of meat on their backs. They had spent the morning hours butchering the kill, laying the meat out on a layer of birch branches by a nearby cold spring to keep it from spoiling, and covering it with the hide and a further layer of branches against sun and flies. Although they had carried 260 pounds of meat for approximately four miles, there were 800 pounds left—six loads.

It is traditional that the neck and back pieces of any carcass, moose or reindeer, are cooked immediately and shared by the team in a communal meal. For this reason these pieces had been part of the first burden brought by Tommy and Gustav. Once all the meat had been carried to Lillselet, it would be butchered and carefully divided among the hunters. The older men, Johan and Gustav, began severing the vertebrae for the hunters' feast while the rest of us made ready for the ordeal ahead.

Shooting the moose is the most elementary part of the hunt. The real work is transporting the meat. Fortunately, eight of the twelve miles from the site of the kill to Lillselet could be traveled by boat. Each of us carried a handmade wooden rack on our back to which we could strap a load of odd shape and great weight. Tommy led the way. When we reached the slaughter site we set about with knives cutting joints so that no piece was too large for the burlap bags we had brought. Each of us had been joking all the way about how little he intended to carry, but now faced with the real thing no one wanted to take less than his full share, and sometimes we squabbled over taking extra heavy pieces. When finally packed it took two men to lift each burden onto a third. It hurt us to do so, but we were forced to leave the hide behind. It would have fit so perfectly on the floor of my goattieh in Staloluokta, but I was not about to add another hundred pounds to my already massive load. Tommy who already carried a superhuman load could not bear to leave the crown behind. We tied it across his pack.

Walking under such a weight was a new experience and a painful one. My legs shivered under the strain with each small shaky step. The limits of balance were much narrower. To dodge a tree in the usual way with a quick leaning side step would be disastrous. We walked ponderously, our only interest to reach the lake shore where we could deliver our burdens to the boat. He who reached the boat first would cruise up and down the lake shore to pick up the others wherever they happened to reach water. Once we had carried the meat to the first boat on Peuraure the rest of the way would be easier as there were trails between the lakes. The long haul continued with one portage at the eastern end of Lake Peuraure and another over the falls until we reached the quiet water of Lillselet between Lakes Peuraure and Karatj—altogether three boats to reach Lillselet. Each time we reached a boat, we collapsed onto a seat and tried to recoup for the next effort. The heavily laden boat rode barely six inches above the water.

We took only a slight pause for rest when we reached Lillselet. The meat had to be divided and frozen as soon as possible. A long sheet of plastic was rolled out onto the grass and the meat was dealt out in equal piles—equal not only in amount of meat, but also in type as far as was possible. Each pile had its rightful share of steak, ribs, marrow bones, and hooves. Butchering demands a great deal of skill. John and Gustav, who were most adept at the art, knew precisely from which angle to attack each joint. Hands and clothing became red and sticky with blood. I was given the job of skinning the legs, an assignment requiring little technique and not too costly if bungled.

When the job was done there was a row of red mounds spread across the lawn. That one moose yielded so much meat amazed me. That we had been able to carry it all amazed me even more.

Gustav came by with a hat in which he shook a number of matches. Each match was marked with a different number of stripes, and on each pile of meat lay another match similarly marked—a lottery with no loser. It remained only to load the meat into the freezer and decide which cuts to smoke, but Amanda called from the kitchen that food was ready. We ate heartily in Saami fashion using knife and thumb. A pan of melted fat stood on the table into which we dipped chunks of moose meat. A chopping block and ax were near at hand for those who desired to split bones and scrape or suck out the marrow.

The hunt was not yet over for us. Our license allotted us two moose and we had one day left to fill our assignment. Johan and I had barely arrived at our tent goattieh on Kavlak the next morning when Pelle reached us by walkie-talkie to tell us that he had just shot a huge sixteen-pointer. Our vista on Kavlak was over. We folded the tent cloth. What had recently been a cozy home was suddenly thrown open to the world. It felt strange to look between the tent poles at our bed of branches. How secure that thin cloth covering had made us feel. We chopped a supply of wood for next year's hunt, hung pots and pans on a tree, and started back to Lillselet.

Pelle had also managed to contact Gustav and Tommy. They were already in Lillselet when we came. Gustav was shaking his head and swearing. Pelle's moose had fallen far from any water route. To carry it all the way to Lillselet would not be wholly impossible, but would demand time and Herculean effort. Yesterday's carrying expedition would seem a picnic stroll in comparison. The only other alternative was to call for a helicopter's services. Tommy, to my consternation, seemed to enjoy the prospect of physical suffering and was assuring Gustav that carrying would be a simple matter. I was relieved to hear that Gustav could not be convinced. After a quick telephone call, we could hear the drone of an approaching helicopter.

The pilot was Martin, my friend from Stalo. He had already freighted fifteen moose today, he shouted, but we had no more time for conversation in the blast from the blades. He had left the engine running and had several other hunters on the waiting list. Gustav would join him to show the way to the spot Pelle had described over the radio, a description based on the shapes of small marshes and streams, baffling to anyone else. The rest of us broke into a loud laugh as the two men climbed into the copter. Martin strode to the door fully upright, while Gustav, who was a full foot shorter, bent himself double under the whirling blades.

They were back in fifteen minutes with the moose dangling in a net under the helicopter. I still ached from yesterday's ordeal and could well understand why so many hunters pay the high price of helicopter transport even if the meat is within carrying distance. We repeated the butchering process and then feasted once again on moose meat. The helicopter had brought the hide with no extra effort. Pelle knew that I longed for a moose hide and had thrown it in the net with the meat. It was huge, requiring three people to help me lift it up against the wall of the shed where I nailed it out to dry.

A little laziness seeped back into Lillselet. We tacitly agreed that we had had enough moose meat for a while. I found myself at the oars, and Johan passed out the net. Tommy, Pelle, and Palle had left for Jokkmokk, their boat filled with boxes of meat destined for the freezer. Every so often we heard a distant shot. The telephone was busy informing us of the success or failure of friends. Sven came from Levik and he and John disappeared with a bottle to celebrate a triumphant hunt. Amanda knitted socks and gloves for winter.

"Hurry up," shouted Johan next morning, and I stumbled out of bed with my usual readiness. "We've got to empty the nets. It's raining and we can't let the fish get wet," he joked. We got wet; the fish instead got drier. We pulled up a good number of gwyniad (similar to a lake whitefish) and a few large, mean-looking pike, a fish Swedes adore but that most Saami toss away like a harmful weed. I could not conceive of a fresher fish breakfast than the one we ate that morning, but Johan commented that they would have tasted better if caught with the *not,* a kind of haul-seine. Those that land in the ordinary net, he explained, struggle to get loose and this gives them a certain taste whereas the ones brought in with the seine are not stressed. They hardly have any time to fight. The best answer to my many questions regarding this seine, Johan decided, was a demonstration.

He may have purposely aroused my curiosity; it takes two to pull the seine.

The seine is an ancient fishing implement. It is an extremely long though shallow floating net that is rowed out from one point of land in a great arc and back to land again at another nearby point. A man on each end pulls slowly but steadily and the fish encompassed by the seine are finally caught in a large bag of net projecting from the center of the arc and held open and straight by a large wooden keel. The fish are able to swim, although in an ever-diminishing area, until the very end when they are trapped in the bag. The seine we used was more than one hundred years old. The ropes on which we pulled were made of twined pine roots and were not only strong, but also incredibly light. The weights were made from rocks encased in pouches of birch bark sewn all along the bottom edge of the seine.

It was quite strenuous to haul the seine and it could easily happen that after much effort the bag at the end would hold only a few tiny fish. Another try somewhere else, however, could fill the bag to bursting. We tried twice, neither time meeting with great success but amassing enough for a substantial dinner. I could taste no difference whatsoever, but Johan and Amanda swore that the seine fish was easily distinguishable from the morning's net catch. I was skeptical, but Sven and John reappeared suddenly, slightly inebriated from their sojourn with the bottle, and as soon as Sven tasted the fish he looked up surprised and asked, "Have you hauled the seine?"

The Saami terminology for fish reflects the same detailed familiarity with certain facets of nature apparent, for instance, in the classification of reindeer vertebrae. In Saami there is not only a different word for each kind of fish, there is a word for each size as well. A big trout is called something other than a small- or medium-sized one. With reindeer there is a term for almost every year of age, color, and antler form, so that with few words herders can give a sketch of any particular reindeer so complete as to pinpoint it in the herd.

John was in fine form. Inspired by the bottle and contented by the fish, he began telling me a pack of lies that made the others smile and wink. "It's not often I find someone who might believe me," he said, "but you wait and see. In three or four months the newspapers will prove I'm telling the truth." According to John, Tuorpon had a secret troll drum, a shaman, and a flourishing heathen cult. They had apparently held a meeting, and the shaman had fallen into trance in an effort to send evil forces against the neighboring Sameby, Luokta Mavas. "We know that they've taken some of our reindeer on the sly [a rather frequent accusation among Samebys]," he fantasized further. "Now they'll have to pay the price." He named no names, but he claimed Tuorpon's shaman to be extremely powerful, more so than the Mavas shaman. The evil sent by Tuorpon would be carried in the jaws of wolves. Only a few wolves were left in all of Sweden, according to the statistics for the last ten years, and there was some doubt whether they still haunted the hills or only the charts. "Ha," snorted John, "no matter how many wolves are killed each year, the experts in Stockholm say there're only a couple left. They can't tell the difference between wolf and rabbit tracks."

The moose hunt, though over for us, was not necessarily over for the moose. The bear needs a heavy meal before crawling off to sleep all winter. I found it hard to believe, but a bear can crush the skull of a moose and knock him over with one punch. Johan's father had once been stalking a moose only to see him downed by a huge bear in a marsh. The bear obviously wanted to get his kill to dry land, but moving a 1,500–pound carcass is not easy. Johan's father watched as the bear suddenly went berserk. He attacked a birch tree, knocked off its branches, tore at its bark, shook and smashed it. With his self-induced fury still boiling, he seized the neck of the fallen moose and dragged it thirty yards to dry land, a feat requiring the strength of twelve men.

The bear, however, was now prey as well as predator. All of September is the open season for bear hunting, although it is rare that any are shot. Not only is the bear skin extremely valuable but the meat is a sought-after item for gourmet counters. Sven claimed bear meat to be not particularly tasty. The price is paid to have eaten it rather than to eat it. I remember Nils-Tomas Parfa, one of the greatest bear hunters, telling me in Stalo that a skinned bear looks so much like a man it was impossible for him to eat bear's meat. Even their cubs are like human children, Nils-Tomas had said. "I'll never shoot a mother with cubs again. It is terrible to hear them cry." He had watched a dying mother bear he had shot try to shoo away her cubs so that they would not fall victim to the hunter as well. The cubs had refused to leave her, even when they saw the hunter approach, and finally the mother before she died had snarled and spanked them to send them yelping into the woods.

Whether it is because of the human or superhuman qualities of the bear, it has always held a special place. The Vikings so admired its frenzied strength that they sought to imitate it. Their warriors, calling themselves berserkers, would work themselves into madness before going into battle. The Saami of old attributed some kind of manliness or extreme sexual potency to the bear that could infect its slayers. Certain observances had to be kept before a bear hunt. When the successful hunters returned with their kill, there was a series of rituals intended to cool them off or return them to the condition of normal men. The hunters had to enter the tent goattieh through a sacred back door. As they crawled inside they would be met by their wives who looked at them through a brass ring and then spat in their faces with the red juice of chewed alder bark. The hunters should abstain from sex for three days. The women were allowed to eat only certain portions of the bear and forbidden to touch the meat with their hands. Instead they had to eat with a pointed stick. The bones of the bear were handled delicately lest they be chipped or broken. After the feast the bones were pieced back together in natural form and buried. It was believed a new bear could then rise from the old skeleton.

Killing a bear by the old method before the advent of firearms was fraught with danger. Those men who dared be bear killers were called *skuorkah*. A Saami would wake the bear from his slumber and wait outside the cave for him to charge. His only defense was a sturdy spear. The enraged bear would rise on his back legs for the final crushing lunge and then the Saami would strike. He would jab the point of his spear into the bear's neck, and holding tightly all the while, stamp the butt of the spear at an angle into the ground to absorb the shock of the bear's full weight. The bear's own downward lunge would kill him and he would die transfixed against the sky like a scarecrow. Death would rarely be immediate, and it took great courage to remain holding the spear while the pinioned bear flailed and gnashed a few inches overhead.

Man and bear have always respected one another as foes. Anta Pirak, a Jokkmokk Saami, dictated to his biographer Harald Grundström in the early 1930s: "One should never say anything ugly about the bear, nor should any bear hunter brag and say that he could easily kill a bear." Should a woman meet a bear she should raise her skirt and say, "Look, I am a woman: Shame, and leave me alone. Surely I don't intend to kill you."

We had no time to hunt bears, however. The reindeer mating season was beginning and with it the sarv slaughter. I had barely enough time to dash back to Jokkmokk, help dig up our potato crop and leave for Valli, the site of the big Tuorpon sarv slaughter, on a mountain plateau just west of Kvikkjokk. As Johan, John and I sped back over Lake Karatj toward Jokkmokk, we saw a large moose standing in the tall grass, browsing lazily by the shore. The moose had already come out of hiding. He watched us blankly, once more secure on his throne, lord of the woodlands.

7

The Sarv Slaughter

New snow sprinkles the mountain tops west of Kvikkjokk although it is still warm in the sun. I have trooped up with the others to Valli peak. In a long line we scrambled up the steep slope to lie in the sun and wait for the sarvs to be driven into the corral. We cook coffee, spy with binoculars, and doze off in the mossy field against colors somewhat browned and faded. It is September 12, and the reindeer rutting season is about to erupt. I have not seen a reindeer at close quarters since the separations at Parka. You will not recognize them I was told. They look different. They behave differently. I am sure to be surprised. This will be the biggest slaughter of the year.

The men out gathering and driving the herd of sarvs to Valli must work terribly hard as we relax and wait. They have had to sweep a huge area, almost the entire summer land, to round up all the sarvs who have scattered with the beginning of the fall and wandered away from the main herd of vajas and calves that spreads toward Parka. Contrary to what one might think, the sarvs have become loners to a great extent as the mating season approaches, although the search for the richest grazing draws them to many of the same slopes. They hope to be able to establish their own separate harems of female deer. The sarvs' physical changes lead to corresponding changes in temperament. They become wilder and more restless. Gathering them together is not as easy as gathering for a calf-marking. Should the herd of sarvs be startled and turn back in the wrong direction, they may run for many miles. Samebys to the south frequently employ helicopters during the round-up and drive of sarvs to slaughter in September. A helicopter can easily outdistance a stampeding herd of sarvs and by flying low turn them back in toward the corral. Using the helicopter, however, can finally make the reindeer so accustomed to drastic, noisy herding methods that they become insensitive to lesser measures. This is a danger with all types of mechanization applied to herding. Eventually the bark of a dog will not bring the least reaction from a herd used to helicopters, scooters, and transport trucks.

But Tuorpon has never used the helicopter for this purpose, and possibly for this reason the wait is long and we have plenty of time to snooze in the sun. Whom should I meet swinging along the path but Henrik Kuhmunen, and we whiled away the time catching up on our comings and goings since we parted last June. I was glad to hear that he had retrieved his tame härks, those that had fled to the mountains last spring. But at the same time he brought bad tidings. Henrik, I learned, stood to lose his entire livelihood. Beneath his charm and carefree manner, I found a worried man. Yet too, I could glimpse a fighting spirit and a stubborn determination I had not seen earlier behind his ever-smiling eyes.

The municipality of Jokkmokk had prospered during what might be called "the water power epoch" during the first half of the 1900s. There were many jobs building the dams and providing the support services for the population influx. Then the tide turned. By the close of the 1960s, most of the watercourses in the Jokkmokk area had been dammed and jobs became scarce. In an effort to maintain the boom epoch, the Jokkmokk municipal board itself offered one of the last untouched waters in the region to the state power board. The lake was Sitojaure, the lake to which the Kuhmunens had fled and built their summer camp after their other homes had been lost one by one to the power company. The municipal board had promised, as always, that this sacrifice would be the last demanded of the Jokkmokk region. Although the damming of Lake Sitojaure and the flooding of much of Sirkas Sameby grazing land—even Sarek National Park land—would give only about one hundred people work for three years, according to the municipal board this would give the municipality a respite to establish long-term, work opportunities in accord with the environment.

The Slav Slaughter

The Kuhmunens stood to lose yet another home, their grazing land and fishing waters. Henrik said that the power company's surveying team had already flown and boated all over the lake to plan "the new site." The damming of Lake Sitojaure would be a terrible loss to many herders besides the Kuhmunens and a defeat for the Saami in general. The board's proposal was also condemned by a small but active local branch of the nature preservation society, composed of both Swedes and Saami in Jokkmokk, but what could these forces offer against the municipal board, the many power company workers, and the state power board itself? When Henrik moved on, I had an even deeper respect for him, and I began to realize what so many of the herders had learned too late—that in modern times, to be a successful herder means being a watchful politician.

Along the same path to Valli peak came many of my friends from Stalo. Small groups of people sat around a number of scattered fires on the plateau, and we all wandered back and forth exchanging greetings and moose hunt stories. Everyone agreed that the sarvs must be slaughtered now. The timing of this event is crucial. At the height of the mating season there is a tremendous release of hormones in the sarvs, and should this release of hormones go too far before slaughter, the meat will have a foul taste. On the other hand, one does not want to slaughter too early, for mating season brings the sarvs to peak weight. The time to slaughter is in the short interval between peak weight and maximum hormone release. The slaughter companies usually refuse to accept sarv meat after September 15. Most of the prime sarvs are killed at this time; only a few are needed to impregnate the vajas.

The mating season makes rivals of the sarvs. They will compete for the vajas and it is for this reason that their antlers have shed their natural sheaths and dried to hard weapons. The rutting season brings the sarvs into fighting form, heavy and inflamed. Then suddenly with the end of the mating season, nature no longer has any need for these dueling champions. They lose weight quickly, their tempers subside, and shortly thereafter, they lose their mighty antlers. It is as if big bullies were reduced to shy children.

Not every sarv follows the schedule exactly. The larger ones usually lead the trend, and therefore should one see a large sarv already past the critical point, it is best to hurry up with the slaughter. Isak Parfa had already seen such a sarv. It was hoped that most of them had not yet reached this stage. "How can you tell?" I asked. Is there not a strong possibility of slaughtering a sarv and discovering only afterward at the dinner table that the meat had turned bad? Isak said there were many signs. One could tell from the yellowish color of the sarv's eyes, from the smell of his urine and breath. One could see in the flatness of his stomach, for once mating has begun a sarv ceases to eat. There are many indicators and a herder knows the cycle so well that he can tell at a glance exactly how far along a sarv has come.

The herd thunders in. While those who have worked take a needed break, others set about covering the wire corral fence with burlap cloth. The thin wire fencing is hard to see against the sky and the sarvs in their heated condition are liable to crash into it and possibly make a hole in the effort to extricate their antlers. The cloth, of course, adds no strength to the fence, but it does make the corral very visible. Everyone is soon in the corral looking over the herd.

I cannot believe the change in the reindeer. They are extremely fat. Their eyes seem swollen and bulging. Their faces are puffed up and their tongues seem too big for their mouths. All the fur is now gone from their antlers, but these are no longer red with blood as I had seen in Parka. They are instead yellowish and brown. Their necks are massive and a loose bag of skin hangs underneath, which reminds me of Brahma bulls from India. All of this has happened in little over a month.

Every so often there comes a crash and a loud rattling sound as two sarvs come together and lock antlers. They lunge against each other with bowed heads, but their encounters are usually short. It can happen, however, that their battle goes beyond the wishes of either contestant. Sometimes their antlers entangle in such a way that it is impossible for them to break away. While hiking in the mountains one can sometimes come upon the skeletons of two sarvs with their bleached antlers still locked in mortal combat. It must be a terrible death.

We must be more wary of our movements in the corral. The sarvs do not step aside fully as readily as before. Now that their antlers contain no nerves, they are not so careful of them. A toss of the head can catch a herder in the face with a sharp point. They are no longer timid. In order to ensure that they do not become hopelessly entangled or injure somebody, the antlers are sometimes sawn off those sarvs that have "gone too far" and are not to be slaughtered. Now that the antlers are dried and bloodless, there is no danger of injuring the reindeer.

Besides the occasional loud crash of two sarvs meeting, there is another constant but lower-pitched sound in the corral, the sound one imagines wind would make blowing through a field of grass if the grass were made of antlers. It is the hard rustling sound of hundreds of antlers clattering against each other in a swirling, churning sarv herd.

A sarv slaughter on this scale is not traditionally Saami. In the past, before the modern freezing and packaging techniques and the transportation routes far into the mountains, large sarv slaughters were hardly possible. Sarvs for slaughter would have to be sold on the hoof, and unless this could be done by the railroad track, where they could be slaughtered and shipped immediately, it was not attempted. At this time of year sarvs cannot be driven long distances over land in a gathered herd. The herders would slaughter sarvs only for family use.

Now, however, technological advances provide mobile slaughter trucks with freezing compartments, and roads left from construction of the many water dams extend far westward. Marketing advances enable reindeer meat to fetch a good price as a delicacy in southern Sweden and even Europe in general. In effect, the herders can "freeze" their reindeer meat in the form of money. There is no lack of buyers. Competition for reindeer among the slaughter companies is fierce, and when the Swedish herders cannot afford them enough reindeer to supply their customers, slaughter companies might even import frozen reindeer carcasses from Russia.

Over the past thirty years, the reindeer slaughter business has grown into a highly modern and profitable industry. This change is largely due to the efforts of John Simonson. He and his family still run the largest reindeer slaughter company in Sweden, a company which has expanded so that it can service almost every herder in the country and offer the best price for their reindeer meat. He has made it possible for the herders to slaughter their deer almost anywhere and at the most advantageous time.

The basic problem associated with reindeer slaughters is transportation. Nowadays roads have been built right to the gates of many corrals. Mobile slaughter units can roll in. The reindeer are skinned and packed on hooks inside the trucks just outside the corral. Or the reindeer may be packed living into specially built two-story trucks and transported to the large permanent slaughterhouse where they are killed and butchered.

Only a couple of generations ago there was another system. In those days the railroad was the main transportation vehicle and Saami would sell entire herds, living, to the slaughter dealers. The dealers would in turn hire their own herders to drive the herd in the vicinity of the track, where the reindeer would be slaughtered and freighted away on the first train. In those days, old people have told me, there were Swedes "who were like Lapps" and knew how to herd and handle reindeer. Long drives to the railway station was not, however, a system suited to the slaughter of sarvs where timing is so crucial. It was rather a system employed during the winter, for the slaughter of ox-reindeer when there is no critical limit for slaughter time. The ox-reindeer, unlike the sarvs, will not lose weight after the rut. In all of these different slaughter techniques, transportation facilities play the deciding role.

Besides timing, speed is also of utmost importance during sarv slaughter. The reindeer must be skinned within five minutes after they are killed. Otherwise the skin gives the meat a bad taste. In the dead of winter when the temperature is −20°F, this effect is diminished and it is not so vital to skin the reindeer immediately. As a general rule, however, the sooner the better. Roads and slaughter trucks have made the sarv slaughter what it is today. The reindeer will never weigh more, and so for the Saami it is the best time to sell.

The corral at Valli peak, however, presented a problem. The road ended at Kvikkjokk. To get from the road to the corral required a boat ride across the river and a long steep climb up the mountain side. By this time I was learning that how-will-you-do-it questions are best answered by waiting and seeing. I did not have to wait long. A small helicopter came flying over the ridge, a signal for the work to begin.

A small part of the corral fence was rolled back in order for the sarvs to be pulled to the outside. The screen of burlap cloth was still stretched across the opening, and the herd within knew nothing about the change. The herders must duck under the cloth and pull the sarvs out from under, one at a time. There is hardly a corral built that holds a herd, especially a herd of sarvs, through brute force. A herd might conceivably stay in a corral made of paper until by chance it was ripped and they saw a way to freedom. Should a herd be frightened and press against the corral it is likely that they will succeed in breaking through. Many times a stray dog, wolverine, or other threat has scared a herd in a corral during the night so that it has torn or pressed down the fencing and escaped. It is best that the helicopter keep its distance. The sarvs will be killed and loaded some distance away.

The helicopter can carry five dead reindeer at once on a heavy wire cable threaded through the reindeer's back leg tendons. The bodies hang like a catch of fish. The trip from the corral to the road end in Kvikkjokk takes the helicopter only two minutes. A large slaughter truck from the Simonson Company waits below with an automatic skinning machine.

Pulling the sarvs out from the corral is exhausting labor. I had thought the work at Parka was tiring, but a tug of war with a sarv in mating fever is something far more demanding. Hands without the protection of gloves are soon raw and bleeding from rope burns. A single man against a sarv cannot hope to accomplish much. At best he can hang onto the lasso and bring the sarv to a standstill in the way an iron ball on the end of a chain might hamper a fugitive. It takes three or four men to win the battle, and even so, only after a wild dance. A number of men dig in their heels and hang onto the lasso while a comrade circles around behind the sarv with another lasso and tries to catch a back leg. The sarv sees the man approach and begins bucking and rearing away to the side, pivoting about the men on the lasso. As soon as a back foot leaves the ground, it is the target for a quick cast, and once two lines hold him, and he has only three legs on which to stand, the sarv is conquered.

He is hauled kicking and straining under the burlap cloth where he is then laid prone. The antlers are grasped and turned like a wheel of an old steamship until the tips point to the ground. This requires a mighty heave. The sarv's head is twisted. He must leave his feet, and once on his side, is easily controlled. One person sits on him, another holds his antlers. The sarv must calm down before he is killed, not out of consideration for the sarv, but for those who will eat him. The reason for this is exactly the same as the reason net-caught fish taste different from seine-caught fish. If the sarv does not stop struggling, his muscles will not have time to recover, and the lactic acid in them will cause the meat to taste awful.

Soon almost everyone is sitting on a reindeer. The sarvs are given their required rest as they await their turn to be among the five dead flown down to the slaughter truck. The helicopter is in constant motion. The wire line with its hook is simply lowered from the sky, and below in Kvikkjokk the cargo is unhooked under the swirling blades. No landing is necessary. During landing and unloading, the helicopter remains motionless in flight like a giant humming-bird.

The actual slaughter, I find, is performed in two different ways. The traditional method is with a knife stab in the neck at the base of the skull which severs the spinal cord. The reindeer collapses suddenly into a loose heap of flesh and bones. A quick heart stab finishes the job, and the last spasms are soon over. It is one of the fastest and, I suppose, least painful deaths possible. Of course, the knife must be in the hands of an experienced person. To lessen the chances of poorly executed and painful slaughters, a special knife is prescribed by law, but no one pays this much heed. All the Saami seem to be expert at the neck stab with or without the special knife. The other method is performed by the slaughter company workers who have come up with the helicopter. They are not Saami, and it is doubtful whether they can execute a proper neck stab. Instead they have come with a special gun which, when placed against the reindeer's forehead, drives a spike into the brain. This is the method preferred by law, for the reindeer supposedly dies faster. Although this may be true from a technical definition of death, of the two forms I dislike the gun more. The gun is foolproof each time, but the neck stab seems at least to cause the reindeer less pain.

The grass is covered with blood, and it is easy to slip. Our clothes are spattered. Once killed, the reindeer's throat is cut open and the food canal tied off in a knot so that the contents of the stomach will not spill out when it is removed. Then the belly is cut open and the stomach, (or I should say stomachs, for the reindeer, a ruminant, has a series of three stomachs) and intestines are extracted and flung aside. The reindeer lie dead on their backs propped up on their antlers. Their stomachs dot the ground like weird, pale gray mushrooms, and steam wells forth out of the open body cavity.

After all the concern for the reindeer, the joy of watching the small calves and working with the herd, I feel that the reindeer have become my friends. Our job has been to protect them, and it is hard to watch them die. Suddenly the reindeers' guardians have become their worst enemies. A herder once commented to me that in modern times with such large-scale slaughtering it was good that herding was so much more extensive than in the past. One no longer knows so many reindeer intimately on an individual basis, and it hurts less to kill them.

At first I help pull the sarvs from the corral, but later I am given the job of tagging each sarv in the ear with a metal number plate and recording the number and owner in a book. The slaughter company people are not able to read earmarks. The earmark system of the Saami classifies the reindeer by groups according to owner, but the number plates give each reindeer an individual identity, an important difference, as the sarvs are each weighed and bought at correspondingly varying prices. It has happened that dishonest people have taken advantage of the slaughter company personnel's inability to read earmarks. They have come with someone else's sarv and sold him to the slaughter dealer, entering their own name in the book opposite the listed tag number. Once the reindeer is skinned, there is no way to uncover foul play. A corral full of comrades, of course, leaves little room for dishonesty, but there are many other opportunities for reindeer theft during the year. Herding together demands much trust, and for the most part this trust is not misplaced.

A couple of families have begun killing and butchering sarvs for their own personal use, not to be sold. They consider the slaughter company's butchering methods wasteful. The Saami make use of nearly everything: intestines for making sausage, blood collected in pails for sausage or pudding, tendons for sewing thread, to give some examples. A rack is put together with fence poles, and the different cuts of meat are hung up off the ground until it is time to send them down with the helicopter.

No more sarvs are pulled from the corral. There are already enough waiting outside to be killed and flown down. It is becoming plain that nightfall will catch us before the work is finished. The last flight leaves in the pale twilight, and we must continue tomorrow. This means I will have the chance to see what is happening at the other end in Kvikkjokk once the reindeer are lowered from the sky. As the helicopter departs down the mountain for the last time today, most of us are already strung out in a long file along the trail to Kvikkjokk, moving at a rapid pace against the fading light. It is completely dark when I reach the river. Boats have come from the other side to meet us, and a voice calls out from the bank, "Here."

I have spent the night in Kvikkjokk and am awakened next morning by the familiar sound of the helicopter. It is only 8:00 A.M., but I see from the window a shipment of reindeer swaying over the woods. I do not envy those who have already trudged up to the Valli corral. The early start, I am told, is so that the Saami and the slaughter truck will have time to partake in another sarv slaughter at Kuorpak. Sirkas Sameby has brought in its sarvs. I doubt if the slaughter company personnel get much sleep during the sarv slaughter season.

The scene at the truck is furious. The workers seem to wade in blood, and some wear fisherman style hip boots. As soon as the reindeer are dropped from the helicopter they are thrown onto steel racks. Some are skinned by hand; others have their hides attached to a machine which with a sudden, powerful jerk peel it off. Whatever the method, it has to be done quickly. One load of reindeer has to be processed and weighed before the helicopter returns. Reindeer carcasses hang on hooks inside the truck like coats in a closet. The hides are spread out round about, and beside them is a large and growing pile of heads entwined in a mesh of antlers.

The reindeer offers goods other than meat, despite the general transition to a cash economy and the specialization of products that tends to result. September sarv slaughter hides are the best and most valuable reindeer hides because they do not shed hair. The hides from the ox-reindeer slaughtered in winter shed heavily. The hard, September sarv antlers are also quite valuable. In Asia the antlers of different kinds of deer have long been prized, and the Asian market now reaches as far as Lapland. Many countries bid for Lapland antler.

Asian interests apply in particular to young, velvet antlers, cut from living deer in a number of countries. Such an antler brings a high price in Asian markets where it is a highly regarded medical item and even thought to enhance sexual potency. In Asia, processed and dried velvet antler is often thinly sliced and used almost as one would a tea bag. In Sweden the cutting of young, so-called wet antler from living animals—that is, blood-filled, June or July antler—is forbidden for humanitarian reasons. However, the Asians are even interested in grinding up hard September sarv antlers, although this product will bring nowhere near the same price on the Asian market as will that of the soft velvet antlers.

Hard September antler has yet another market, a local market. Saami handicraft artists also want such antlers, with which to make a variety of utilitarian and beautiful objects. The Asian market and the local Saami handicraft artists are locked in competition with the herders in the middle. While Swedish law forbids the cutting of velvet antler from living deer, the profits from the antler market are so attractive that some herders consider slaughtering especially early (thus cutting the velvet antler from deer already dead), sustaining a loss in meat quantity, for the sake of the antler quality. This practice means fewer hard antlers will become available to the handicraft artists, although fortunately for them it is a practice hardly developed. At this time of year, June and July, the reindeer are usually far west in the mountains where quick transportation of meat in the summer heat is not feasible. Reindeer slaughter in Lapland is still timed predominantly out of consideration for meat production. Nonetheless, to their chagrin, the Saami handicraftsmen have found that they now must pay considerably more for their raw material, because the Asian market drives up the price. The competition for hard reindeer antler has become so fierce that Saami artisans are finding it difficult to obtain material for their work.

Stimulated by tales of antler-induced sexual prowess, Per-Henrik Labba had managed to procure some "medicine" from an Asian buyer. He reported no effect, but the other herders were still curious and distrustful of Per-Henrik's results. After all, Per-Henrik was single and lacked a partner with whom to conduct an adequate experiment.

The slaughter company is, of course, concerned with big business, and as most of its customers in the south do not like the idea of eating blood, intestines, head meat, and marrow bones, these things are frequently thrown away. Before leaving Kvikkjokk, many Saami took a few reindeer heads, which lay in the pile free for the asking (once the valuable antlers were sawed off). When the slaughter truck pulled away packed with meat, Kvikkjokk was once again a dreamy little village at the end of a road.

The sarv slaughter has become something of a demarcation point in the yearly herding cycle. Once it is over there is a long pause. People take up odd jobs or turn to all those other things that have been postponed over the spring, summer, and fall. When active herding once again demands attention, it is well into the winter season. Still, there are a number of things that must be attended to before freeze up, the time when winter first takes hold and overnight covers the lakes with a thin layer of ice. Initially there will be a period when travel along the waterways either by boat or snowmobile will be impossible. The nets must be cleared from the lakes and mended. A new supply of shoe grass needs to be cut before the grasses wither. Boats must be pulled ashore and sheltered. It would be a shame not to pick the ripe blueberries, whortleberries, and cloudberries. Soon travel possibilities are not only restored, they are also greatly expanded, but then the snowmobile has replaced the boat and the ground is covered with snow.

A few days after the sarv slaughter, Johan and I were once again sitting in the boat bound for Lillselet to collect shoe grass. Amanda had fresh fish, coffee, and cake for us when we arrived. Sven had come from Levik to join our little expedition, and he, who had not shivered for over an hour across Lake Karatj, was eager to get a move on. It seems that people have special shoe grass places the same way they have secret berry-picking spots. Sven and Johan discussed the merits of the grass in different areas until it was agreed where we would go. Soon we were on the move, Sven taking his rifle. He had seen what he called a "good luck bird" and favored his chances of bumping into a bear. Or, he added, he might have the good fortune of mistaking a moose for a bear. (Bear could still be hunted legally at this time of year, but moose season was over.)

The grass used in shoes instead of socks is a special type of sedge that grows in wet or soggy ground where there is plenty of light. That which grows on open marshes and around lake sides, though of the right species, is not good to use, being both too dry and fragile and usually not long enough. The best shoe grass is found growing in dense willow bushes. Here the grass is long, tough, and sheltered from too much sun. Fortunately, Johan and Sven knew exactly where to go for the best quality grass. It is interesting to see how the grass changes texture, toughness, and length from one spot to another, even if separated by only a short distance.

Johan and I set to work with our knives while Sven departed to investigate what a bunch of crows were circling over. Should he find a reindeer killed by some carnivore, he is entitled to fifty crowns from the owner. The owner receives a sum from the state in compensation for his reindeer, and it is from this that he pays the finder of the carcass. One need only cut the ears from the dead reindeer and send them for identification to the Sameby. The owner is extremely thankful, for he can then collect compensation rather than suffer a total loss. Most of the victims are never found, and Sven returned empty-handed. Smart birds that they are, the crows moved their circling to trick him.

Once I had put together a few large handfuls of grass, Johan showed me how to twist it into the first unit of production, the *snuftu*. One picks out all burrs and hard stalks, beats the root end against a tree, and winds the top around itself so that it remains in a bundle. Sven had a huge fire and pot of coffee ready for us when we were tired. Snowflakes encircled us. When our packs were filled with *suojne-snuftus,* altogether about fifty sheaves, we headed home to Lillselet.

After dinner Johan and I hurried out to the woodshed to comb and braid the grass before it got too dark. The comb consisted of a board filled with spikes in a tight cluster. We sat on each side of the board and took turns whacking the sheaves into the comb and pulling them through. We worked like a team of old-time pile drivers, banging the grass onto the board with a steady beat until the grass was shredded finely and evenly. Then it was time for the next unit of production, the *pil'ka.*

A pil'ka of shoe grass is made from two or three snuftus braided together at the top in such a way that the grass can be hung over a stick or a rope for drying. Saami almost always carry a pil'ka or two with them in their packs. There is even a further unit of shoe grass production called the *vierra,* composed of about thirty pil'kas wound and packed together into a tight ball. The vierra lasts a long time and serves generally as a resource for an entire household. When finished I had only seven pil'kas, but this would prove to be enough to last me through the next summer.

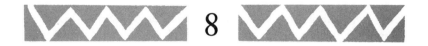

8

Autumn Migration
to the Lowlands

I t is October, and reports come almost daily of different lakes that have newly frozen over. The deeper the lake, the longer it remains open in the early winter, and the longer it remains frozen in the early spring. Fluffy new snow sits on the evergreens. A slight wind stirs the branches and sends a silent cascade of crystals down through the last low sun rays. Morning and nightfall creep closer and closer together. Soon the sun will cease to show itself at all and the days will pass in a blueish twilight. I can understand the bear's desire to sleep through it all. Not that these short days lack beauty, but the darkness and cold make the body heavy and tired. Everyone is yawning and blowing his nose. Oddly enough, it is the temperature just below freezing that seems to cause the most aches and pains. Yet the same darkness and cold that follows the fall of the sun heralds the rise of another light, the aurora borealis, or Northern Lights.

The Saami have now moved into their winter quarters, homes that at first glance are like any other home in the far north. Houses are usually small but well insulated. The largest and most central room is the kitchen with a trapdoor in the floor leading down a ladder into the potato cellar. As the family grows and the herd prospers additional rooms may be built on. A closer look uncovers many signs of the outdoor herding life. Long, broad Saami skis lean against the wall; handicraft materials, antlers, and birch knurs may be strewn about, and frequently a tent goattieh used for smoking fish or meat stands out back. Here one smokes the meat that will then be eaten, dried, in the summer. It is the time for handicrafts and tarring skis. Many of the more extensive herders have managed to find part time jobs. Some work at building new tourist cabins along the main hiking trails. Others find jobs with the timber industry. For the intensive herders, however, the late fall–early winter pause is short. The members of the Blind group have hardly enough time to move into their winter homes in Stenträsk before the men fly with Lundqvist back to Stalo. A few weeks later seaplane travel will be impossible.

The Blind or Stenträsk group still has the main part of its herd in the summer land. Their reindeer are scattered at the western end of Lake Virihaure. Some of them have even crossed into Norway, though the steep, clifflike drop of the mountains toward the coast inhibits scattering too far. Henrik Blind and his brother, Nils-Anders, Per-Henrik Labba, and Lars-Anders Blind landed on Virihaure in early October. Their job: to gather the herd together and when the snows permit, begin the long, hard autumn migration down to the winter land.

Not so long ago each Saami family migrated with its herd, and a few tame härks would pull the sleds carrying the entire family and their provisions. The caravan used to be the only means of transportation for the families, but nowadays the women, children, and old people can fly to and from the mountains. A small number of men on skis with dogs and a greatly reduced caravan to carry only those supplies needed during the migration itself are all that move with the Blind herd eastward. This group is one of the last that still migrate with the herd from the summer land using the old caravan.

Autumn migration is not a leisurely move. Only the hardiest men take part. No snowmobiles can be used. There is not yet enough snow for their passage. The caravan, or rajd, carries the food and gear, but the men must travel the whole route on skis. I doubt if the Saami can be matched in their skill at overland skiing. The migration takes them over mountains and lakes and through thick woods. Once moving, the migration is fast. No matter how interested and earnest he may be, a tenderfoot cannot hope to follow. One cannot simply jump off if the going gets too rough. Each person bears the responsibility of ensuring that he is no burden to the others. It is terribly easy to die in the mountains during the winter.

I felt quite frustrated my first winter in Jokkmokk. I knew it was out of the question for me to follow the migration. I had hardly stood on skis before. Nonetheless, it hurt to stay behind while the others set out on what I dreamed of as the greatest adventure. It is easy to dream on a real bed in a heated house. Now that I have participated in the autumn migration, I doubt I will ever want to do it again. It took many months for my toenails, which dropped off from the cold, to grow back again. Fortunately there is a whole year between each autumn migration, and in that time the toes may have forgotten the cold they felt while the eyes can never forget the beauty they saw.

During the winter of 1973 the men were gone about six weeks before a phone call in November over the emergency rescue line in Stalo reached the police station. The police relayed the message to the families in Stenträsk: the migration was underway. By this time I could shuffle with some confidence on skis and I was all excited and eager to meet the herd as it came down. The best place to wait was Lillselet. A reindeer herd is extremely difficult to keep together and drive through a thick forest, and therefore, once in the lowlands, frozen lakes make the best transportation routes. About thirty miles of the Stenträsk group's migration route traversed the Peuraure-Levik-Karatj Lake chain. Lillselet lay athwart the path. Henrik, Nils-Anders, and Per-Henrik would ski past their childhood homes. Only Lars-Anders had not grown up there.

Once again I rode with Johan up to Lillselet, only this time we traveled by snowmobile, not boat. Johan drove and I lay on the sled in a bundle of coats and blankets. Gustav had painstakingly marked the snowmobile trail along Karatj Lake with small birches stuck in the ice. I was reminded of watching an endless row of telephone poles from a car window, but these birches serve an entirely different purpose. A storm might obliterate the trail and leave only the birch branches to show the way in the dark night through the whirling snow. It was preferable that all the traffic stick to the same trail so that it becomes hard packed and lasts far into the spring when the rest of the lake surface turns wet and soft.

The day did not seem so cold, but once one begins speeding over the ice with the cold air blowing hard in the face, it is easy to freeze. I had smeared my face with fat, but even so had to peek timidly above the edge of the blanket when I wanted to see. It was −12°F. My pack served as a pillow, and besides warm clothes, contained a supply of cigarettes, snus (ground wet tobacco), and cognac for my friends when they came with the herd. The police had not failed to inform us of the essential shortages in their supplies.

Everyone in Lillselet waited anxiously for the arrival of the "Saami." Although the people of Lillselet were themselves Saami, they reserved the term for the active herders. John had joined their party, so now there were five Saami with the herd. There was no way of knowing when they would appear. Not so long ago there was no emergency phone in Stalo, and it was impossible even to know when they were beginning the homeward trek. Once, the weather had forced them to wait in the mountains for three months, until January, before leaving Stalo, and a huge rescue operation was undertaken to save the lost Saami. When the helicopters found them, they were alive and well and somewhat disturbed by all the commotion, headlines, and pictures. Saami had been living like that for hundreds of years and never thought themselves in need of rescue. Now suddenly they had become celebrities, and Henrik Blind, then a young boy, was offered large sums of money to pose in mosquito spray advertisements.

I had to wait only a week in Lillselet before they came. During that time I heard many old stories: buried Saami treasure with ghostly guardians; stories of Lillselet's past, when the death rate of children was so high that baptisms had to be hurriedly performed in the absence of a preacher to save the dying from eternal darkness. I skied to Alte Dievva, the sacrificial mountain, where countless heathen memories lie buried with the piles of reindeer antlers, gifts to the spirits. And I listened to Gustav swear at the Arabs and the rising cost of oil. Saami swearwords, I learned, are almost all borrowed from Finnish and Swedish, accessories to the avowal of the Christian God. As always there was much to do and learn in Lillselet, but I was impatient for the migration to sweep by. The arrival of the herd meant reindeer meat for everyone in Lillselet. Arthur and Gustav were itching to buy ox-reindeer for slaughter.

There were already a number of scattered reindeer around Lillselet, those belonging to the extensive herders. These reindeer were the same we had separated and driven to the winter land last August in

Parka. They had now drifted further eastward, out of the birch woods into the pine and fir forests. A number of the extensive herders had been trying to gather them together, but this had proved difficult. Reindeer belonging to extensive herders are not so used to being gathered into herds for long periods, and once the snows have set in they are prone to scatter everywhere in search of food.

One of the herders engaged in the thankless task of trying to round up the scattered deer around Lillselet leaped from his snowmobile to join Amanda and me in a cup of coffee before he had to hurry back to work. It was Isak Parfa. He had seen wolf tracks and was anxious to see if any reindeer had been killed. "The state simply does not understand the needs and problems of the Saami," said Isak. Everything works against the herder. "Not only is our grazing land taken a bit at a time, but our children are kept in school when they should be learning to be herders. Lots of Saami children today would not recognize a wolf track from that of a dog. Herding is a year-round project and cannot be learned during the summer vacation. To make matters worse, the Swedes have decided to pity the wolf and turn Tuorpon into some kind of a zoo where the worst reindeer predators must be protected. I wish they cared as much about Saami as wolves." At this rate, Isak considered, "real herding" would disappear in a generation.

Isak had just left when the phone rang. It was John calling from Njunjes, another emergency line in the Tarra Valley. He had made a detour to tell us they would be reaching Lillselet in a few days, and more important, to hear what grazing conditions were like where we were. "Dry powder snow and such easy digging for the reindeer that even the laziest will become fat," we told him. He was also most concerned about the location of the extensive herders' flocks. It could prove disastrous to drive the Blind group's herd into the same grazing area. The Blind group's reindeer were used to more intensive care, used to the presence of men, and used to being driven for long periods as a herd. The extensive herders' reindeer were far less tame, and should one of these mix with the more intensive herd, much trouble could result. The wild temperament or fright of one reindeer can infect hundreds of others. If one reindeer tries to break from the herd, it is almost certain to pull many others away with him. Having received the information he needed, John hurried off to catch up with the herd.

Three days later at an early hour, we were awakened by a call from Sven in Levik. The men had reached him late at night, rested for three hours, and continued on their way. I gulped a cup of coffee, grabbed my pack, and skied toward Levik to meet them. I did not get far before I saw John coming toward me. It was strange to see him so thin. The herd was nowhere in sight. "You had better hurry as fast as you can to Luovaluokta if you want to catch them," said John. "We've decided to bypass Lillselet—too many other reindeer about. So we're leaving the ice and heading through the woods directly from Levik Lake to Karatj Lake. We've broken up the rajd at Levik and left the sleds behind. I've come to pick up my snowmobile in Lillselet. It can pull the sleds and replace the härks now that there is plenty of snow. Hurry if you want to see them pass. They are moving fast to lessen the chance of mixing. Hurry!" I turned around and set out at my top speed, which unfortunately was rather slow.

Luovaluokta, a small inlet of Karatj Lake, was a few miles eastward from Lillselet down the lake. On a flat, open lake there are no trees, rocks, or buildings to measure movement against. I skied furiously and never seemed to move at all. I stayed in the same relationship to the mountains around the lake. After days of waiting, the thought of coming too late, combined with the feeling of skiing without progress, filled me with a sense of hopelessness. I wanted so much to see reindeer on the ice that my mind began playing tricks. I was convinced that tiny dark dots far ahead on the white surface were reindeer. I was positive that I could see them move. They bobbed up and down like reindeer, and they seemed to be moving ahead of me, for I could not catch them. Actually it was my own motion which lent them movement. When the real herd came into view, it suddenly became plain what was a reindeer and what was merely a bouncing figment of my imagination. Yet I had been sure. There is undoubtedly more than just folkloric tradition behind the appearance of ghost herds.

I heard them long before I saw them. Shouts and barks rose from a steady clanging of bells. I skied toward the shore where the woods roared with commotion, life, and movement in an otherwise still, frozen world. I could feel them sweep by me invisibly until finally they broke from the cover of trees and spread onto the ice. Per-Henrik was out in front leading a tame härk that in turn led the entire herd. I handed him a cup of coffee from my thermos and shoved a pack of cigarettes into his pocket. He looked dead beat. His face was pale and his eyes sunken. Besides the short stop in Levik, this last stretch had kept them going for two days. Even now he must hurry. He downed the coffee and skied on, he and the tame härk plodding together in the same steady, tired rhythm. They did not want to spend any more time than necessary in a region with scattered, half-wild reindeer.

Two thousand reindeer followed Per-Henrik. Their walk spoke of eighty hard miles, and yet gave the impression that they could go on forever. Three heads stuck above the sea of reindeer. Nils-Anders came directly behind and Henrik and Lars-Anders on the flanks. They yelled and shouted to drive the herd forward, all the while watching carefully for the least sign of scattering. Reindeer were constantly flaking from the edges of the herd, and if the men behind were not in a position to stop them, a quick command to one of the dogs soon brought about the desired result. For the most part the dogs did not need to be told what to do. They were constantly skirting the herd. The dogs also showed signs of the journey. They were terribly thin and looked like skulls with tails.

I fell in behind, and the herd passed as Henrik, Lars-Anders, and Nils-Anders puffed contentedly on cigarettes and diluted the coffee I gave them with cognac. It was −-20°F and almost painful to rest— better to keep warm by skiing. I handed over the supplies I had brought them, and they flung their half smoked cigarettes into the snow. They had no more time to spare. Now on the open lake, free from the trees, they picked up the tempo. I straggled along behind as best I could, surrounded by the sounds of a moving herd: the shouts of the herders, barks of the dogs, and muffled thundering of several thousand reindeer hooves on snow. For half an hour I felt the thrill of migration before I stopped to rest. They had already pulled well ahead of me. I watched them draw further and further down the lake. The sounds grew faint. The entire herd shrank to a dark speck in a white world. It was a silent and lonely world they left behind them. I turned and dragged myself back toward Lillselet in the failing light.

I depart here from the account of my first year in Jokkmokk to move ahead two winters. In the interest of depicting the full year's herding

cycle, I must describe the autumn migration from an active participant's perspective, and I was not able to follow the Stenträsk group on
this difficult trek until the winter of 1975. In late November I started
skiing up the Tarra Valley toward Stalo in hopes of meeting them on
the way down with the herd. By this time I had already accompanied
them on spring migration in the opposite direction, a far less haz-
ardous move, back to the summer land. Moreover, I had improved
sufficiently on skis so that I could take care of myself and stubbornly
reach the finishing line even if somewhat slowly. I knew the territory
better; I had a better idea of what I would be facing, and most important, the others knew me better and had granted me permission to
follow. Although I would probably be of little help, I would at least be
no burden.

Everything had happened much as it had the first year I met
them in Luovaluokta. They had flown to Stalo on October 9 to
gather the herd. This time, however, Nils-Gustav replaced his
brother, Lars-Anders, and Lars-Henrik Omma had joined the group,
making John's presence not necessary though nonetheless missed.
The snows were late in coming this year, and the men were gone
almost two months before the call from Stalo alerted us that they
would start down soon.

It was unknown which route the migration would take. I hoped
they would choose the same way we had gone in the spring. Otherwise
there was a good chance we would miss each other, unless, that is, I
reached Stalo before they began to move, a doubtful prospect. Should
they migrate down the route we had followed in the spring, I would
encounter them somewhere along the way in Tarra Valley. Birgit,
Henrik's wife, had heard from the police, however, that they were
thinking of taking the Varvek route in hopes of picking up the few
belled härks whose accompanying flocks they still missed. They
thought the chances of finding them around Varvek better than in
Tarra Valley, but what they did not know, said Birgit, was that the
Luokta Mavas Sameby herders had gathered in the Varvek area and
swept it clean. Birgit propped me full of messages and news of other
herd movements for "the boys." "Remember snus and cigarettes," was
the last she had said. As I would be carrying the load, they would have
to do without cognac.

Autumn Migration to the Lowlands

When I had tarred my "Saami skis" and cut rubber band like bindings from the inner tube of a car tire to stretch from the ski-binding's simple toe loop to my heel and prevent my foot from slipping out, when I had stuffed my boots with grass (from the supply that I had collected with Johan last autumn in Lillselet) and wound my trouser legs tight to the shafts with shoe bands, and when I had crammed my pack full of food and clothes, Johan drove me to Kvikkjokk. I planned to follow the summer trail up the valley, stopping at the empty tourist cabins for shelter. Everyone had warned me to stay off the lakes and rivers in the valley as the ice was as yet too thin. I was eager to start, but at the same time rather nervous. I had never before attempted to tackle the Lapland mountains in the dead of winter alone. I did not know where, when, or even if I would meet the herd. I shall let my journal continue the narrative.

November 26, 1975

Most of the way across the Kvikkjokk River delta I could follow an old snowmobile trail and avoid thin ice. Once I was on the main trail, however, I found the going terrible. There is too little snow, and what there is, is too loose to carry me over ground obstacles. The snow serves only to hide the trouble spots and lure me into rocks or raised planks put across marshes for the summer tourists to keep their toes dry. My pack is ridiculously heavy. The slightest lean to one side pulls me over in a way reminiscent of carrying moose meat in Lillselet, and on one such occasion, when one of my ski poles snapped, the pack shot over my head and jerked me into the snow face down where I remained a good while, dizzy. I will have to leave things behind at the cabin if I am to continue.

It gets quite dark by 3:00 P.M. In the −20°F air my heavy nylon coat sounds like a paper bag with a kitten inside. All the streams are open, and I must walk a good deal of the way. Fortunately the night sky is clear and the stars bright. The snow is glimmering white through the dark trees, so I can pick my way along where it looks as if a trail has been cut.

The Holmbom family had once lived in Njunjes all the year round, and I collapse in what must have been their wash shed. It is little more than a mile to the cabin with bed and stove, but I am too spent to move any further. It is impossible to start a fire with icy wood at this temperature in the open, so I must melt snow with a candle. I have not eaten all day, but vomit when I try. Obviously I'll reach the cabin tomorrow and recover, but at this rate I am a fool to try to reach Stalo. The snow conditions may be equally bad further up the valley. I crawl into my sleeping bag and am able to get fairly warm although the ice lumps in my beard refuse to melt.

November 27

I rise a new man, with enough energy and morale salvaged to persist in this foolishness. It is snowing. The sky is white and the wind has sprayed the mountains with white powder from one angle making interesting shadow effects. At the top the mountains merge with the hazy sky. I reach the Njunjes phone, the same phone on which John called us at Lillselet two years ago. I talk to Amanda in Lillselet, Gunborg in Jokkmokk, and Birgit in Stenträsk, telling them what conditions are like in Tarra Valley should they get the opportunity to pass the word on to the boys. At the cabin I build a good fire, drop a bucket on the end of my lasso into the rapids below the cliff for water, cook coffee and bacon. The cabin's logbook shows no entries for over a month.

I unload half of my food supply, hoping that this will enable me to move on tomorrow. A major problem, I realize, is to make it from one cabin to the next, an average of ten miles with the meager six hours of pale light. Had skiing conditions been good, this distance would take no time. But this is not skiing, it is plowing. I must find a good stick to use as a ski pole.

November 28

It has snowed heavily during the night and is still snowing. It took a vigorous push to get the front door open against the drift. It is impossible to see more than a few feet ahead, and I am therefore confined to quarters. I chop some wood for the stove, fashion a new ski pole, and improvise a crude webbed hoop from an old wire egg beater I have found in the cabin.

November 29

The weather has turned worse, not better. I am forced to spend another lonely day singing songs to myself in the dark. The speed with which my candles disappear has caused me to enforce strict rationing. I have found reading materials left in the cabin for the daylight hours: the New Testament and old pornography, though I would have preferred the reverse.

November 30

Am now recovering from the grueling trip to the Tarrakaise cabin. I arose this morning in Njunjes when it was still dark out and was underway with the dawn. Although the distance is short, I did not reach Tarrakaise until dark. Unfortunately the snow that has fallen the last two days is unpacked, and skiing is still next to impossible. Most of the time I could see only the tips of my skis. Uphill I have had to walk to my waist in snow. Coffee is strange cooked with melted snow water. I understand why the Saami might add salt.

December 1

Saw the first living thing since I entered the mountains, a crow. Have decided to rest here another day to reassess my position and let my blisters heal. They were extremely painful yesterday and made my boots sticky with blood. The worst part now is the psychic—not knowing where the herd is, or even if they have started, and at the same time realizing that if I do not meet them soon I will have to turn back. I simply cannot take the risk of going down to my last bite in one direction. I must always be sure to have enough food to get back

should I miss them. Even waiting requires food. At this rate of progress it could take me a week to reach Stalo, meaning that I must carry
two weeks worth of food at a minimum. Even so, this would mean
reaching Stalo and leaving immediately should I meet no one there. I
doubt if I can stretch my food so long. The best plan I can work out,
taking all factors and hopes into consideration, is to move on to
Såmmarlappa, the next cabin up the valley, and wait there. If they
have decided to take the Tarra Valley route before branching off
toward Staika, they must pass the Såmmarlappa cabin. Directly opposite the cabin is the low pass that offers the herd a route over the steep
valley wall.

December 2

Såmmarlappa is nearly twice as far from Tarrakaise as Tarrakaise is
from Njunjes. Nonetheless, it did not take me twice as long to ski the
distance. Snow conditions were better, and the terrain more even. I
reached Såmmarlappa in nine hours, only the last three of them in
darkness. The occasional paint spots or blazes on the trees that mark
the trail are more than adequate for the summer hiker, but in the
winter darkness they do me little good. Lost the trail only once when
crossing a wide open area but soon found it again. Another major
problem with night skiing is that although it is a simple matter to see
the snow as opposed to the trees, there is great difficulty in discerning
contours in the field of white. It is easy to ski head on into a snow-
covered rock that juts fully two feet above the normal level, or to fly
suddenly down into a deep gully. During one such unexpected descent,
I broke my ski pole again. Odd, but I am constantly hearing a kind of
droning noise that fills the otherwise perfect silence outside as if a
plane were passing far in the distance; but the sound never fades, is
continuous. I celebrate my arrival with some soup.

December 3–5

Which way I intend to go always seems to depend upon how I feel
rather than any reasonable argument. But now snowstorms and food

shortage make the decision for me. I must turn back. There has been a severe storm. The snowflakes fly horizontally and sweep over the drifts like sand blowing over desert dunes. I want to wait here a few days anyway to see if they come. I chop wood in the light hours, a project the Saami always say warms twice, once while doing the chopping and then again as the wood burns. I need all the warmth I can get. The water bucket contains a block of ice each morning, and the pots and pans creak and whine with the heat change when I light the stove and they thaw loose from the counter top.

December 6

Once again it is blowing strongly down the valley, but I am so tired of staying alone in one place with my food dwindling and my last candle getting shorter that I have packed up and left despite the weather. I head back toward Tarrakaise. At least I have the wind at my back. I am also in much better shape. Not at all so tired, and feel able to push on to Njunjes tomorrow. I can call Birgit from Njunjes and hear the latest news, although I am almost certain that if they have moved, they have taken the Varvek route.

December 7

The wind has shifted and now blows directly in my face so that I am covered with white and my frozen beard makes me look like a great white owl. On the high slopes the wind has blown away most of the snow and I must walk over fields of rocks carrying my skis. I take only a short rest at the Tarrakaise cabins. At Njunjes I find that an ermine has broken into the food supply I had left behind. He has been kind enough to leave me some bread and coffee.

I had been there only fifteen minutes, pulled up water with lasso and bucket, and made a fire in the stove when in tramped Henrik, Per-Henrik, Nils-Anders, Lars-Henrik, and Nils-Gustav. I had given up all hope of meeting them and was so unbelieving that it took me a while to recognize the faces under the hats, hoods, and new beards. But who else could it be in the mountains during a winter storm? My spirits were scooped from the depths and thrown high in the sky. My plans spun around. I had joined the migration.

"Dark in here," said Henrik and spread five new candles around the room—incredible luxury. "Cold too," he added, and from somewhere produced a jug of white gas, poured some into an empty bucket, and flung in a match. Nils-Gustav reappeared with a huge pot and Nils-Anders set about chopping up a whole side of reindeer meat. They had slaughtered one of the herd just before leaving Stalo. At last I was freed from soup and bacon. For me this was the Thanksgiving feast I had missed in America. The horn (or rather antler) of plenty was the rajd. It was the tame härks that had pulled the supplies. "Tomorrow you can put your pack on one of the sleds," said Henrik. This would relieve me of a heavy burden. Just the sound of a human voice lifted a great weight. "You are the first people I've seen in about ten or eleven days," I commented. "You're the first new face we've seen in about two months," they replied.

I spilled forth messages, greetings, and news from Jokkmokk as we ate. It was good that the Mavas herders swept the Varvek area, they thought. "Now we just have to pull out our reindeer from their herd sometime this winter in the separating corral." "If they reach the corral before we get down, Per and Anders will cover it," said Per-Henrik. I waited for a few expectant glances before hauling forth cigarettes and snus. Clouds of satisfaction hung over the table.

The next item of curiosity was how this meeting had come about. "How did you get here if you didn't come down the Tarra Valley?" I asked. "But we did come down Tarra Valley; where were you?" When it was all straightened out, it became plain that for the past two days we had been moving parallel to each other down the valley, separated by less than a mile. I had been on the trail. They had moved over the river and lake ice. I had been unable to see them in the dark and unable to hear them in the howling storm. "It was good to have an extra man on our left flank," said Henrik, and smiled. "On the other hand, it was lucky for you it did storm, or else we would not have stopped here."

Tomorrow we would move to Vuoka, I was told, not a very hard haul, but the next stretch to Levik would be the toughest of all. "There is good grazing here," said Henrik, "so we can leave the herd. They won't scatter far in one night when there's food close at hand. There is good grazing in Vuoka too, but after that there is no good grazing for thirty-five miles until we reach Levik." Henrik and Nils-Gustav prepared to ski the extra mile to the telephone booth, spread the word of the migration's progress, signal Sven in Levik of our approach, announce that I had joined them, and hear of other herd movements and grazing conditions ahead. All the while I had huddled in Såmmarlappa during the storm, the migration had also been held up. By now everyone would be wondering where we were and why we had not already come.

Nils-Anders set about repairing his ski. It had split, but by reenforcing it with a thin plate of reindeer antler it might hold until he reached home, Stenträsk, where the migration ended. Per-Henrik made a last quick search for his dog, which had failed to keep up with the herd and was still missing. When the others returned from the phone we received the bad news that it was out of order. There was no way of breaking our isolation. We stoked up the stove for the night, hung our mittens high above and piled our damp shoe grass round about to dry. My blisters looked ghastly. Nils-Anders produced a vial of iodine, and I crawled into my sleeping bag swearing through clenched teeth.

December 8

Arise about 6:00 A.M. Coffee is ready. Nils-Gustav, who claimed to be such an early riser last night, was last one up this morning. We fry meat, pack, and stuff our shoes with grass, this last such a careful art for all but me that I am sure they took close to half an hour putting on their shoes. I began to wonder how many feet they had. I suppose their patience with shoe grass stems largely from past blisters like mine. I can see, or rather feel, that the proper stuffing of shoe grass is a skill I should rapidly perfect, and I have been delinquent in not having it fully mastered already.

The wind has howled all night. We start out with a few stars still in the morning sky and cross the river to where the three tame härks stand tied beside the two sleds. We load our packs into the sleds. I feel like a sprinter freed from his weighted training shoes. Henrik stuffs birch branches all along the sides of the sleds, cut ends toward the front. He says this hinders twigs from catching in the gear when the sleds go through thick underbrush, and helps keep the supplies securely fastened.

Since there are only two sleds or *pulkas,* only two of the härks do the actual pulling. The third is a trainee, only five years old and inexperienced, but he is sometimes harnessed to pull as it is important that young härks learn to replace the others when they become too old. A single line is led from the small yoke, between the legs of the härk to the front of the sled, a method some anthropologists claim demonstrates evolution from the sled dog teams of other Arctic peoples. On steep downward slopes, one of the härks is tied behind the last sled to act as a brake. In this way the sleds will not slide too fast forward into the back legs of the pulling härks. A strong well-trained härk can pull extremely heavy loads. On steep uphill climbs they may go down on their front knees to pull better.

Nils-Anders is in command of the rajd. Not everyone has the calm, steady hand suited to this task. I have been given orders to stay with the rajd while the rest of them go to round up the herd. So I remain behind the rajd, skiing in its wake as it loops in long "S" curves up to Vuoka. The rajd moves fast, and I must hurry to keep up. Nils-Anders is expert at finding the easiest route. He stops occasionally to spy with binoculars. The skill with which these men can spot reindeer alive or dead many miles distant always astounds me. Far below lay a dead reindeer, killed during the night by a predator. I could hardly see it even with Nils-Anders directing my gaze. Apparently this was what had frightened the herd and caused the reindeer to scatter despite the good grazing. Gathering the herd, therefore, took many more hours than planned.

We move like one huge animal snaking along the mountain crests. We seem to be the only thing moving in this wide waste land. The Vuoka cabin lies like a tiny match box between large mountain waves, a lifeboat in a sea of white. Nils-Anders and I reach the cabin first with the rajd. The lock is frozen tight and we must build a fire around it with a bundle of birchbark kept for such purposes in one of the sleds before we can even insert the key.

Nils-Anders unhitches the härks and then tethers them, each on a long rope, to rocks, separated so that their grazing circles do not overlap. There are no trees here. We have left the birches behind in Tarra Valley. The white landscape is unbroken except by rocks, and the wind blows unhindered. The ground seems to boil. Vapor pours over the rocks as if rising from a huge hot spring. Odd that cold can imitate hot so convincingly. The vapor is really fine snow powder.

The air becomes abruptly empty as we step into the cabin. We experience the same type of silence one notices first when a neighbor finally stops his lawnmower. We have moved out of the wind. Frustrated by our escape, the wind occasionally grips the cabin and shakes it. We would roll like a tumbleweed if not for the steel cables strapping us to the cold rock foundation. I cook coffee on the kerosene burner; a woodstove is useless above the treeline. Nils-Anders gulps down a cup, rubs his freezing hands over the burner and leaves again, out into the cold to take the ears from the dead reindeer he had spotted way back.

I hear shouts in the night and soon all five men tramp into the cabin accompanied by five dogs. Per-Henrik has found his dog sulking near Tarrakaise. Nils-Anders hangs on a nail the bloody reindeer ears he has cut from the carcass. All agree it is Lars Hotti's mark. The herd has been left under Rakkas mountain. I have yet to see it as something larger than a stamp on a great white envelope. I am sure to get my fill tomorrow, I am told. Weather permitting, we will drive nearly half the total migration distance in one day.

Besides the lack of good grazing between Vuoka and Levik, there is another factor adding pressure to tomorrow's trek. We will be moving through the birch woods and down into the thick, dark evergreen forest. It is hard enough to drive a herd through pine and fir forests, but at night it is twice as difficult. We will be in a great hurry to reach the ice of Peuraure Lake before 3:00 P.M. This means twenty miles at a fast pace with hardly a pause, no food, not even time to cook coffee. We must race the sun down.

We build a blaze outside in lee of the cabin with the last of the emergency wood pulled by the rajd. We tar our skis in preparation for the big push. The tar in the can freezes a few feet from the flames. "How did you ever manage before the Sameby built these cabins?" I wondered. Nils-Gustav explained that before cabins dotted the mountains the rajd carried a tent goattieh, the goattieh poles being dragged on a special runner behind the last sled. Single herders often carried small cotton tents. They would first cut a large pile of birch branches, burn them, spread a thick, fresh layer on top of the smoldering embers, and then put the tent on top of that. In this way they obtained enough warmth to sleep for a few hours. It did feel a bit strange to consider myself pampered under the circumstances, but there was no denying that compared with the recent past, the Vuoka cabin represented the height of luxury.

December 9

We rise at 5:00 A.M. The wind shakes the cabin as we pack, eat, and stuff our shoes. Henrik and Per-Henrik head out to the herd in the dark. The rest of us doze until pale blue dawn. Then Lars-Henrik and Nils-Gustav join the herd, and Nils-Anders and I hitch up the rajd and start out. Along with the brightening of the sky we can hear bells and barks drawing closer. Soon they are upon us. Per-Henrik is in front leading the whole herd by himself with a bell strapped across his shoulders. The herd contains a härk that, to use the Saami term, "follows empty." This very valuable animal will follow the sound of the bell alone and does not require that it be hanging from the neck of a lead härk. The rest of the herd follows the härk following Per-Henrik with the bell.

We stopped the rajd until the herd had passed and then fell in behind. Nils-Anders now has a double job; he leads the rajd and at the same time helps drive the herd. Lars-Henrik and Nils-Gustav are on the right flank, Henrik on the left. It is all I can do to keep up, usually following in the wake of the sleds where the snow is packed. I manage to stay with them in spurts and have some periods of usefulness, but on the whole I am an observer. It is extraordinarily clear and bitterly cold. The sun tops the mountains pink. The herd obscures itself by kicking up a cloud of snow dust and travels in a moving fog. Sometimes I drop so far behind that the herd moves out of sight below a ridge and the only sign I have of its whereabouts is the mist hovering overhead.

We move hour after hour at a terrific pace. Fortunately, experience from spring migration has taught me to carry raisins in my pocket which I chew when hungriest without breaking stride. Six miles above Peuraure we make a single, brief pause. We have entered the birch woods and see the evergreen forest drawing near. It is no longer enough to lead the herd "empty." We must lasso one of the tame härks to follow with Per-Henrik out front. The change-over from the high tundra with its wide views and white horizons to the lowland forest with its restricted views and dark contours naturally makes the herd uneasy. The reindeer feel safer following a lead härk.

Nils-Anders stopped, leaned against his ski poles, and rolled a cigarette. The rajd stopped behind him, strung out like a long tail. Härks can be ornery and hard to catch. An old trick is to urinate into the snow and lasso the härk when he is lured forth by the salt content in the urine to eat the snow. This härk, however, was caught with disappointingly little effort. We were moving again sooner than I had hoped. Nils-Anders tossed away his cigarette and we began the descent to the woodlands.

As we hit the dark evergreen belt, the herd became noticeably more nervous. Attempts to dash from the edges and turn back toward the high plateaus became all the more frequent. The year's new calves especially began going wild. I could well understand them. They had been born in the highlands seven months ago, and had never encountered anything so dark and menacing as the evergreen woodlands. The woods stood before us like a vast black wall in the waning light. Moving below the treeline brought us into a new world.

We shouted ourselves hoarse and swore at the dogs, which in their excitement often made matters worse. They were prone to pursue unnecessarily, heightening the tempo of nervousness. "Biergalla, biergalla, biergalla"—damn, damn, damn. All the calves were cowering at the end of the herd. They shot from the sides in wild panic, torn between the threat of the woods and the relative security of the herd. At Skaite all hell broke loose and the herd dashed through our ranks. Regaining control of the herd was a grueling task; thick juniper bushes trapped our skis and sharp branches clawed at our heads. At last we brought the herd out on the ice of Lake Peuraure just as the trees blurred with their shadows and colors disappeared.

We could have found shelter in Skaite, where there was a herder's cabin in which we could have been quite comfortable. But the reindeer would have scattered throughout the forest looking for food, and it would have taken far too much time to bring them together next day. It was better to keep going now that the herd was gathered. Both the herd and the herders would find ample food in Levik.

I was thankful now for my struggles in Tarra Valley. Otherwise I would never have been in any condition to continue on to Levik, twelve miles farther on at the other end of the lake. I was exhausted and hungry, but found I could keep going. Everyone had a job to do; everyone was tired. No one had any extra energy to look after anyone else but himself. Each of us was on his own in a different corner of the herd within his own island of visibility.

The temperature dropped steadily. Soon no amount of skiing could keep me from freezing. My hands were too numb to untie the rope that strapped an extra wool shirt across my back. If only I could free the rope, I could put the shirt on. I reached for my knife to cut the rope, but my knife was frozen in its sheath. I could gain the necessary dexterity to overcome these difficulties only by freeing my hands from their mittens. In just the short time they were exposed, my hands froze so that in days to come all the skin was to peel. That night on the Peuraure ice later caused my toenails to drop off. Probably I should have taken boots of a larger size than those I now wore, and moreover, I should not have stuffed my shoe grass so tightly. I had been glad of the adventure despite the effort and the cold. I had thought of the stories I could tell—but after a couple more hours on the lake, experiencing and learning were crushed by exhaustion and hurt. Had a helicopter lowered a rescue line I would have grabbed it. All I cared about was reaching Levik, to eat and thaw in Sven's kitchen.

In places the ice on the lake had cracked enough to let water seep to the surface. If possible it was best to skirt these spots. Wet skis fasten immediately to snow and in no time become unbelievably heavy with ice underneath. All glide disappears. Many times we had to walk through the water carrying our skis, or if they were already coated with ice, time had to be spent scraping the ski bottoms clean with the big Norwegian chopping knife each had in his belt. I dropped farther and farther behind. I could hear them ahead, but I could no longer see them. I followed the wide trail they left. Their pace never slackened.

The sounds of the herd finally stopped, and shortly thereafter a fire appeared off to my left. I had not been far behind. The fire led me to Sven's house. The others were glumly standing around the blaze melting the remaining ice from their skis. We were out of luck. Sven was not at home. He had had no idea we were coming and had probably gone to visit Amanda in Lillselet. The house was locked and the emergency phone on the wall outside was out of order. All the emergency phones were apparently on the same line. None was working. The herd was released in the rich grazing land and the rajd was unhitched. Our only concern now was for ourselves. It was obvious to all of us that we had only one course of action.

We stood tired and silent absorbing the last warmth of the dying fire. My appearance must not have inspired confidence. The others were plainly concerned as to how well I could stand the added strain. "What do you think we should do?" said Henrik at last. What he really meant was: Are you ready to move? "Nothing to do, I suppose, but push on to Lillselet." I tried to sound matter-of-fact although the thought of the added distance, only about four miles, pained me considerably. There was no use waiting. Each of us pulled his pack from a sled and started off.

Luckily there was a good snowmobile trail from Levik to Lillselet and I had only to follow it. Gradually I moved deeper and deeper into home territory. Alte Dievva, the old sacred knoll, was a welcome sight, rising black against the starry sky. I knew I would find the old nomad school goattiehs a bit further up on the right, and just around the bend I would catch sight of Amanda's welcoming light.

In Lillselet we are treated like conquering heroes. Our tribulations are over. Amanda places all kinds of food in enormous amounts in front of us. Mattresses are found for all. Sven and John would like to talk all night, but we are exhausted and soon asleep. The rajd is ended. The snowmobile takes over. John will drive up to Levik tomorrow and bring down the last of the gear. The sleds will be leaned against Sven's storage hut wall until next March or April when they will once again cover the same ground, back to Stalo on spring migration.

We plan to rest a day or two here. The herd needs rest and food as well. John, Gustav, and Arthur will buy some slaughter deer before the migration continues down Lake Karatj and on to Stenträsk. It will be a changed migration. Back in October, when the herders reached Stalo to round up the herd for the long eastward move, the ground was still bare. There were then no snowmobiles to use, and even had there been one available, it would not always be usable over the mountain terrain with the first, loose snows. But now in the lowlands the snowmobile will carry the rajd's load. A tired herder need only attach a lasso and be towed along behind like a water skier. When we reach the road at the eastern end of the lake, Birgit will undoubtedly arrive with the car. The fellows can ride home to Stenträsk and drive back to the herd in the morning. We have reached "civilization."

There were still some miles to travel, but to me autumn migration ended with the rajd. In the next few days we would experience the changes of the last hundred years in compressed form. I would enjoy riding in a car and watching TV, but I wanted to end this day in the atmosphere of the past. For the first time I was glad that the telephone line was ragged. No one outside of Lillselet yet knew that we had arrived. Tomorrow would be soon enough to step into the technological world.

9

Winter in Jokkmokk

As we drove the herd down Lake Karatj, past Luovaluokta, I remembered the time two years ago when I had stood alone on the ice watching and listening to the migration shrink in the distance. Once again Per-Henrik and the lead härk were in front of the weary herd. So accustomed were they to each other now that the härk's four legs kept perfect pace with Per-Henrik's two skis, and even the bell that clamored weakly in rhythm with the walk seemed tired. Everything looked as it had then, just as frozen and white, just as close to the edge of darkness. Nothing showed the least trace of time. Time must have frozen too.

Somewhere here I must have moved through the exact spot I had occupied before. It made me feel as if I was finally completing something I had promised myself then. Watching the same slow struggle and knowing that it would be like this again next year and had been like this for many, many years made me incredibly tired. Some of the reindeer would be slaughtered before next autumn migration; the calves would grow to take their places. With time, some of the herders would drop out and be replaced as well. The migration was a kind of being in itself, a most demanding master.

I wanted to come skiing up as I had two years ago and hand myself a cup of coffee laced with cognac. That would have hit the spot. Here, where time is least important, I will return to the description of my first year in Lapland. I switch skis and go back to that first winter when I had met the herd on this same ice, at this same time of year. The herd, then as now, continued on down Lake Karatj without a break in stride, and I returned to Jokkmokk.

I found the shop windows there filled with Christmas presents and pictures of a jolly Santa Claus leading his own rajd of reindeer over the roof tops. Santa has not been spared study, and the learned claim that he derives from a hodgepodge of cultural motifs, many of which originate in Lapland. That jolly smile he has while leading a reindeer caravan, however, must have been a Christian influence. The presents Santa's rajd brought me all followed the same pattern—heavy sweaters, coats, woollen socks, until I was swamped by the generosity of thoughtful friends and relatives. To those in America who were only dreaming of a white Christmas, winter in Lapland sounded miserable, and I received more winter clothing than I knew what to do with.

Of course, they were right, the Lapland winter is severe and extremely long. Metal is dangerous to touch with the bare hand. People say that words freeze and do not come forth until the spring thaw. Cars race on the frozen lakes, a favorite teenage pastime—where the ice is many feet thick. Anyone driving long distances without an extra warm coat and a pair of skis on the car roof is a fool. Getting stuck in the deep snow by the roadside is common, passing traffic is not, and one must be prepared to strap on skis and leave to find telephone and help at the nearest house. It is rarely all that near.

The penalty for not taking winter seriously in Lapland is far worse than that awarded the same mistake in a more populous or southerly area. Almost every year someone is missing. Like words, he often thaws forth in the spring. Several Jokkmokkers, Saami and Swedes alike, have told me stories of being caught by snowstorms in the mountains while hunting, and being forced to huddle for shelter in some tiny cave. When the weather cleared with the dawn they found they had been crouching over a human skeleton. Such graves dot the mountains. Many will never be found. Johan Turi, an old Saami, has left us this account of migrations in the old days:

> It is just as difficult for the weak, old folk, they get exhausted on the long journeys and then they have to spend the night out in the wilds, and then they freeze terribly and some have died on migrations, and

there hasn't been time to look for them, and many years afterwards folk have seen their bones, but no one has bothered about them any more than if they were reindeer bones. (1910; English edition, *Turi's Book of Lapland,* 1931:40)

In modern times it is more usual to find that the skeletons bear traces of old World War II army uniforms. During the Nazi occupation of Norway, refugees poured over the border into neutral Sweden. With the help of the Saami and the Swedish rescue teams, many survived winter mountain crossings. Others were not so fortunate, especially German deserters, who were often unaware of the winter's harshness.

Although as Turi says there might not have been time to look for missing people during migration, it was more common that deaths occurred with the caravan or at camp. In the winter the bodies could be transported by sled to the churchyard in the lowlands, but if a death occurred during the spring or summer, migration would be going in the other direction, toward the mountains. The only course of action was to give the body a summer burial and uncover it again later in the fall or early winter for transportation down to the churchyard by sled. Piles of rocks, hardly noticeable against the general rock rubble, might mark such summer graves. Some of the skeletons have never been moved to holy ground and remain lying there, often in the sled that served as a coffin. Once at the churchyard, the waiting was still not over. The snow and ice which had solved the transportation problem created more difficulties. Graves were difficult to dig in the frozen ground, and what's more, the soul could not be laid to rest without a preacher, who was usually spending the winter in a sunnier clime or off on a circuit miles away. The old church in Jokkmokk was therefore furnished with a thick wooden wall around the churchyard, in which the bodies could be stored as in a row of lockers until spring or when the preacher came, the ground thawed and the smell grew noticeable.

The winters are just as cold as before, but the death rate has decreased considerably. For one reason, there are fewer people wintering in the mountains. For another, rapid transportation and communication networks have spread to the most desolate corners. One can ride from Stalo to Kvikkjokk in a matter of hours by snowmobile. Or, a quick call on the emergency phone can bring a helicopter to Stalo in a matter of minutes. New equipment, however, involves new dangers. Passengers have been thrown from snowmobile sleds and the reckless or drunken driver has driven on for miles totally unaware. The driver can also be bucked off the snowmobile, and if the gas throttle has frozen in open position, the snowmobile will continue on. A tiny mistake can lead to more than a common cold.

Although mistakes can be very costly, winter life is now hardly so rugged as it once was. As the winter homes are in the lowlands, and the lowlands are always the first opened to technological advance, we cook our coffee on an electric stove with water from the faucet and watch TV. Seen from the surrounding hills, Jokkmokk is a small hearth in a vast and frozen wilderness.

Once the reindeer had left the mountains I thought at first that there would be a pause in the herding cycle and that I would settle into the slow pace of long, dark winter days. I could not have been more wrong. Not only is the herding cycle far from a pause period, but the long, dark days are also far from being slow. Jokkmokk is bursting with activities, courses, exhibits, folk dancing, ski racing, and much more. Winter extends over half the year and people launch into it with enthusiasm. Everyone is at last gathered together in one area after having been spread across the mountains. As for the reindeer herding, I was to find that the real work was about to begin.

No sooner had the Blind herd reached Stenträsk than it was attacked by wolves during the night. The wolf tracks Isak had spotted were no idle threat. Four reindeer were dead. Three other badly torn and partially eaten reindeer staggered aimlessly among the trees, dazed and dying. Flayed skin hung from the back of a vaja and dragged behind in the snow. Her back legs were only half there. These poor reindeer had to be killed immediately to end their suffering. The herders patrolled the woods round about looking for other dead and wounded strays. Tracks showed that there had been two wolves, one of them quite young and most likely inexperienced in the art of killing.

An experienced wolf does not leave half-dead reindeer in its path. It has a well-refined system of slaughter differing with the strength and size of his victim. For a large reindeer, Anta Pirak, an old Saami herder from the Jokkmokk area, gave the following account of the wolf's procedure:

> When the wolf has caught up with the reindeer, he bites him in the lower part of the back leg at the tendons at the base of the muscle. . . . He holds tight there . . . a big reindeer drags him along a good way. The wolf brakes the movement with his feet. . . . When the reindeer gets tired, he falls. Then the wolf jumps forth and bites the reindeer under the neck. (*En Nomad och hans Liv,* 1933:64)

Because of the presence of wolves, instead of resting and recovering from the long migration, the men would have to take turns guarding the herd day and night. A herd need but catch the slightest scent of wolf to break into wild panic and scatter in all directions, making it impossible to guard and protect them. It is an old Saami saying that the wolf has the strength of one man and the cunning of nine. It has many tricks. Nils-Anti Pirtsi, who has tangled with many wolves in the days when wolf attacks were the rule rather than the exception, told me that when a wolf pack nears a herd the wolves may communicate by putting their noses under the snow before howling. This muffles the cries and leads both reindeer and herder to believe that the pack is far away.

Anta Pirak describes how Saami in the past sent warning to each other when wolves entered the area. Men would come together from many different villages to join in a "wolf run" (to hunt the wolf down on skis). In those days Saami used only one long ski pole, which doubled as a wolf spear. A wolf would be trailed hour after hour through the deep snow until, exhausted, it turned at bay and the run was ended with a well-aimed thrust. But wolves are not always so easy to kill. Turi gives a number of instances when wolves have joined forces against a hunter and injured him severely. The first thing a wolf bites is the hands so that the hunter is unable to use either spear or knife.

Saami once believed that the devil created the wolf. Anyone prone to evil, a thief or a murderer, could be turned into a wolf by a shaman, or nåjd. This is why, Turi explains, when the nåjd arts ceased, there began to be more Saami thieves—and, he might have added had he known what the future would bring, fewer wolves. Today the Swedish so-called experts claim there to be hardly any wild wolves in all of Sweden. This pronouncement seems to hold in spite of the number of wolves sighted each winter, and in spite of reindeer casualties occurring in widely separated tracts at the same time. It is, however, incontestable that the wolf is a dying breed in Scandinavia. It is generally accepted that the wolf attacks occurring in Sweden today are due to wolves which have entered the area from Russia via Finland. They are gone as mysteriously as they came, until next winter.

Conservationists the world over have banded together to protect the wolf. It is illegal to hunt wolves in Sweden, and although by law the herders are allowed to protect their reindeer, they are forbidden to carry their rifles and their rifle bolts together on snowmobiles. If the rifle is on the sled, the bolt must be on the snowmobile. Nor is one permitted to pursue on snowmobile a wolf that has ravaged the herd. It must be caught in the act—something that hardly ever happens—and it must stay in the immediate vicinity while the herder assembles his rifle. In effect, the modern herder is almost helpless against wolf attacks.

Although the wolf is the most hated enemy of the Saami, most herders are considerate of the conservationist viewpoint. The "save-the-wolf program" in Sweden is agitating in favor of a vigorous wolf stock in a wild state, but in seeking to correct what they term "the wolf myth," the pendulum has swung to the other extreme. Wolves are now portrayed as poor, misunderstood creatures who kill only what they need, and then only the sickly or feeble reindeer. So they say. The hundreds of years of Saami experience in dealing with wolves is frequently ignored as totally biased.

Those Saami with whom I have discussed this matter are willing to share the world with the wolf if they must, but they rightfully consider it unjust if they are forced to carry alone the burden this involves. The conservation expert in Stockholm suffers no consequences from a wolf attack on a deer flock in Lapland. As it is today, the herders are given improperly poor compensation for all the reindeer Sweden's "one" wolf is able to kill each year. It may be true that a wolf hunting caribou in Canada is best able to take the sick and feeble individuals, but in a land with a practice of tame reindeer herding, such observations carry little weight. No wolf that comes upon a gathered herd of hundreds of animals is going to run about asking the reindeer how they are feeling. On the contrary, it chooses the healthiest and fattest victims. During the winter it ignores the scrawny sarvs in favor of the härks. As a rule, the wolf takes the best it can get.

It is no fun to work for weeks only to bring your herd of reindeer from the mountains into the jaws of a wolf. After his misfortune, Henrik shocked newspaper reporters by saying he would shoot any wolf that came into his sights. The wolves seemed to know when it was best to go, and they disappeared toward the south. I recalled what John had told me during the moose hunt. He had spun a great yarn about rivalry between secret shamans of Tuorpon and Luokta Mavas Samebys, each seeking to send wolves against the other. He laughed uproariously at me for remembering this nonsense, but now that events had in part borne out his prophecy he could act mysterious and say "told you so." The only flaw in his prediction was that the wolves which were to strike Mavas struck Tuorpon instead, but this was a nonessential to John who could not remember the finer points of his pronouncement anyway.

As soon as possible, the Blind herd was driven toward the large separation corral at Rahanåive, a short distance from Stenträsk, and word was circulated that the separation would take place very soon. By far the majority of the reindeer brought down by the Stenträsk group belonged to the members of their group, but as the summer land is open to all reindeer, the herd contained hundreds of animals from other groups as well. Once the reindeer have reached the lowlands, it is desirable to get them separated and brought to their proper grazing territory quickly. Whereas the separation at Parka might be classified as an inter-Sameby separation, those occurring during the winter months are primarily intra-Sameby. Of course, members from a number of Samebys are always present at each of the many winter separations, but on the whole they function basically as family members.

The reason behind this separation into small family herd units stems from the changes in herding procedure and winter grazing demands. Winter grazing is usually the weak link, and therefore crucial in the year-round grazing program. If the summer land can support 20,000 head, but the winter land only 10,000 head, the herd will not exceed 10,000 head (aside from those deer that are slaughtered in the autumn). Winter grazing is also much more fragile and susceptible to weather fluctuations and snow conditions. The reindeer dig through the snow with their cloven front hooves to reach the food on the ground. Should a rise in temperature after the first October snowfall bring a temporary thaw, a hard, icy crust can form on the moss, which may prevent the reindeer from reaching it. Or, icy moss can ruin the deers' digestion. Sometimes, although they can reach the moss, they may have difficulty in loosening the moss from an ice bed. Herders must constantly move their herds and make use of the little available winter grazing land. There must be a far more intensive form of herding than that needed in the summer. In many respects the extensive herders carry on the same type of winter work as the more intensive herders. Should grazing conditions prove bad for a long spell, emergency methods must be used to try to prevent mass starvation. There are a couple of alternatives I shall discuss elsewhere, but in the case of a normal winter it is rarely advisable to permit a herd to scatter and fend for itself in the winter as is the case in the summer.

Besides a more demanding grazing situation, the winter brings a far greater threat from predators. Apart from the wolf, winter predators include the wolverine and the lynx. The wolverine takes by far the heaviest toll. The bear has gone to sleep, and the eagle has moved toward the warmer coast. They return to the scene in the spring to feast on the newborn calves. The slow-moving wolverine sneaks about the upper snow crust and leaps down on the neck of a reindeer that has dug itself a deep hole in search of food. A herd that is scattered cannot be guarded and protected from danger. For these reasons, each family or small herding group tries to assemble all its reindeer in its own well-recognized and respected winter grazing area. The winter land is not open to everyone; each group has its territory within the wider boundaries of the Sameby's lands of traditional winter usage— hence the winter separations. The breakdown of winter land within the Sameby is a matter of internal agreement by the Saami herders themselves, whereas the realm within which they extend this collective rule is firmly controlled by the authorities. The further east one moves the more the grazing lands of the herders fall under seasonal legal restraints. Sameby lands of traditional winter usage often have hunting and building restrictions whereas Sameby lands further west (usually west or "above" Agriculture Line) are more available to the herders. In these "year-round lands," the herders enjoy a greater variety of rights that are also more firmly held legally. I participated in four or five separations in my first winter in Jokkmokk, and there were many more that I missed.

The days are short, so it is best to start the separation early. The Rahanåive corral, like most lowland winter corrals, is approachable by road, and the parking space is filled with cars already at daybreak. Those Saami who have come from other Samebys sit in their cars to keep warm and wait for the herd to be driven from the large grazing corral into the separating corral. Those more intimately connected with this herd might enter the grazing corral to mark any "whole-ears" belonging to them. Whole-ears born last spring are young enough still to be running with their mothers. Some calves have always managed to avoid the summer marking knife. Preferably one should not mark in the cold. The ears have a hard time healing and are prone to shrivel in such a way that the mark becomes unrecognizable. If it is not too cold, a white powder containing iron sulphate and alum can be blown into the cuts to stop the bleeding and aid healing, but in the coldest weather it is better to use the tag system. A typical tag is made from a piece of wood or plastic shaped crudely like reindeer ears incised with the owner's mark. This is simply tied around the reindeer's neck until next summer, when the tag can be removed and the real ears marked instead. Besides knives and extra ski-binding thongs, one can often spot these tags hanging from belts ready for use at any time. It is a simple way of marking property in general, and it is not unusual to find these tags adorning gas tanks, boat motors, or key chains.

Before the herd can be driven into the central corral enclosure, the fencing must be checked and fallen boards replaced. The winter corrals are invariably made of wood, most of them being roughly circular with the large central area forming a hub and smaller booths, *kontor,* lining the circumference. A couple of long alleys connect the central corral with the outside, breaking the ring of booths. Now that a road leads to the corral door, the slaughter company need no longer employ helicopters to freight dead reindeer. The huge truck stations itself at the mouth of one of the long alleys, and any reindeer sold to the slaughter company can be hauled down and loaded directly into the truck. Sometimes the reindeer are killed at the corral, sometimes they are freighted away alive in the two-storied transport trucks and killed later at the main slaughterhouse.

The grazing corral has a fairly wide section of fence in common with the central, separating corral, and when the time comes, this fence is dismantled and the herd ushered into the separating corral. The herd pours in like water from an opened dam. Curtains of mist are immediately thrown up around the reindeer as they swing into their counter-clockwise run. It feels strange that a herd of such number and force should be so quiet. The snow stills the thunder. The thousands of stamping feet are hushed. Thick separation lassos are in the air.

No one can really say from the beginning how many separate units the herd will be broken into, how many of the booths will be in use. Some families may decide to "pull together" (pull their reindeer by lasso to the same bunch), and separate only later at another corral after driving their reindeer closer to home ground. Some may have too few reindeer to warrant a booth. They might simply pull their reindeer out of the corral along one of the long alleys and load them into the back of their pickup trucks for the drive home. Most often there are numerous booths in use and one can get an excellent idea of how a Sameby is divided and grouped by taking a walk around the corral's edge. Each group will be hauling and wrestling reindeer into its own corral partition.

Although the mist turns the corral into a beautiful impressionist painting and the powdered snow provides a magic silence, it causes quite a problem when there is work to be done. Only the vajas and a few of the härks still possess antlers; it is hard enough to catch an antlerless sarv with the lasso, but this is nothing compared with the difficulty of pulling him through the often deep and slippery snow. By now everyone has switched to Saami winter footwear. Furry, curly-toed shoes sewn from reindeer leggings when stuffed with shoe grass cannot be matched for lightness and warmth. However, their smooth bottoms cause them to act like water skis when powered by an angry sarv on the end of a lasso. The härks are even more troublesome, being heavier and stronger at this time of year. Soon the corral is filled with people going for unwanted rides.

The hauling seine is an ancient piece of fishing equipment. The one we used was more than a hundred years old.

The sarv herd has been driven to the Valli peak corral above Kvikkjokk.

Pelle on the way to the freezer with moose meat on his back.

The helicopter is in constant movement; no landing is necessary during loading and unloading. From the time the deer are killed at the Valli corral, it takes only two minutes before they are down in Kvikkjokk.

The animals destined for slaughter are pulled from the corral. Help is needed to deal with a full-grown sarv.

The reindeer herd continues along Lake Karatj. The dogs are thin as skeletons.

The reindeer herders often take the opportunity to slaughter deer for their own use and to butcher them in the traditional manner. Here a rack has been erected out of fence posts to hold the different cuts of meat.

Nils-Anders stops now and then to spy with his binoculars.

We move like a big snake over the terrain.

Winter separation.

In a circle around the edge of the large central winter corral, there are many smaller *kontor* (booths) into which the different winter groups pull their deer.

Two Saami women in traditional Karesuando dress pause for a chat in the corral.

Heavy logging puts a major strain on reindeer herding. Yet a common argument for logging irreplaceable forests is that jobs are thereby created.

During the fair days, the municipal government arranges for a reindeer caravan to drive through town.

In protest against the municipal government's support of new hydroelectric dam projects, the reindeer caravan boycotted the fair of 1977. Instead, there was a protest march. On the sign carried by the herding dog is written: "Even we demand employment security."

In February the sun returns.

The reindeer recognize the striped bags containing artificial fodder and begin to break in for a snack.

A spoiled freeloader.

Henrik's dog, Rick, knows precisely how to deal with deer.

If a flock of deer gets past the dogs, one can quickly drive them back to the main herd with the help of a snowmobile. The snowmobiles are used mainly for transporting supplies and for giving a rest to those who have been skiing.

Nowadays there are cabins spread along the migration route for the herders.

The reindeer gather together in the highlands under Staika mountain for continued
migration.

The snow-covered goattiehs of Stalo.

Nils-Henrik and Nils-Anders knew almost every crack in the Sulitjelma glacier.

It is almost hopeless to handle a big reindeer alone when it is impossible to dig your heels in and stop him. Weight plays almost a greater role than muscle. Two men, however, can reverse the situation and drag the stiff-legged resisting reindeer into the booth. Not owning any reindeer, I am one of the few free hands and get calls of "Hugge" from all sides. I have hardly time enough to extricate the lasso from one reindeer in the booth before another friend is calling from the central enclosure as he glides by clinging to a rope.

There are a number of effort-saving techniques. If you catch a reindeer on the far side of the corral from the booth to which you must pull him, it is not the straightest distance that will get you to your destination with the least effort. On the contrary, to pull a reindeer across the counter-clockwise circle of motion, or even worse, to pull against the current, is to take upon oneself a most furious and unnecessary battle. The best thing to do is let the reindeer continue running in the circular arc with the rest of the herd. One simply runs alongside with the lasso slack until reaching the booth gate. Here the herder must exert himself, for the reindeer will want to keep going.

The older men need help most. In the past they had hired hands (even apprenticed herders who lived for many years with the family, amassing reindeer as pay). Now the Swedish employment tax (devised by the welfare state to cover employee benefits, such as health care) has made this financially impossible for a reindeer herder whose wealth is in reindeer, not money. Moreover, new young herders today may find it easier to accumulate a herd by working in some other industry at a high wage and then buying reindeer outright. Eighty-four-year-old Petrus Gruvisare is still struggling with härks in the winter corral. I switch lassos, take Petrus's reindeer to his booth, and meanwhile let Petrus take my lasso to catch his next reindeer. So it goes, reindeer after reindeer, hour after hour, until one slumps in a snowdrift tuckered out.

There was a sudden loud cracking noise from one corner of the corral. I groaned. The wall of one of the booths had collapsed from the weight of a hundred packed reindeer bodies. In a few seconds the work of a few hours was wasted. Before anyone could stop them, the reindeer that had been so painstakingly separated were once again mixed in the central enclosure. There was no recourse but hurry to do it all over again before it got too dark. Some of the larger corrals near electric supply sources (or with generators of their own) are equipped with floodlights. The work can continue into the night, although the lights cast strange shadows from many different directions and make the earmarks hard to distinguish. Rahanåive, however, had no such lights; we would have to work fast.

Happily, there are always a number of fires going outside the corral where one can rest and warm up after a long bout on the end of a rope. Hungry and tired workers can buy coffee and reindeer-meat soup. Children are usually scurrying in and out of the corral. Their mothers are swatting reindeer gently with birch branches or "scaring" them in the direction of the gate. Winter separations have something of the holiday spirit even though there is much work to be done.

A good many reindeer can be packed into the back of a pick-up truck or into a small trailer with home-made removable walls and roof. They are crammed together tightly so that there is less room for them to shake around during the bumpy ride. During a separation, the road from the corral is full of cars pulling these boxlike trailers with their kicking and lurching load. It is not the most comfortable mode of travel. Groups with an equally long road home but with a large flock to transport have two alternatives: They can drive the flock overland or truck them in huge, rented double-storied vans. These vans make the private trailer seem like luxury accommodations. First of all, the reindeer are going to be packed so tightly that all remaining antlers must be sawn off both to provide space and to prevent injury. Then they are driven up ramps and jammed into tiny compartments on two levels like chicken in cages.

As the lowlands become increasingly developed, it becomes both more difficult to drive a herd long distances overland and at the same time, much easier to transport the herd by truck. Truck transport of herds is very much a consequence of the extensive form of herding that mixes the reindeer from widely different areas together in the summer land. Unfortunately, trucking the herds is not merely a consequence, it is also a cause. Reindeer that have been jostled over the highway for many miles in a truck frequently become totally disoriented and are much more difficult to handle. In some Samebys entire herds are freighted from summer land to winter land by truck. The reindeer transported in this fashion soon lose all sense of their old migration routes. Trucking can become habit forming.

The Samebys in the Jokkmokk region have no roads in their summer grazing land, and therefore trucking has not come to replace migrations. Instead, trucks are used only for transportation of reindeer from the winter separation corral to the various groups' winter grazing land. This is one reason why it is preferable to complete the winter separations early. The later the separation, the further the vajas are advanced into pregnancy, and the more damaging and grueling a truck ride.

Besides the big trucks, the trailers and the cars of the herders, there is another category of vehicle parked outside the corral, those belonging to hopeful buyers. The price of meat is so high in the stores that it is a considerable saving to go to the corral and try to buy a "slaughter reindeer" directly from the herder. Of course, the herders themselves often take the opportunity to slaughter a reindeer for their own use at the corral where there is handy road access. Car roofs are decked with bloody skulls and antlers. The fresh hides have frozen hard in oddly twisted shapes, most difficult to fit into the truck. The slaughter company naturally wants to buy as many reindeer as possible, and so there is a good deal of bidding and bargaining going on both inside and outside the corral. Herders are usually in no hurry to sell. If the coming winter looks as if it will be a bad one, the herders are especially loathe to sell stock and undermine their ability to reestablish a decent herd should many head be lost. The personnel of the various slaughter companies must often actively campaign for every reindeer. At other times there might be only one slaughter company attending the separation, and it would therefore be in a better position to set terms and do good business.

It is not the sarvs that are slaughtered now, but the ox-reindeer. The once proud and magnificent sarvs are now without antlers and lean. The ox-reindeer, with their fine layer of fat, are the prime choice. Even a good calf-producing vaja might be sacrificed, however, if she is what is termed a "wandering vaja," one which roams too far from her owner's district. If he does not slaughter the vaja when he has her, the owner may never get the chance to draw any benefit from her whatsoever. She will simply wander far, far away, and he will never be able to mark her calves. Such considerations require a knowledge of a reindeer on an individual level, beyond that of simply recognizing its mark. This is the type of knowledge that is being eroded by the trends of modern herding.

The reindeer that were driven across into the winter land last August in Parka are generally later in entering the winter corral for further separation. They have not been driven eastward as a gathered herd on migration. They have wandered eastward, and have had all fall to spread far and wide. It is quite a job collecting them together in the forest land and bringing them to a corral. Herds are gathered and brought in for separation one after another. In January the incidence of separations is so high that two may occur on the same day in different corrals. Such situations may cause families to split up and send representatives to each. The further the winter progresses, the harder it becomes to get the reindeer into the separation corral. If they find a good spot to graze in deep snow, they generally do not want to move. If the herd has not been gathered by late winter, February or March, it should probably be left alone to wander westward in spring. The reindeer will do better in scattered condition if grazing becomes scarce in the winter. However, herders find it difficult to protect their deer from predators when the deer are widely dispersed. December and January are usually the months of hardest winter work.

With the separations over, and the reindeer dispersed in small family herds, the winter work enters a new phase. The watching, guarding and occasional moving of the herds begins. I joined my friend Jova Spik one morning in early February to help him move his herd from one grazing spot to another. The area they grazed now, said Jova, was the best grazing he had, and he wanted to save it for later. Farther up the slope was an area good for the time being but likely to deteriorate from crusting with the returning sun, and it was here Jova wanted to drive his flock while the pasturage there was still available. "It will be easy for them to dig on the slope," said Jova, "They can scoop the snow downhill."

We plowed in among the evergreens on skis in search of reindeer tracks. Jova knew exactly where to look. We began circling, keeping left of the tracks we found. The tracks grew more and more frequent until we came to areas completely trampled and with deep trenchlike holes in the snow—"craters," reminiscent of a battlefield. "These holes mean good grazing," said Jova. "When the reindeer take the time to dig this deep, there is plenty of food underneath." Although we had as yet seen no reindeer, Jova knew where they were and soon we could hear faint bells. A herder can tell from the sound of reindeer bells if the animals are running, walking, grazing, about to rest, or just getting up from a rest. "I'm here almost every day," Jova continued, "so they're used to me, but its never a good idea to surprise them. I always give a loud call to let them know I'm coming." And with that he let out a long whoop of greeting to his reindeer.

The herd accepted our presence without the slightest nervousness and moved obediently in the direction Jova drove them. Heavy machinery pounded in the background as we crossed a frozen lake. The form of the lake would soon be altered. The water power company was at work on a new site. A truck full of dirt roared down the road, startling the herd temporarily, but they seemed used to this as well, and the road crossing went calmly despite the banging and digging nearby. It struck me at first as strange to see a reindeer herd, representing an age-old life-style, against a setting of bulldozers and trucks. But, although it never ceases to seem odd, I have since found it most common. Herds graze along highways and in the shadow of thousand-volt cables.

Coexistence is not always so harmonious. Hundreds of reindeer are killed each winter by trains, and many by cars. The real threat, however, is to the grazing land. Their ruin by flooding and heavy logging will undermine herding to a far greater degree than immediate reindeer casualties.

When driving through Lapland in the winter one can usually spot plastic bags tied to poles or trees along the roadside. These serve as scarecrows to keep reindeer from straying too far out of bounds or out onto the road. Passing motorists are also alerted to reindeer in the vicinity. A fluttering bit of plastic scares reindeer quite effectively. In fact, Jova mentioned that he sometimes used a "plastic dog" to help with his herding. He would tie a black plastic bag on the end of his lasso and drag it behind his snowmobile. His reindeer were much more respectful of the plastic dog than of the snowmobile alone.

Before the advent of the snowmobile, all work had to be done on skis. A sled, or pulka, pulled by a härk was a common mode of transportation, but it was simplest for a herder out with his flock to lasso a härk and be towed along behind on skis. Of course, steering in this situation is almost impossible, but if the härk was given a trail to follow, there would be no problem. They would even follow after a dog's tracks, I was told.

Among the tightly packed trees, neither snowmobile nor plastic dog was of any use. At times it was difficult to maneuver even ourselves through the tree trunks on skis, and if we so much as brushed against a tree, we would be covered by a cascade of snow. We spent all day in the woods moving the herd. For Jova, this was a normal winter day's work. Herders have often told me, "You have to be a little crazy to be a reindeer herder." I knew they were right.

The winter is terribly long, but it is not all work. The first week of February brings the Jokkmokk Winter Fair, an event so important that "before the fair," or "after the fair" are the most commonly heard time references. The fair began in the seventeenth century and has been held every winter since, without interruption. The one in 1973 was Jokkmokk's 369th. The fair originated as a period when missionaries held a Church holiday, married, and baptized, where taxmen made their collections. It was expedient to bring as many Saami together as possible at one time for the Church and government officials to spread their influence along with that of the businessmen. The Saami would also come to the fair to exchange wares, buy supplies for the year, and meet friends. In recent times the fair has become a great cultural event and a major tourist attraction.

In the old days the long caravans streamed into Jokkmokk. The Saami would sell reindeer hides, skins, cheese, and handicraft work in return for coffee, sugar, salt, tar, and, to the churchmen's dismay, "fire water." Squirrel skins were sold for twenty cents if shot through the body, thirty cents if shot through the head. Fights that had arisen during the year were frequently postponed until the fair so that they would not interfere with the work. The fair's romance of one year led to a fair wedding the next. People from miles around, Swedish pioneers as well as Saami, flooded to Jokkmokk. Amanda, Johan's mother, said that it used to take them three days to make the fair run from Lillselet to Jokkmokk by horse-drawn sled. They would spend the night with friends along the way, and next morning their hosts would join the ever-growing train. A favorite pastime on the journey was to race with each other. The stakes were often high: many a horse that went to the fair did not return to the same stable when it was over.

One of Johan Märak's favorite childhood memories was going to high mass at Jokkmokk's church on Fair Sunday, not necessarily to hear God's word as one might have expected of a preacher-to-be, but to see if the dogs would start a commotion. In those days the Saami dogs were allowed into church. Trouble would begin with a few slow growls during the sermon. The growls would grow louder, but still no one would want to interrupt the solemn process by admonishing the hounds. Then it would be too late. Two dogs would lunge at each other in full fight, and soon they would be prancing and frothing over the altar, and the preacher would be wielding a heavy candlestick. The only thing more fun than a dog fight was if a male and a female dog got together in a corner, and everyone pretended to ignore it.

As for the commercial part of the fair, Johan remembered tricky businessmen who sold Saami all manner of radios and electric shavers long before they would ever see an electric socket. Bath tubs were popular one year, and that summer people could be seen sitting in tubs on the mountainside with fires underneath. Many Saami bought cars when they made their first appearance, although no one knew how to drive. Once they got the car in motion they would be continually stopping at curves, getting out and running around the bend to see if anyone was coming.

The commercial contribution to the fair nowadays is basically the same as that which might be found at a fair in Stockholm. Apart from the stalls erected by the local people selling handicraft of different kinds and qualities, there are the usual hot dog stands, candy trays, and toy counters. Various clubs and organizations sell lottery tickets with all kinds of prizes. A section of Jokkmokk is closed to traffic, and the streets are lined overnight with booths. People from all over the world crowd into little Jokkmokk. Reservations at the hotels must be made a year in advance.

What brings most people to the Jokkmokk Fair are the truly fine cultural programs, the folk dancing, the yoiking, the storytelling, the lectures and slide shows—and, of course, the lure of seeing real live

Saami and maybe reindeer. Many people come hoping to find primitive people with quaint manners engaged in strange rituals. Instead they are met by such eye openers as the Kautokeino school brass band, about twenty young Saami dressed in full Kautokeino Saami regalia, equipped with saxophones, clarinets, and trumpets playing "Anchors Away." The older Saami might shake their heads and sigh, but many of today's yoik performers accompany themselves with guitar or accordion.

Although many Saami are saddened by the passage of familiar traditions, those I have talked to realize that traditions must grow and change if they are to endure. The yoik has survived years of religious persecution; some sects today still frown upon it. Olof-Johannes Blind told me once that his grandfather continued to yoik even though he was himself convinced that it was sinful. He loved yoiking so much he was willing to jeopardize his soul at Peter's gate. He simply could not refrain, but practiced the art as a man might relish a cigarette, knowing that it is not good for him. Yoiking today might not be what it was three hundred years ago, but it is strong, the song of a strong people.

In February the sun makes its glorious reappearance. It is shy at first, peeking above the hills, casting long shadows and lowering its gaze all too soon. As it gains altitude at a rapidly accelerating pace each day, the shadows shorten, and the light reflected from the snow shines back from the faces of the herders. The Northern Lights still decorate the night sky with flaming, shifting colors. Streaks of green and rose shatter a crystal sky; a diamond dome cracks. Sometimes like an animal, it rests, usually in the form of a green snake. According to the old Saami it was powerful enough to make you crazy if you failed to show it due respect. The old men squint at the night sky and say they can see what the weather will be like in the dazzling lights or in the soft, starry clouds of the Milky Way. A study of this channel of stars, the Winter Street as it is called, can reveal what kind of a spring and summer it will be.

At some time during the winter the herders must confront the job of the reindeer count, or census. It is most convenient to keep a running account at each winter corralling, but when the deer are expected to be in the corral a number of times during the winter the count may be late in starting, as it was this year in February. This count is not at all a traditional Saami herding practice, and has nothing to do with the care of the reindeer. Although it is not such a bad idea to know how many reindeer one owns and how many new calves have been added to the herd, this is information instinctively kept to oneself. But Saami too must pay taxes. They have been taxed for more than four hundred years. When I first joined the herders, a household was taxed not according to how many reindeer it owned, but depending on how many new calves were born to it each year. A calf was counted as income, and when it grew up and was sold to the slaughter company, it was taxed once more according to the money it brought.

In order to establish what was termed the "calving percent," which usually reached between 15 and 30 percent of the herd (after subtracting winter losses to predators), the herd had to be counted each year. The reindeer were again corralled. Since they were generally separated beforehand, the herds to be counted were not large. Makeshift corrals could be set up for them on the spot with wire and burlap cloth. Often the count was conducted in conjunction with a separation or slaughter, whenever the figures had a chance of having validity and it was convenient from a herding viewpoint. There was still a possibility of finding a reindeer that did not belong with the herd in question, but this does not account for the popularity of the various reindeer counts. Nearly everyone in the Sameby could be found at each count, especially the later ones. They came for the fun of it, to help out and to exchange news. Corral occasions of any kind have a social as well as a practical side.

The Blind herd was driven into the Rahanåive corral, but this time lassos were idle. Instead, Henrik and Per-Henrik, each equipped with a long wooden pole topped with a paint brush, strode searchingly through the herd. Both men could read a couple of hundred reindeer marks, and they would count any reindeer belonging to others as well as their own. Henrik would make a sudden jab with the pole, and a reindeer would scamper away with a streak of red on his rear. He would shout out owner, sex, and age of the reindeer, and his wife, Birgit, who held the clipboard with the names of all Tuorpon herders, would put a check in the appropriate place. The paint would wear off in a few months, but served the purpose of letting the counters know that this reindeer had already been noted. The census was complete when every reindeer had a painted rump.

I was surprised to find a pair of policemen at my first census. They could not read reindeer marks and wore city uniform shoes in the middle of the snow-covered corral. They could not have looked more out of place. Their assignment was to make sure that no herders cheated on their income tax by miscounting. Of course, the officers had no way of knowing, and they returned to the station rather quickly with frozen toes. Reindeer herding is not something that can be easily transcribed into exact monetary terms.

Efforts by the government to regulate, count, control, and legislate the herding of, at best, semidomesticated reindeer were difficult for all involved. Strict regulation at the corrals was hard enough for the authorities, but it was hopeless in the field, even with the best intentions of the herders. There were always reindeer loose in the mountains. During a bad winter especially, thousands were missed by the census.

State taxation policy for the herders has always been one of the main methods of implementing general herding policies and Saami minority policies. Today the herders are taxed according to income, like any Swedish business firm. Although this form of taxation of herding may be just, herders resent the imposition of economic laws that may force them to give up their livelihood or at least conduct it in a way foreign to their desires and customs.

The time remaining in the lowlands, March and usually the first part of April, can be quite restful if the grazing is good. The herders need only go out in the morning, gather the flock together loosely from the night's roaming, and look them over. Now that the sun is so intense, one is forced to wear sunglasses. The days can be warm, but the nights are still extremely cold. It is the time of the big cross-country ski races, and the time when the lakes are dotted with sport fishermen sitting on the ice staring at small holes they have drilled. Not many warm days in Lapland are mosquitoless, and to have snow and ice left for skiing and snowmobile expeditions makes this one of the most popular times of the year. Of course, winter has not totally given up. Stig Lindberg, one of Jokkmokk's most renowned fishermen, earned his reputation not so much from the size of his catch, but from the time he refused to leave his hole in the ice during an unexpected blizzard. To keep his worms from freezing before he could affix them to the hook he sheltered them in his mouth.

Of the ski races, probably the best known in the Jokkmokk region and most interesting historically from the Saami point of view is the Nordenskiöld Race. The origins of this race are dramatic. Aldof Erik Nordenskiöld, the Arctic explorer, was accompanied on an expedition to the interior of the Greenland Ice Cap in the late 1800s, by two Saami from Jokkmokk, Pavva-Lasse Tuorda and Anders Rassa. When supplies ran out, and it was obvious that he would have to turn back, Nordenskiöld decided to wait for one last effort and send out the two Saami on a reconnaissance mission. Their instructions were simply: Go as far as you can and be back in a couple of days. When they returned, 57 hours later, they claimed to have skied 138 miles into Greenland's inner ice sheet, 276 miles altogether. When Nordenskiöld returned, he was laughed to scorn. His claim that Tuorda and Rassa had skied so far in such a short time was dismissed as fraudulent. Nordenskiöld stood by his comrades, and in April 1884 organized a race from Purkijaur to Kvikkjokk and back, a distance of 132 miles, the longest ski race ever. Besides Tuorda and Rassa, many other Saami competed, it being a point of honor to show the disbelievers what real cross-country skiers could do.

The first Nordenskiöld race is now legendary. Tales are told of reindeer herders who skied for many miles out of the woods, arriving at the start long after the race had begun and without a pause setting off in pursuit only to be among the first to finish. The skis they used were heavy, thick, and homemade. There was no plowed path for them to follow with sugar water and soup at stands every few miles. After only 21 hours, 22 minutes, Pavva-Lasse Tuorda crossed the finish line, first.

Although the annual commemorative Nordenskiöld race is now only thirty miles long, for me it was a great test. I had practiced all winter on skis and swore to myself that I would finish the course. I had no illusions about being speedy: my only concern was endurance. If I could prove to myself and to the members of the Stenträsk group that I could indeed take care of myself on skis and keep going for long distances, then maybe I would be able to accompany them on the coming spring migration. Out of the two hundred to cross the finishing line I was last, a placement that won for me a huge sausage, but most important, I was not one of the fifty who had collapsed and given up along the way. "Anyone who can win a prize in the Nordenskiöld race should have no problem following us on migration," said Henrik.

Unfortunately, the winter of 1973–74 was not a good one. It began very well indeed, but trouble began soon after the reindeer were brought to the lowlands. The snow crusted, grazing was scarce, and the reindeer were half-starved and sickly. The bad effects of the first half of the winter became evident in the second half. The weakest reindeer began to die. The different herding groups met the situation differently. The extensive herders let their herds disperse, the subsequent increased losses from predators being outweighed by the improved chances of finding enough food. When food is sparse, it is best to let the reindeer scatter and move freely through a wide area. The extensive herders do not migrate with their herds. When the returning sun causes crusting on the top snow layer, the extensive groups normally release their reindeer to make their own way to the summer land. The poor winter grazing this year merely hastened this event.

The intensive herders of the Stenträsk group chose the more costly and laborious alternative of feeding their herd with commercial fodder. Whereas the extensive herders gave their reindeer nearly complete freedom, the intensive herders tightened their control yet further. In this way, they hoped to feed their herd while at the same time guarding and protecting their reindeer. Come the spring, the Blind group would begin the migration back to Stalo and the summer land. It would not do to let their herd scatter and mix or they would never be able to separate them from the others and collect them again in a single herd in time for the migration.

The choice of how to react to the winter was not free for each kind of herder, but rather, the form they were practicing before the advent of poor conditions determined how best to survive them. If the herd is already spread extensively when poor grazing conditions strike, it will be almost impossible to bring the reindeer together, and it is certainly inadvisable to try. If the herd is already "in the hand" intensively, however, the use of artificial fodder is feasible.

I visited the Blind herd in March at Stenträsk both to confer about spring migration and to learn something about the feeding process. As the grazing in the winter land grew steadily worse, the reindeer naturally wanted to scatter far and wide in search of food. It was no longer possible to leave them loosely guarded in the woods. They had therefore been driven into the large grazing enclosure connected to the Rahanåive corral to keep them from spreading. The central corral in which they had earlier been separated and then counted was now converted into their dining hall. Long, wooden feeding troughs were scattered throughout the corral. I helped Per-Henrik carry heavy fodder bags from which we poured a stream of dried food as we walked the length of each trough.

Henrik had circled behind the herd, Nils-Anders was busy dismantling the fence separating the reindeer from their newly served meal. It was afternoon feeding time. Henrik did not have to do much coaxing. The reindeer had spotted the big red-and-white-striped bags and dashed to the troughs as soon as Nils-Anders had the fence removed. Most of the reindeer crowded eagerly around the troughs jostling for space, but some sick animals merely stood and watched. There is as yet no commercial fodder that suits all reindeer. There are always some that refuse to eat it or become sick from it.

Twice a day, morning and afternoon at feeding time, the men carefully inspected the herd. Any reindeer not eating could often be induced to do so by forcing a little salt into its mouth. But others were seriously ill, suffering from what Per and Anders termed *skvalpmage* ("slosh stomach"), a blockage in the intestinal track stemming from an inability to digest the artificial fodder. The bacterial colony in their stomachs needed for the digestion of food had died. If discovered soon enough many of the reindeer with skvalpmage could be cured.

A tightness of skin along the backbone was an indicator of trouble, and if one shook the reindeer's stomach a bit and heard a "sloshing" sound, this was a sure sign of blockage. These reindeer would be made to drink a bacteria brew from plastic squeeze-bottles. If administered in time, this medicine would enable the reindeer's stomach to digest the fodder. Health and appetite would return. Reindeer that had been ill for too long frequently died. Sickly vajas often "threw their calves," aborted the fetus. Those reindeer that had passed the point where medicine could help were taken to a special corral partition. A small amount of real reindeer moss had been scraped together and saved for the critical cases. These reindeer were often too weak to stand. Anders fed the sickliest vajas butter to ease their abortion.

Hunger and sickness had made the herd unbelievably tame. They were now totally dependent upon the herders for survival. When they had finished the fodder, we supplemented their diet as best we could by beating down the lower branches of pines with long sticks. The branches of old pines were often thick with a hanging "beard" moss loved by reindeer. As soon as one of us took a step with a pole in hand, he would be followed by a score of hungry reindeer. They would eat from our hands and nudge us if they thought our pace too slow. This moss takes many years to grow and only minutes to eat. In a few days all the accessible pine branches in a wide circle had been knocked down. The amount of hanging moss they yielded was just enough to justify the effort. For those unwilling or unable to eat the artificial food, this moss was a life saver.

The timber industry, which has made great inroads into the Saami winter grazing areas, does replant the forest it destroys, but it is more economical from the perspective of rational wood production to cut and plant frequently rather than permit the trees to grow to great age. Yet it is only on the very oldest trees that the hanging moss has enough time to develop. Before the days of commercial reindeer food, the intensive herder might chop down a pine whenever it was feeding time. Now there is nowhere near enough hanging moss, and what there is must be hoarded.

Two reindeer died while I was in Stenträsk. Altogether they lost eight reindeer that March and a number of calves were thrown. Yet these losses were relatively light considering the severity of the winter. It hurt to see the reindeer so scrawny and weak. The casualty rate would multiply the longer this situation persisted. They could not hold out this way much longer. Luckily it looked as if spring would be early. I knew that Henrik and the others would not want to spend a moment longer in the winter land than necessary. Patches of bare ground would appear first in the mountains, on the southern and eastern sides of the treeless slopes where sun and wind could join forces. The sooner the herd reached there and could return to a natural diet, the better. The calves would be born soon, and they would be too small and weak to dig for food. Their mothers must be healthy and well fed to supply the milk they would need.

No two groups handle their winter work exactly the same. Nor does the same group follow the same pattern each winter. Herding must always be as flexible as the weather. As I began to understand the various factors involved, I found I also began to comprehend the decisions and their timing. I began to see the meaning behind the favorite word of the Saami, "maybe." Maybe a few patches of bare ground were already growing on the mountain sides. When I returned to Jokkmokk, I brought out my hard-bottomed spring skis, specially made for use on crusted snow.

10

Westward with the Spring

On March 28, the phone rang. It was Birgit. "Are you ready to go?" "When?" "I'll pick you up in two hours." "When will the herd start out?" I asked, hoping to gain more time. "Start! They're already half way to Lake Karatj."

A few hours later I was back in my mountain clothes speeding over the ice of Lake Karatj on a snowmobile sled. I was still dazed by the quick transition and was belatedly reviewing my check list as I braced myself against the bumps and held tight to Benno, the dog placed in my charge. Let's see: sleeping bag, sunglasses, food for a few weeks, skis, camera, and film. If I had forgotten anything, it was too late now. Birgit was probably doing the same thing up front as she drove through the night: cigarettes, snus, extra tanks of gas, three sacks of commercial fodder, one dog, one American.

I was wondering why we had stopped, until my ears readjusted to the calm, and I could hear Birgit talking to someone up ahead in the dark. We must have caught up with them, and I peered ahead into the blue-gray darkness. Two thousand animals were in front of me, moving together like a gray shadow over the ice. A fast cloud in flight across the sun would have given a similar effect, but the sun was long since set. The silhouette Birgit was talking to was Per-Henrik's. He kicked off his skis and handed me the poles. "I need a rest," he said and sat himself with Benno on the snowmobile sled. "Just ski along behind and yell at them when they try to scatter." Things were happening all too fast, I felt, as I set off in pursuit of the shadow. I was still wondering if I had cleared up all the correspondence a month's absence required.

Saami appeared and disappeared in the darkness, a head higher than the other, big shadow. All moved forward at a steady pace. Everything was absolutely silent except for the crunch of the snow under cloven hooves and skis and the constant clicking of thousands of reindeer hoof tendons. Occasionally out of the dark silence came a curse directed at a dog, or a shout to a part of the shadow that had begun to separate from the rest. I began to fit voices and silhouettes together. It must be old Anders in the lead with the bell, Per off to my right, and Henrik to my left. I wondered if they could guess who I was.

Three snowmobiles were behind us loaded with supplies, eliminating the need for a rajd. Birgit drove one. Who drove the others I could not know. A snowmobile is not particularly successful in driving reindeer, which are often frightened by the high whining sound of the motor at too close quarters. Snowmobiles, though faster, are less maneuverable than men on skis, and men certainly need nowhere near the amount of repairs required by the snowmobile. The Stenträsk group preferred to let men on skis with dogs drive the herd. This practice gave the herders better contact with the herd. The snowmobiles kept a respectful distance. At times a noisy snowmobile would penetrate our silence, move forward, and relieve a tired skier. At other times it was the driver of the snowmobile who wanted relief from the cold. Skiing certainly kept me warm. The men would switch, and the snowmobile drop back again into the darkness.

Suddenly, the sky lit up with a dazzling stream of shifting lights as if someone had struck a match in a closet. Clouds of light waved in a kind of solar wind, and rays shot out from a central light explosion. These were the Northern Lights as I had never seen them before—the magic of the Lapland twilight. I almost expected the thunder after the flash, the crackling roar of fireworks. This made the silence, and the crunch of the snow even more enchanting.

It was no longer possible for my thoughts to be anywhere but along on migration. There was something about the reindeer herd which arrested my attention. The herd, now far from a corral, moving in a semi-free state though kept together and guided, was more than a collection of two thousand individual reindeer. Like a flock of birds, a reindeer herd seems to have a nervous system of its own. The Saami know how to anticipate its movements and be on hand to head off sudden thrusts in the wrong direction. During the many miles across Lake Karatj under the Northern Lights, I began to see the herd as one large animal the feelings of which I could in part read. Emotions could be seen rippling across the herd in the way wind can be seen on a wheat field. Driving a herd means being attuned to these emotions. The herders worked together in beautiful harmony without a word to each other, all part of the same nerve, and I began to learn my job from their example.

A snowmobile roared by us in a wide arc toward the black rim of the forest, and a little while later we could see the glow from a large fire. The fire was still several miles away, but it had become very cold, and the thought of the imminent coffee break was heartening. The rosy rays danced across the ice and greatly magnified the shadow of the man in front chopping wood. In a restricted circle around the blaze the trees took on form and color.

Another snowmobile pulled up beside me. It was Per-Henrik, now on his own machine, which he surrendered to me. He wanted some exercise he said, to warm up, but most likely he thought I needed a rest, and he was right. Per-Henrik was already back on his skis up with the herd when it struck me that I had never driven a snowmobile before. Luckily, the mechanics involved are elementary, and the skill that snowmobile driving can ordinarily demand is negligible on a flat lake.

It was 2:00 A.M., when skiers and snowmobiles converged on the fire. The herd was left lying calmly on the ice. For the first time I was to meet those whose silhouettes I had seen and whose voices I had recognized. It was Nils-Anders who had made the fire and who now had a pot of coffee ready for us. Altogether we were seven: Henrik, Birgit, Anders, Nils-Anders, Per, Per-Henrik, and I. In a few hours it would be light. We would pass Lillselet in the early morning. Travel would be best in the early hours before it got warm and the snow loose, and then again in the late hours as the snow froze once more to a hard surface.

A doctor told me once that Saami have the ability to withstand cold better than others because of an adaptation in their blood circulation, but this was nowhere near enough, I felt, to explain the fact that they were all soon sleeping peacefully while I was shaking with cold, though nearly lying in the embers. At this rate, I thought, I would be long dead before we reached Stalo, at least 150 miles ahead.

I was glad to be moving again with the dawn. Better warm and tired than cold and rested. Soon we were enjoying Amanda's hospitality, long enough to gulp down a cup of coffee as the herd passed Lillselet. She had thoughtfully baked my favorite cake, a large piece of which I downed on the run. When we reached Levik, we stopped to let the reindeer feed. There is no food to dig for on a frozen lake, and a herd being driven gets little chance to eat. Stops must be made for their sake as well as ours. In the woods around Lake Peuraure we found a spot abundant in hanging moss and let the herd partake of this delicacy, although it meant strict watching. They had little more time to enjoy their moss than I had for my cake. We drove them out onto the Peuraure ice where we could see them easily and would not have to watch so diligently for strays.

With the reindeer lying at ease on the ice, we were quick to follow suit. We built a fire, lay down in a circle around it on the ice, and dozed. The sun grew in power as the fire burned itself an ever-deepening hole. Last night's cold was forgotten with new-found comfort. I awoke an hour later to find that the reindeer had not been idle while the herders slept. They had recognized the red-and-white-striped bags of commercial fodder on the snowmobile sleds and broken one open for a snack. I poked Nils-Anders, "Biergalla," he muttered. "Well, it's time to feed them anyway," and he dragged the torn bag across the ice leaving a long trail of food behind. The reindeer lined up on both sides of it like soldiers in a mess hall. "They know right away when you're asleep," Nils-Anders commented. "I should have set the alarm." The alarm clock he referred to, I learned, was set by lassoing a härk and tying him to your belt. When the herd starts to move anywhere, the härk will try to follow and tug you awake.

Sven was at home in Levik, and the two sleds (pulkas) left there last December on autumn migration were brought out of his storage hut. They must be conveyed to Stalo now so that they could serve in the rajd down next winter. The sleds, which carry all the supplies in the winter, are themselves baggage in the spring. This spring migration, however, was slightly different. One of the yearling calves was so weakened from the poor winter grazing that it obviously could not survive the trek. Instead of having to walk, this little reindeer was bedded down in one of the sleds and towed behind Nil-Anders's snowmobile. I had to laugh seeing this calf there looking so contented and even a bit ashamed at its privileged status. Ironic, I thought. Reindeer who once pulled sleds now ride in them. In days to come our pampered passenger was to grow strong and healthy. When released to return to the herd and advance on its own four feet, the calf hesitated and then clambered back into the sled to continue its free ride.

A cold wind swept across the lake in the early afternoon, hardening its surface. We could move on. No one said anything about it, Anders simply lassoed the lead härk and began skiing. The *tjuovvos* reindeer, those with the special characteristic of following the lead, came along behind, and soon the whole herd was in motion, spread out in a long, thin line. We scrambled to throw our gear back on the snowmobile sleds and take up our positions at the rear and flanks of the herd. The fire was left to burn down through the ice and extinguish itself. Anders and Per, the two old-timers, both of them sixty-five, scorned to ride a snowmobile. I skied for the fun of merging with the herd and helping with the work.

The trick, I learned, was being at the right place at the right time with a strong voice. Running reindeer are much faster than a skiing man. The only way to keep them from scattering was by anticipation. Yelling and pursuing from the wrong angle only makes matters worse. Once the opportunity is lost for the skier to contain a scattering flock, it is up to the dogs alone.

Henrik's dog, Rick, won my full admiration. He was worth four herders. He prowled up and down the edge like a marine drill sergeant inspecting his troops. The reindeer had respect for him. He seemed to be everywhere at once and could sense the reindeers' impulse to scatter long before it became manifest. Henrik did not have to tell him what to do. Should a flock break away completely, Henrik could just point, and Rick would skirt the outermost reindeer to bring them all back in.

We drove the herd past Skaite, left the reindeer in a broad valley where they could be easily gathered tomorrow, and doubled back to the reindeer herders' cabin, built by the Sameby. It was a tiny but much appreciated refuge. Gloves and boots were soon crowding the rafters where they would dry out fastest, and shoe grass was tucked into all free corners. There were four beds and three of us made ourselves comfortable on the floor. Birgit resumed the crossword puzzle she had left last year. The dogs jealously guarded the territory of their master's bed and were suspicious of anyone who so much as happened to sit on "their" bed.

We were all tired and wanted to make the most of the little time we had to sleep. Everyone grew quiet, and I was just about to fade away when I heard someone yoiking. It was Anders. I had asked him about yoiking once and received the strange answer that he never yoiked while awake. Sure enough, he was fast asleep. The yoik came and went like a shy dream and was soon accompanied by a loud snore from another end of the room. I had nearly managed to overcome these hurdles when Henrik, lying next to me, joined the symphony with a wild fight, punching and twisting his blanket. Everyone else was infuriatingly fresh and bouncy in the morning. Not only had I shared cabins with a well-known sleep yoiker, I was told, but Henrik had quite a reputation for killing bears in his sleep. Fortunately, each performance is rare, I was assured, and both at once an unprecedented event. They practically had me feeling honored to have been audience to the show.

We moved out early to gather up the herd in the valley ahead. Those of us on skis *tolked,* or were towed behind the snowmobiles from lassos. Although the snowmobile supplies power, steering is still left very much to the skier. One must dodge bushes and be ready to let go of the line at any moment should the ski catch. Nils-Anders showed me how to hold my ski poles both together under my left arm and to loop the lasso around them, relieving the squeeze on my hand. After looping around the poles, the lasso is gripped by the right hand so that rope and poles form a "Y," and the skier between the two forks can regulate the tension on each side. On long, steep downhill slopes, the skier might pick up more speed than the snowmobile, be forced to release, and continue under his or her own steam until the snowmobile swings by again. I learned to fish up the trailing lasso and wind it around my poles without requiring the snowmobile to stop.

Henrik drove high up the valley wall to get a good lookout. He stood on the snowmobile seat to gain a couple of feet and scanned the white expanse below with binoculars. We had left the evergreens. Leafless scrub birches speckled the white bowl with black. Unable to grow thick and tall, the birches seemed to have redirected their growth energy into creating a colony of thin shoots. "Small birch hedges" would be a more apt description than "birch trees." The untrained eye is often unable to distinguish a reindeer from a scrub birch at great distances. Both are a dark dot against the snow. "Where are they?" I asked. "There," said Henrik sweeping his hand over twenty-five square miles. He and Nils-Anders unhitched their sleds and sped off with their snowmobiles to round them up.

Per-Henrik was having snowmobile difficulty. I doubt if I have ever encountered a snowmobile without some type of problem. One had to be an amateur mechanic to keep them functioning. But this time the trouble was of a more serious nature. At every campfire, after the coffee pot was put on, one of the men was always throwing a lump of iron into the embers, and after a leisurely cup, the red hot iron was lifted out and used to solder some wire or other. Per-Henrik and Per were now kneeling in a snowbank with a piece of motor spread out on a plastic bag. It was a familiar sight, and snowmobiles provided a recurring topic of conversation. No amount of swearing and head scratching solved this problem, however, and Per-Henrik decided that the only course of action was to limp in to Kvikkjokk and get it repaired.

The herd Henrik and Nils-Anders brought together was bigger than the one they had released the day before. Besides those we had brought, other reindeer from extensive groups, or even reindeer who had wintered in the mountains, had been swept in with the gathering operation and joined our ranks. I began to notice that the reindeer were not responding as readily to shouts as they had before. A shout was no longer enough to turn a straying flock. They demanded escalated action. Now to achieve the same response I had to yell, stamp my skis loudly, and wave my ski poles. I wondered what I would take to once they got accustomed to this display.

The farther we went, the hoarser I became and the more tired and hungry. When finally we reached the Vuoka cabin I was asleep before coffee was ready. When I awoke, Birgit was immersed in her Vuoka crossword puzzle, and Nils-Anders had left by snowmobile for Njunjes to use the phone there. Here we were miles out in a snowy wasteland with a herd of reindeer, and yet a quick jump over the mountains could connect us to civilization. "He probably wants to tell Per-Henrik to bring an extra gas filter and most important a case of beer," said Henrik. A snowstorm was raging full blast when Nils-Anders returned. It took a while for his jaw to thaw loose so he could tell us who had won the last big ski race. The headlight on his snow-mobile had gone out, and he had been forced to hold his mini-flashlight in his teeth the whole way back.

The storm blew all the next day and night. We hardly budged from the cabin. Henrik dug a seven-foot well through the snow, hit-ting precisely the small brook he knew to be underneath, and thereby spared us the task of melting snow and expending valuable fuel. Per-Henrik was back as soon as the weather cleared with a temporarily well-running snowmobile. It was time to move on. The storm had given us a rest and a chance to dry our socks and boots, but it had also let the reindeer scatter. Fortunately, the grazing was good around Vuoka and the topography of the area was such that the reindeer would not scatter far. I joined in gathering the herd together again, but made sure before putting my pack on the sled that my pockets were stuffed with cheese and raisins. The chances were that we would not stop to eat for another twelve hours.

We fed the herd our last bag of commercial fodder. It was unnec-essary to haul them along any farther. We had reached the first patches of bare ground, and from now on grazing was good. We had only to slow down every few hours and give the reindeer a chance to eat. The next few days I experienced as one long, continuous job on the left flank, waving and shouting. The trek was broken by campfire stops and several more cabins, but these were the small incidents attached to a grand journey.

Besides the incredible beauty of moving the herd through these snow-covered mountains, the most memorable events were encoun-ters with new people. At one point we ran into a squad of policemen on snowmobiles involved in practice rescue operations. According to operational code, they pretended to be looking for "the Saami John Andersson." This set us all laughing as everyone knew John. If there was anyone who could take care of himself in the mountains alone it was he. The real John was now in Lillselet, but the police made a note of our route, which spared them from searching for the mythical John along the same stretch.

After they had gone we discovered a bag full of apples they had forgotten. Fresh apples in the winter in the mountains are an unprecedented treat. "Can't leave them here to rot," Nils-Anders said as he passed them around. We cooked coffee and munched apples. Whoever cooked the coffee made sure he took the first cup, there being a saying that he who drinks the first cup will be the one to turn the reindeer herd and save the day once they begin to scatter.

A while later two police snowmobiles reappeared. "The bag is still here," the first policeman called joyfully back to his companion as he leapt from his snowmobile. There was a guilty silence. Nils-Anders swallowed his last bite of apple and said slowly, "The bag is here, but it is empty." The faces of the policemen drooped. "Just after you left," continued Nils-Anders with a wink, "a fellow came skiing like a madman over the ridge. He said he was John Andersson, stuffed all the apples in his jacket and left that-a-way in a great hurry." The policemen smiled knowingly.

The closer I approached Stalo, the more familiar the mountains felt except for the essential difference that they were all clad in white. I seemed to be meeting old friends in different moods and feeling I was getting to know them much better because of it. A blizzard hit us a day's journey from Stalo, and the mountains were veiled from view. In fact, I could hardly see my skis. This must be what is called a "white out," I concluded, and decided to sit down until it cleared up. When I touched the snow I was thrown with considerable force. I had been totally unaware when I tried to sit down that I had been making good speed down a long slope. It could work the other way, too. I might be crouched in skier's stance thinking I was moving at fantastic speed with the wind whistling around me only to find when I put down a ski pole that I had been standing still.

After the storm cleared I was in for another trick of the senses. We crossed a high ridge at an angle that I knew afforded the first view of Lake Virihaure. Instead of seeing a wide expanse of ice disappearing in the distance, I saw only a band of ice that rose straight up in the air like a huge, long snowdrift. I knew that was the lake, but it refused to lie down as a lake should. I had no sense of depth. I rubbed my eyes and tried to think it down, but it stayed the same. Bit by bit as we neared Stalo the mountains turned toward us their old familiar faces and stood in the same relation to each other that I remembered from last summer. The next time I looked, the lake lay flat. When I finally spied the snow-covered goattiehs of Stalo in a field of empty white, I felt the warmth of coming home as never before.

Migration was over. For the next month, until the calves were born and able to run, the herd would be guarded daily against attack from predators. Then the melting snows and lake ice would force us back to the lowlands with the snowmobiles before they became stranded in the mountains. The mountains would then be closed to travelers by the massive spring floods, and people would not return to the summer land until late in June when the trails would be open and the lakes clear of ice to permit seaplane landings.

"What now?" I wondered stretched out on the moose hide inside the Blind goattieh. I enjoyed the feeling of having an entire month stretch ahead into the unknown. I knew only too well that it would be overflowing with work and adventure, but I had dropped the habit of trying to find out in advance what lay in store. Time would answer all questions if my curiosity could stand the wait. Already I was suspecting one problem to contend with. The last snowstorm had spread a clean white sheet over the mountains. Both my eyes felt as if there was something in them. The bright sun on the fresh snow made them water, and I had to consider the possibility of going snow-blind.

Birgit, back in her goattieh, had everything unpacked, cleaned, and functioning in no time. Henrik dug up a large wooden box from under the snow. Inside it, packed with snow, were cuts of meat from the reindeer he had slaughtered last November before embarking on autumn migration. We could celebrate our arrival with a feast of reindeer meat. Per-Henrik produced beer, and Birgit made a roaring blaze to drive the chill from our snow-covered home.

The billows of smoke from the damp winter wood stung my eyes terribly and forced me to lie on my stomach with my face to one of the goattieh vent holes. The sun outside and the smoke inside combined to swell my eyes shut by morning. I was miserable: I could see if absolutely necessary for a few seconds at a time by opening my eyelids with my fingers, but the pain was prohibitive.

All the others had been snow-blind before, and their descriptions made me glad I had such a mild case. Suggested treatment ran from bathing my eyes with human milk, unavailable, to rubbing them with fresh snus, unthinkable. Per and Per-Henrik had moved to their own goattieh up the hill, leaving us still crowded but less so, and Birgit advised me to join them. They had installed a small woodstove in their goattieh, which would free me from the billows of yellowish smoke from the open fire. Henrik guided me over, and I lay in the Labba goattieh for a couple of days like so much useless baggage. The little stove was indeed a godsend. When my eyes finally did squint forth through puffy lids, they were not punished and walled up again by a cloud of smoke. The stove had simply been placed over the hearth stones, and the chimney pipe run straight out through the smoke hole. In the summer it could be lifted out in a couple of minutes.

When finally back in action, I helped Per-Henrik haul birch trees from the woods for the coming summer's wood supply. When the requirements of one season were met, there was always a long list of duties for other seasons awaiting attention. Chopping and splitting a large supply of birch now would give it time to dry out before the families moved up at the end of June. Luckily, Per-Henrik had a chain saw, but unluckily, I yanked the start rope out and pulled loose the recoil spring in a moment of misguided strength. For three nights before going to sleep, Per-Henrik and I delved into the nuts and bolts. Slowly and carefully we would rewind the old spring and ease it with bated breath into its niche. Each time it ended the same way. Half a millimeter from its rightful place the spring would leap like a rocket from the motor and slash the air. Per-Henrik and I would dive for the far wall. With our nerves shattered we would lie like hunted rabbits wondering if the shooting was over. The only sound would be a soft "Tshshss" as Per, totally unaffected by the sudden release of flying steel, continued to unwind his shoe bands and spit snus juice against the hot stove.

On one occasion we were equally surprised when there was no whirling burst. The spring sat snuggly, and with a few screws it was whole and functioning again. We had completed the woodpile with handsaw and ax, but Per-Henrik was pleased to have the saw in operation again so that it could be used, he said, on tomorrow's fishing expedition. I refrained from asking the obvious question, deciding instead to wait and see.

Henrik, Per-Henrik, and I departed next morning by snowmobile for a small lake, Keddijaure, famed for its fat spring char. Besides the chain saw, we had two long nets with us. All the lakes were, of course, still covered with a thick layer of ice, and I was wondering how they would get those nets spread out underneath. The chain saw was used to cut a large hole in the ice a yard square and just about as deep. Per-Henrik had to pull the saw away fast once he reached water. What had at first been a deep pit was quickly flooded with water to the top. The last of the bottom ice layer was knocked out with a heavy iron rod. Per-Henrik considered the length of a net and paced off the same distance across the ice for the next hole. When done, there were three holes between which the two nets would be strung.

"I suppose you swim with the net between the holes," I said, unable to contain my curiosity any longer. "No," said Henrik, "*we* don't. That's why we brought you along." Their joke left me none the wiser. They enjoyed leaving me ignorant. Henrik walked to the middle hole and jammed a ski pole in the ice beside it. Per-Henrik produced a loglike contraption from the snowmobile sled. "This is what will do the swimming," he said. He called it the "ice-horse." It was a two-foot plank, made very buoyant by a number of corks nailed to it. There were two small steel runners across the top, and when the ice-horse was put under the ice, it would slide along the ice bottom like an upside-down sled. It was propelled by a lever with a nail at the top. By attaching a string to the other end of the lever, one could move the ice-horse in a series of jerky thrusts by intermittently tugging on the line. The nail worked like a mountain climber's pick ax.

"The only trick now is getting it aimed properly," said Henrik. He plunged the ice-horse into the first hole and sighted carefully toward the ski pole twenty yards away. After each short tug, the horse drew the line further and further under the ice. I stood between the holes and could hear it creeping along underneath. "It seems to be holding course," said Per-Henrik. A little while later the horse resurfaced in the middle hole. With a line between the holes, there was no difficulty pulling the net across under the ice. The horse was once again set swimming from the the last hole to the middle with the same perfect aim. After pulling the second net across, we checked the first one before returning to Stalo and found to our delight an obliging five pound char for dinner.

A great snowstorm made Stalo's goattiehs look like a row of sugar domes. Someone went out to the reindeer in all weathers to keep track of their movements and watch for wolverines or lynxes. Other jobs could wait until there were better working conditions. The fish might have to wait a while in the nets. I remember awakening to the Norwegian morning physical exercise program on the radio, which drove everyone crazy but effectively roused us. Snow had driven into the goattieh through the vent holes. The outhouse seat had to be shoveled open and even the inside walls were plastered with snow. We took little advantage of the privacy it afforded. The radio push-ups were followed by news and the weather report. Sweden was on the whole blessed with good weather, but Norway had miserable rains and snows. Stalo was close to the border, and it was always the Norwegian report that tallied.

The longer we stayed in Stalo the closer we got to the bottom of our food provisions. A supply run to the Swedish lowlands meant much travel, and moreover, the good weather everywhere in Sweden, except in Stalo, had surely melted so much snow that it would be hard on the snowmobiles. Contrary to what one might expect, the break up of the snow cover is not necessarily welcomed with open arms by the Saami. Sun crusted snow is ideal for travel, but as the sun gains in intensity, the wonderful maneuverability of early spring is forfeited. It was far better to cross the border and head for the little town of Sulitjelma only thirty miles away. Crossing the Norwegian mountains would be no problem, since they were full of snow. Much of the way we could ride along the Sulitjelma glacier. Nils-Anders and I made plans for the "Sulis" trip as we waited for the weather to clear. We took shopping orders from everyone. Tobacco, coffee, snus, bread, and butter were most prominent on the list. It was understood that we would return with Norwegian moonshine. Not a house in Sulis, I was told, lacked a still.

Before access to the Norwegian side was severely restricted for Swedish reindeer in the early 1900s, contact across the border was much more common. But even though relations between Sulis and Stalo were no longer so regular or frequent, there was not a Saami in Stalo who did not have good friends and a welcome bed waiting in Sulis whenever he or she happened to drop in. Sulis is a copper-mining town with a railroad and a new highway under construction. Its stores were, therefore, as well stocked as those in Jokkmokk. Moreover, the baker in Sulis, I learned, was famed for his raisin bread, "Sulis loaf," which remained ever fresh and was guaranteed not to crumble under rough treatment.

When the blizzard died, Nils-Anders and I were ready to leave for Sulis. Just then, two more snowmobiles roared into Stalo. Johan Parfa, Karin and little Per-Jonas came with one snowmobile, Nils-Henrik Gunnare with the other. They had freighted up some supplies for the summer and planned to stay a few days preparing the wood-pile. Johan brought me mail and Easter eggs from the Märaks. When Nils-Henrik learned we were bound for Sulis, he joined us at once. I was glad to have the opportunity to resume my summer's conversations with him. Nils-Henrik had once been offered a job in Alaska teaching reindeer herding to Eskimos. He had been unable to tear himself away from Lapland, but he had ever since read almost everything printed in Swedish about Alaska and knew far more about the American North than I.

Nils-Anders and Nils-Henrik knew the location of almost every split in the Sulitjelma glacier, though new ones are always forming, and we had to be careful. Entire herds of reindeer have been swallowed by glaciers, and avalanches in the steep mountains can gain such force that they continue for miles and even climb up smaller mountains and crash back down the other side! In places the snow was so deep we had to crawl uphill on hands and knees pulling the snow-mobiles up behind with lassos. Hard work was pleasurable in these surroundings, and in what seemed a short time we were peering from a high mountain ridge at a small, "toy" village below. Sulitjelma lay at the base of a large forested valley; at least it had been forested, but all the trees were now dead from poisons emitted by the copper smelt works.

News spread quickly that "the Saami had come," and we were surrounded by friendly faces. Our snowmobiles were repaired and refitted by the local mechanic. Moonshine was thrust upon us, and the baker promised to make a special effort. En route back to Stalo I lay on a sled with twenty-five enormous Sulis loaves.

By the end of April there was little to do but wait for the calves to be born. Only I still struggled with a woodpile. I was seriously considering another summer in Stalo. I shoveled out the snow that had driven into "my" goattieh and slowly began sawing logs. I did not dare use the chain saw again. Later, when I showed Birgit some pictures from Stalo that spring, her method of dating the scene was by the height of my woodpile. Stalo was finally beginning to thaw, and occasionally one could hear the ice of Virihaure give a deep groan. At times the reindeer could be seen crossing the blackening ice in long strings, seeking their old calving land on the western end. Biegolmai's shovel was broken, and the winter snows were waning. We had to hurry from the mountains while there was snow left for travel, but we wanted to stay until the calves were born, until they were up and running and stood a chance against the trials ahead.

Most calves are not born until the middle of May, but already on April 28 Anders announced that a calf had been born. In almost no time it can stand and take wobbly steps toward its mother. In a couple of days it is almost impossible to catch. Just after birth is the most dangerous time for the calves. Should a strong blizzard strike before it is licked dry and can rise, the calf will freeze and die. The bears have awakened with an awful hunger. They can simply watch a vaja until she gives birth and then saunter forth and collect their meal before it can run. Eagles are about the worst calf-killers. Even large and fleet calves are not safe from sudden attack from the air. Ravens will also kill small calves. A raven will first render its victim helpless by pecking out the calf's eyes.

The little calf did not seem in the least worried by the approach of people, but the mother was naturally nervous. The reindeer should not be disturbed on the calving land, but it is wise to watch and make sure that predators know there are men about. It seemed impossible that this tiny awkward calf had the slightest chance of survival. Yet, the endurance of the reindeer calf is baffling, and the speed with which it develops is amazing. It must grow fast, as winter is never far away. A reindeer calf's chances of survival are still quite good.

As we feasted on a fresh Sulis loaf I consulted my "Saami thermometer," the butter. It was rather soft, meaning warm weather and melting snow. I knew it was time to contemplate the return to Jokkmokk. The others could stay a few days longer to guard over the newborn calves. They had snowmobiles; I did not. Already there were two persons per snowmobile, and along with the sleds and other gear they would have a heavy load. I could not add myself to their burden. I would have to ski where I could and walk when no snow remained. When I mentioned these plans to Nils-Henrik, however, he changed my mind in seconds by offering me a ride on his snowmobile sled. Johan, Karin, and Per-Jonas would accompany us with their snowmobile as well. Should one have trouble with the difficult descent, the others could help.

We decided to take the Tjuolta Valley route instead of the more usual Tarra Valley route. The Tjuolta Valley was higher than the Tarra Valley and thus had more chance of preserving snow cover. My companions had come up the Tarra Valley only a week ago, but they said it was almost bare then. Now after a week of soft butter, there would be no snow left at all. Although bare ground appears early in the mountain zones, the snow remains long after it has disappeared further east. In the highest mountains it was still full winter. Yet, spring was touching Stalo, and in Kvikkjokk, the others told me, summer was in full bloom. Our journey into summer would gain in difficulty with every step.

The first twenty miles were easy. There was plenty of snow on the high tundra. We stopped at various small lakes, chopped a hole in the ice with an ax and pulled up char for lunch. When one char was caught, its eye supplied bait for the next. After a few long stretches of bare ground, Nils-Henrik's snowmobile began having difficulty. We were forced to stop, and Nils-Henrik tipped the snowmobile on its side to inspect the tread. Maybe the tread had slipped from the wheels. Tipping the snowmobile brought more trouble. The extra gas tank slid out of its rack and was soon bouncing down the mountain with terrific speed. We watched it slide for miles over the snow far below until finally it disappeared. The gas it contained was vital for the trip to Kvikkjokk. When Nils-Henrik had readjusted the tread we began the search to recover the gas tank. Johan had had the good sense to watch its course with binoculars and was able to mark the spot where it vanished. It had slid more than three miles and was badly battered, but it still held the valuable gas.

The runaway gas tank seemed to mark the beginning of our problems. We dropped steeply from the mountains onto the valley floor and found ourselves staring summer in the face. The snow ended abruptly. Ahead of us lay brown fields and marshes. "If we can manage to take ourselves past this to the evergreen forest we'll be all right," said Johan, "There'll be more snow there because of the shade." The ordeal began. The snowmobiles pounded over dry land and splashed through marshes. I walked. When we hit the birch woods our troubles increased. We could not always dodge obstacles in this terrain, and I had to clear the way ahead with an ax. Waist high birch trunks cluttered our path. They had been chopped once before at snow level to create a smooth snowmobile trail, but now the snow had melted down.

We struggled along, step by step, often having to unhitch the sleds and pull them by hand. We rested briefly every four or five hours. Our progress was so slow I remember standing by one campfire and seeing faint smoke from our last camp fire smoldering near at hand. It was strange to see a snowmobile with sled churning over a brown meadow, as strange as someone skiing over a green golf course. Four-year-old Per-Jonas was so exhausted he lay bundled in the sled asleep no matter now hard it knocked and screached over rocks. Along the edges of streams where there was some snow left, I could still ski. I awoke once with a start to find that I had dozed off leaning against a tree; still standing up on skis.

Nils-Henrik's snowmobile could no longer withstand the strain. The back axle broke, and we were forced to abandon the machine. After each hard stretch we were convinced that the going could only improve, and little by little we were led into a hopeless situation. "We were fools not to have taken the Valli peak route," said Nils-Henrik. He explained that we would have run along a high mountain ridge most of the way, over the sarv slaughter corral, and dropped only at the very end, an extremely steep but short drop down to Kvikkjokk. But for each step we dragged ourselves along, the more loathe we were to retrace our steps back to the pass leading to the Valli peak.

I had to carry my pack now to lighten the load. Nils-Henrik and I scouted for the best path and hauled the heavy sled. We could see the evergreen woods only a mile away. The moon was full, so we could struggle on into the night. Finally at 1:00 A.M., after two hard days of work, we could go no farther. Not only had the snow vanished, but the fields and marshes came to an end. Ahead was only a broad band of rock rubble. We were all quiet as we looked out upon this last devastating hurdle.

Johan finally spoke as we warmed ourselves around a last fire. "There's nothing we can do but turn around and go back the way we've come. With the gas from Nils-Henrik's snowmobile we should have enough to take the Valli peak route. There's no need for you to go with us if you can make it to Kvikkjokk on foot from here. With luck you can still wade over Kamajokk. When you reach Kvikkjokk, wait a couple of days, and if we haven't made it down, borrow a snowmobile and take an extra tank of gas up to Valli peak to look for us." After a final shared pot of coffee, they turned back. The last I saw was the snowmobile's red taillight fade in the twilight.

When it was light enough, I crossed the shelf of rock. In less than a mile I had reached snow and could ski once again. Kamajokk was in full flood but surprisingly enough I could see a narrow ice bridge underwater. The old snowmobile trail had packed the snow so hard that it had withstood both sun and water. The bridge could not hold for long, but maybe if I waded across it on skis I could distribute my weight enough to make it over. It was probably foolish, but I was already so wet and tired, a swim in the stream I felt could make no difference as long as I got across. The water reached my hips, but the bridge held. A short while later I was in Kvikkjokk drinking a beer with friends, giving news from the mountains, and catching up on events in the lowlands.

I reached Kvikkjokk on April 30, and, as is Swedish custom, a huge bonfire was built at night to welcome back the sun. It is an old pagan rite, and the fire was as tall as a man, drying my trousers most effectively. In the cold of the early morning a snowmobile roared across the river to Kvikkjokk. Nils-Henrik, Johan, Karin, and Per-Jonas had made it down. They had timed their crossing carefully. Half an hour later, the morning ice was gone. Although it would not have supported their weight had they been stationary, the ice was just strong enough to hold them during the rapid crossing. Henrik, Per-Henrik, and the others in Stalo were all down within the week. Although they had taken a different route, their descent had not been less difficult. The mountains were definitely closed until the flood water would run off at the end of June. The calves would have to do the best they could on their own. We would not see them again at close quarters until marking time, late June and July, in the corral.

May and most of June are an intermission in the Tuorpon herding cycle, even for the intensive herders. They may find a part-time job or spend their days repairing nets, varnishing the boat, or preparing handicraft work for the tourist invasion. The ice darkens as the snow melts and begins to break up. The time of no travel sets in again.

When Lake Karatj finally opened, and we were able once more to visit Amanda in Lillselet, I caught sight of a lone sarv moving slowly toward the mountains. His new antler shoots were already more than a foot long. The year flashed by me in a whirl of moves, packings and unpackings, gatherings and separations. Nothing ever stood still. If those antlers would just slow down for a little while, I felt, I could regroup my forces for another galloping year. For me, the awful time of decision had come.

It had been a year since I had first come to Jokkmokk. The herding cycle would begin all over again. My moose hide would make a welcome addition to the goattieh floor in Stalo. I was sure to become an even more proficient baker, I told myself, if I could practice for another summer. Nils-Tomas and I had already considered some repairs to be made on my goattieh with the premise that we would combine our efforts. After all, the improvements were for my benefit. Maybe it was not so important for me to be somewhere else. Perhaps I could enjoy another summer in Stalo. Should some kind of explanation be demanded of me by my career-oriented past, maybe I could appease these voices of reproach with arguments about the value of "fieldwork" and the need for in-depth anthropological participant observation. The truth of the matter was that I could not bear the thought of leaving.

In a short while I could hike up to Parka to join in the gatherings for the early calf-markings. Always there were new things to see and learn. My friends, who by this time were expert in how to manipulate me, never failed to point them out. The hike to Parka from Lillselet would offer me the opportunity to view the early calf-markings of the Nuortvalle group on the birch tree line as their reindeer moved westward. And from Parka, I was told, I should continue to Stalo along one of the old migration routes for another summer in "my" goattieh. Johan Märak presented me with a hand-crafted wooden pack frame "to carry our next moose." How could I leave? There is no fitting place to end the herding life. My heart moved westward with the reindeer toward Stalo. I thought of the times when I came home to my goattieh sweaty and tired from a calf-marking to find fresh fish and glödkaka left for me by thoughtful neighbors. I remembered the bed of freshly cut birch branches surrounding the open hearth. How delightful it is to drift off to sleep watching the faces of friends in the night wink and flicker to the dancing flames at the center. Perhaps I should awake from this boyhood dream. Maybe harsh realities will shatter it. But until that time I wish to be caught up in the herders' cycle, tucked away in a mountain corner where all good plans begin and end with a "maybe."

Epilogue

The thought that this book will soon be published in America fills me with mixed feelings. On the one hand, the professional anthropologist within me would like to tell all that has happened to change the life I have described. Admittedly, much could be learned from a detailed analysis over time. On the other hand, this book was not designed to be an anthropological record. It was intended precisely to describe my experiences as a guest of the Saami.

Although I have pursued new field assignments, among them a year and a half working as a reindeer herder in Alaska, I always return to Stalo and Padjelanta as the reindeer to their favorite grazing grounds. I have settled permanently in Sweden. My work, currently an investigation of the long-term social effects of the Chernobyl nuclear disaster on the Swedish Saami, gives me ample opportunity to join old friends in Jokkmokk, and even if I am no longer a part of their daily lives, I am no stranger to it. The prophecy of Lars Kuhmunen's trolldrum has come true—I have found a wife. Annie enjoys sharing the goattieh life with me in Stalo, and we pop up now and then for the moose hunt in Lillselet, for the winter fair, or for no reason at all but to drink coffee, join in the current conversation, and maintain the continuity that makes one feel at home.

Seventeen years have passed since I ended the account of my time with the Tuorpon Saami. On the large canvas, decisive changes are brewing for the Saami concerning their rights as a native minority.

Some of these most recent changes are important enough to warrant commentary.

The Swedish government's Saami policy is finally moving toward a break with the occupational perspective that has characterized it for so long. According to present Swedish law, so-called Saami resource privileges fall to only 10 percent of the Saami, those who practice the reindeer-herding occupation. It is true, as the state maintains, that the greater Saami majority possesses Saami resource rights; but one must bear in mind that by legal sleight-of-hand only a small percentage of those granted these rights are allowed to *practice* them. While there are about 900 active herders in Sweden today (counting family members at most 2,700 people pursuing the herding life), there are fully 8,000 Saami still living on their ancestral lands who have been denied the use of their Saami resource rights.

According to state policy, the Saami (but only certain Saami) are permitted to practice reindeer herding in order to maintain their distinctive culture. This distinctive culture is then simplistically equated with reindeer herding, and should a Saami herder come to receive the greater part of his or her income from a nonherding source, that person is to be deprived of the herding privilege. According to the same philosophy, the Samebys are not permitted to engage in any economic activity other than herding.

With the increasing pressures of extractive industries (mining, timber, hydroelectric power), the available grazing lands continually decrease. By extension, so must the Samebys' reindeer numbers. At the same time, the minimum number of reindeer needed for subsistence per family continues to increase. Thus the herders are hit from both ends. Not only have many Saami had to quit herding, but large numbers have been forced to seek employment in the big cities to the south.

In 1982 a Swedish Saami Rights Commission was established to investigate ways to improve conditions for the Saami and to make recommendations to the government for new legislation. During its almost ten years of activity, the commission has taken the first halting steps to implement an ethnic rather than a purely occupational base to Swedish Saami rights. Besides suggesting changes in the current Reindeer Herding Act of 1971, the Commission has advocated the creation of a Swedish national Saami Parliament or "Sameting," whose Saami electorate is ethnically defined.

Despite a number of useful, legal adjustments, many of the changes recommended by the commission remain, in my opinion, less than adequate. The Sameting is still not a reality.

The state claims that its Saami policy is devised to help preserve the unique Saami culture. Yet this policy is devastating for the Saami. A policy where "the reindeer-herding business" is tolerated only for its roll in cultural preservation is doomed to failure with respect to both culture and business.

One does not save the Saami culture by promoting business rationalization methods which result in a continual decrease of the reindeer herding population. One does not save the Saami culture with laws that divide the Saami collective into different judicially defined camps. One can save no culture by trying to legislate its status quo. One can give it a chance only by granting possibilities for it to become, or to remain, what it wants to be.

Dark clouds swept over Tuorpon and all of Lapland with the Chernobyl nuclear disaster of April 1986. Tuorpon was not at all so heavily hit by fallout as were some of the Samebys farther south. Nonetheless, come the autumn time for slaughter, cesium-137 concentrations in reindeer over the whole of Sweden were considered high enough to warrant controlled inspection before the sale of their meat. My phone grew hot with calls from distant lands. Journalists and filmers were avid to document the demise of the Saami. The story of a small, native minority pursuing a life close to nature only to be ironically snuffed out by the collective sin of the industrialized world was undoubtedly a scoop. The situation held mythic proportion and obvious political relevance to the nuclear power controversy. Naturally such attention was in its place, but frequently the need for a good story drove some reporters to make ungrounded pronouncements of doom.

Unfortunately, when it comes to any evaluation of the health risks from consuming meat and fish with different becquerel levels, we have no real baseline with which to compare. The long-term statistical studies necessary to judge the effects of radioactive contamination have been (often purposely) neglected. Lack of detailed and scientifically proven knowledge, however, is not the same as lack of risk. It is certainly not my desire to belittle the eventual health risks of the Chernobyl nuclear disaster, only to point out that the Saami herders are not about to perish from this earth as a result of it.

The social effects of the disaster among the herders are far more evident than the health effects for the individual. Herders have been forced to purchase nontraditional foodstuffs to compensate for the lack of "good" reindeer meat. Frequently the timing of slaughters has been changed in an effort to harvest the reindeer before they have consumed so much of the heavily contaminated lichen grazed in winter. In the harder-hit areas far to the south of Tuorpon, herders have transported their reindeer many miles by truck in order to bring them to cleaner grazing lands. Some people have been forced to leave their families for many months and to stay with the reindeer on foreign pastures far from home. Thousands of reindeer all over Lapland have been "junked," that is, declared unfit for human consumption and then thrown into earth pits or ground into fodder for animals at fur farms. It is disheartening for the herders to see the fruits of their labor disposed of like this, notwithstanding the monetary compensation they get from the state for their confiscated animals.

Many of the most significant aspects of the Chernobyl disaster for the Saami in principle stem from the policies made in reaction to it. Here, however, we enter the realm of my current research. How, for example, did one determine the initial control limit (300 becquerels of cesium-137 per kilo), over which reindeer meat could not be sold? Why was it raised to 1,500 Bq/kg, and why raised for reindeer meat and inland fish, basic foodstuffs of the northern population, when it remains at the old level for the basic foodstuffs of the average Swede? As it turns out, cesium levels in Lapland reindeer had been well above the current marketing limit because of atmospheric atomic bomb tests in the Soviet Union long before the accident at Chernobyl. Why was there no limit set for meat contamination then?

The questions go on and on. What effect does this blow to reindeer herding mean for the recruitment of new herders? What can be done to reduce the contamination in the living animals and how can one prepare the meat so as to minimize radioactivity? If such measures have little effect, will there be long-standing changes in Saami dietary habits? What changes will result in the herding cycle of work and grazing land utilization? With a half-life of thirty years, cesium-137 will plague the northern economy for a long, long time.

The special absorption properties of the reindeer lichen and the sensitivity of the northern environment have placed the Saami herders at the forefront of a dreadful problem for all of mankind: radioactive pollution. Our environment does not absorb radiation uniformly. Nor does radiation spread uniformly in the food chain, and different peoples do not have uniform food habits or access to the same foodstuffs. Politically derived regulations and marketability limits set for dealing with contamination of this sort should not solely and simplistically be based on the food habits of the average Swede. One can only hope that the rest of us will heed the warning sounded by the situation of the Saami. I cannot imagine people meeting the fear, adversity, and concrete deprivations entailed by this most modern of nightmares with a greater degree of fortitude than they have.

Striking as are the developments concerning Saami resource rights and the upheavals of the Chernobyl disaster, it is the particular changes on the local level that have touched me most deeply. The following few pages contain my personal comments on a highly selective view of these past years.

Before everything else, I think of the old ones who have died. Petrus Gruvvisare, the timeless herder and figure of a hundred local legends has come to rest. Jova Spik, with whom I nearly had an unexpected cold bath one autumn while fishing in Tjaktjajaure, is gone. Per Pavval can no longer tell me about herding "in the old days." Abmut Tuolja, with whom I had shared an equally unexpected but so very welcome sauna on the trail en route to Staloluokta, is also gone. These four and I shared a few strong memories when we met, but our paths then led us to different summer camps and different herding groups. I knew these old men only well enough to realize what a treasure of information and potential good times were lost with them. The deaths of closer friends like Per Labba, Sven Larsson, Anders Blind, and Henrik Kuhmunen are more difficult to accept.

Working the same herd, being part of a migration together and living as neighbors in the same village made me appreciate Per Labba enormously. He was a small, modest, but terribly tough herder whose wry sense of humor still draws a smile as I think of him. The herders in the western Virihaure group have suffered a great loss with Per's departure.

Sven, or "Suorva Lasse," lived alone to the end as he wanted in Levik by Lake Peuraure. His relatives grew anxious when he did not call or answer the phone one winter, and driving out by snowmobile to check on him, they found him dead and frozen on the ice. His old dog had died a few days before, but apparently Sven had forgotten and had been out trying to find him. The dog's leash was in his hand. Lillselet's neighboring homestead to the west is now empty. Sven was one of the last full-time hunters, a type of person that will never come again. He seemed to fill the whole Peuraure-Karatj Lake area. His home in Levik was the natural stopping spot for the Stenträsk group during migrations east and west. I shall miss my fellow bald head.

Henrik Kuhmunen, my first Saami companion, holds a special place in my thoughts. He was always so totally unpretentious and big of heart. Yet he was also incredibly shrewd despite his seemingly simple, backwoods manner. Over the years my respect for him increased steadily, not just for his fighting spirit, herding skill, and traditional knowledge, but mainly for the way he was as a person.

Anders Blind, shortly before he died, sent me word through Birgit that he would like to tell me about his life. For years he had said he would tell me "everything" one day, but he had always put it off. When I got his message, I dropped whatever I was doing at the university in Uppsala, took the train to Jokkmokk, and spent a week in his company. I knew he must have felt near the end. When he started to reminisce, he regained his old flair. What a time we had together! Once he had passed on the story of his remarkable life, knowing that it would be available to any of his family and friends, he felt at peace. Soon thereafter he was gone.

Per, Sven, Henrik, and Anders were old men with full lives behind them when they died. This was not the case with Per-Henrik Labba, Per's son, who died suddenly one autumn while gathering reindeer west of Virihaure in preparation for the eastward migration. He collapsed of heart failure and died soon after with his comrades around him. They had all grown up together and took it very hard, of course.

In a small, tight-knit group as this one, such a blow can be devastating for the herding work pattern. Per-Henrik's calm hand with the lead reindeer will no longer bring the herd through the forest out onto the ice. Nor will his even temper and gentle resolution in the face of adversity encourage his comrades. Fortunately, Sven-Ingvar, Henrik and Birgit's son, has grown to full competence as a herder and can help fill the herding gap. Bosse Svensson, a Swede who has married into the Blind family, has with hard work also become an excellent herder. Bosse and his wife, Marianne—old Anders' grandchild—now have two small boys. Sven-Ingvar and his wife, Annelie, are also parents. The Virihaure group is recouping its losses in personnel, but it will be a problem bridging the gap between Sven-Ingvar, the youngest active member, and these small children.

Tuorpon, once jokingly known as the bachelor's Sameby, has experienced an explosion of marriages and births. There seem to be children everywhere, so many in fact that Karin Parfa has started a summer preschool group in a tent goattieh by the shore of Virihaure. The children converse in Saami, learn Saami traditions, and hear tales of the Stalo troll. For a field trip, Johan drove them once all across the lake for a hike to Stalo Rock. I enjoy watching them practice with their parents' lassos on some old loose reindeer antlers or trying to whittle on sticks with small wooden knives that their parents have made to get them used to the feel of a knife before feeling a real edge. Problems of discipline generally revolve around stopping them from duplicating the more dangerous aspects of adult work.

I am pleased to report that even the most inveterate bachelor, John Andersson, is now married and has three children, my godchildren. His wife, Maria-Teresa, comes from Chile and met John on the bus to Kvikkjokk where she had planned a vacation. John was on his way into the mountains to repair some of the Swedish Tourist Association cabins for hikers. As usual, he was talkative, and, imitating the most professional of bus guides, took it upon himself to treat all the passengers to a running commentary of the countryside, complete with tall tales and Saami lore. I am sure he made quite an impression. In fact, it is remarkable how many people I have met who have only passed through Jokkmokk but who carry glowing memories of a talk with John.

Maria-Teresa is a dark-haired Latin American beauty. She felt flattered, as few would, when an irate Swedish driver once shouted "damn Lapp" at her. When in Lillselet with Amanda, her mother-in-law, Marie-Teresa has heard all kinds of Saami folk tales and myths. She is an excellent artist and has painted scenes and symbols from these stories in a way both true to the Saami culture and expressive of her own feeling. She is soon to open an exhibit of some of her work in Santiago, Chile.

Staloluokta has not only been changed by the presence of new children, it has also altered drastically in appearance as well. Whereas before only turf goattiehs and storage huts dotted the shore, now there are numerous full-fledged cabins as well. These are great improvements for the herders, who no longer have to unpack and repack their goattieh gear each time they arrive or depart. They are much warmer in the winter and much roomier. Many of the old goattieh homes have become guest quarters for visitors like me. They are used to smoke fish, and a harried parent can escape there from the turmoil loosed by one of Stalo's new children. Of course I, who come like a visiting summer bird and no longer share the hardships of migration and do not spend months gathering the reindeer, want no substitute for the arran and bed of birch branches.

One might wonder at the flurry of cabin construction in Stalo. It turns out that according to law only active herders are allowed to build cabins there, but these can be inherited by their children, even if they do not become active herders. Every herder, both young and old, appreciates the comforts provided by a cabin, but it is understandable that especially those approaching retirement from the more trying aspects of herding work, who might be unsure about the future commitment of their children, would want to guarantee them a cabin in Stalo. Cabin construction has, therefore, been rapid. The Saami are also used to sudden changes in the law, so many feel it is best to build when they can. There are those who refuse to trade the goattieh life for that of the cabin, but even these have often modernized their goattiehs in preparation for old age. A wooden floor might be laid, for example, to do away with the work required to cut a birch-branch floor.

Other changes have been inspired by a more experimental curiosity. Anders Blind mounted solar cells on the outside of his turf goattieh, and with their help a car battery supplies electric lighting indoors. Not to be outdone, Henrik and Birgit next door have erected a small wind-powered generator on the top of the wood shed. Biegolmai, the wind god, is active enough to power lights and even a small TV, Stalo's first. Newer still is the advent of cordless telephones. These resemble the old walkie-talkies, but are really more like the mobile car phones used by many executives. A number of wireless telephone masts have been raised in the mountains, and via them the herders have phone access not only to each other but to all other phones. The herder out gathering the herd for a calf marking in the evening can stop for a quick call to his girlfriend in Jokkmokk. If necessary, a rescue helicopter can be alerted from the scene of an accident. I remember the problems we had on the eastward autumn migration when the emergency police telephones in Njunjes, Skaite, and Levik were all out of commission. These problems are over for the Tuorpon herders. In their packs, they each have their own phone with an individual number. I really could not believe it until Sven-Ingvar demonstrated it for me in Stalo, and I could not keep myself from laughter when I heard Henrik on the phone to Stenträsk speak as he would with a walkie-talkie. "How is the weather there? Over." Can you send some new spark plugs for the boat motor? Over." "Over and out!"

Changes to the autumn migration are not only due to the phones. Little did any of us know it then, but it turned out that the migration eastward I was on in 1975 was the last one undertaken with reindeer caravan. Snowmobiles have taken over here too. Why did they not before? I think a good part of the answer can be found in the changes in tax law for the herders. Herders are now taxed as small companies and must account for not only their incomes but also their expenditures. The old rough-cut taxation by estimated calving percentage and herd size has been replaced. Most herders are not versed in the keeping of strict financial records or in thinking in terms of filing receipts for the purchase of a lasso or a pair of skis, but they have been forced to learn. Such necessities for work can now be deducted from their taxable income, and so can a snowmobile. Earlier, when the snowmobiles were private and not "company" vehicles, the terrible wear they suffer on the thin powder snow and rocky terrain during autumn migration was reason enough to use reindeer caravan. Now, when it is a good idea to limit taxable profits, one can buy a new snowmobile yearly.

Travel expenses in the line of work can also be deducted from the herding company's taxable income. Now when the reindeer are gathered from the mountains around Stalo, the trail to Jålli is no longer thronged with herders. Many of them have flown up to the corral. Even the young people who might have walked regardless of a possible tax deduction might fly simply because the plane is not full, and it does save time and strength. There are often calf markings booked night after night in different corrals. Even the gathering procedure itself is largely changed. The Sameby as a collective organization pays often for gathering by helicopter, a sizable expense covered in large part by a herding fee extracted from the herding members per head of reindeer owned. The helicopter is quicker and somewhat more certain. On occasion Stalo's own motorcycle team, consisting of Sven-Ingvar, Nils-Gustav, Anders-Ivan, and Per-Jonas Blind, scramble over the tundra in their dirt bikes to help gather the herd. It is a rough ride, to say the least. In these mountains a man over thirty should never even try it. Accidents were common during the learning phase, but even if the boys have proved it possible, I doubt it will gain much permanence here as it seems to have done on the flatter Finnmarks vidda of northern Norway.

It is quite a scene to see the herd driven into the corral by a line of growling motor bikes followed by the air support of two helicopters. One feels as if one were watching a war film. Conservationists and animal lovers are jumping with indignation. They claim that the motor bikes tear up the tundra and that the reindeer are heavily stressed. Of course one can question the penny-wise-but-pound-foolish attitude of many conservationists who fume at a few herders but swallow the ravages of the modern timber industry, for example. And who is to say that the modern reindeer herder should be forced to hold himself to an out-dated technology when no one else does? Then again, every side in this controversy has justified points. It will take time to get it all sorted out in a proper balance.

Despite all of these changes, there is still a deeper, basic, unchanged core of life in Tuorpon. Had I been gone all the while and returned suddenly after seventeen years, I would probably have been primarily struck by the contrasts. For me, however, having grown older with the same people and places before my eyes, it is the continuity that is most striking. By following events as a participant, one gains a different perspective, which I feel is more deeply satisfying. Yet beyond all these variable insights of continuity and change, that which matters most to me is simply a sense of belonging.

I could not help but feel proud when a newly arrived tourist to Stalo wandering among the goattiehs asked to take my picture as I was chopping wood. Johan Parfa rushed forth to wave the camera aside for an instant, insisting that my lip bulge with a real plug of snus for the event. The photographer grew a bit suspicious of the authenticity of her motif at this point, especially when I turned down Johan's already open snus box (as he knew I would). "I am no Saami," I told her so that she could save her film, but Johan shamed her into taking the picture nonetheless: "He's been practicing with us for a long time now, and anyway, he's just as good at chopping wood!"